COSMOLOGY IN ANTIQUITY

The widespread interest in recent discoveries and arguments, and the popularity of books by such writers as Stephen Hawking and Paul Davies, have made this the 'golden age' of cosmology. Many of today's problems awaiting solution are more sophisticated versions of puzzles discussed by the philosophers and mathematical astronomers of ancient Greece over two thousand years ago. They too worried about the limits of time and space, the elements that make up the whole, how (or if) the universe began, and whether cosmic events are random or meaningful, chaotic or maintained by balance and order.

Cosmology in Antiquity is a comprehensive introduction to the origins and development of cosmological thought in ancient times. It examines the main themes of the subject, starting where appropriate with the Babylonian and Egyptian forerunners, and continuing through the Presocratics to Plato, Aristotle and the Hellenistic schools of the Stoics and Epicureans. Their impact on the intellectual life at Rome along with the scholarship developed at Alexandria is also considered.

M.R. Wright is Senior Lecturer in Classics at the University of Reading, and formerly of the University of Wales, Aberystwyth. She has previously published books on the Presocratics, Empedocles and Stoic ethics in Cicero, as well as articles and review essays on a wide range of subjects in ancient philosophy.

SCIENCES OF ANTIQUITY
Series Editor: Roger French
Director, Wellcome Unit for the History of Medicine,
University of Cambridge

Sciences of Antiquity is a series designed to cover the subject matter of what we call science. The volumes discuss how the ancients saw, interpreted and handled the natural world, from the elements to the most complex of living things. Their discussions on these matters formed a resource for those who later worked on the same topics, including scientists. The intention of this series is to show what it was in the aims, expectations, problems and circumstances of the ancient writers that formed the nature of what they wrote. A consequent purpose is to provide historians with an understanding of the materials out of which later writers, rather than passively receiving and transmitting ancient 'ideas', constructed their own world view.

ANCIENT ASTROLOGY
Tamsyn Barton

ANCIENT NATURAL HISTORY
Histories of nature
Roger French

COSMOLOGY IN ANTIQUITY

M.R. Wright

London and New York

First published 1995
by Routledge
11 New Fetter Lane, London EC4P 4EE

Simultaneously published in the USA and Canada
by Routledge
29 West 35th Street, New York, NY 10001

Typeset in Garamond by
Ponting–Green Publishing Services, Chesham, Bucks
Printed and bound in Great Britain by
T.J. Press (Padstow) Ltd, Padstow, Cornwall

British Library Cataloguing in Publication Data
Wright, M.R.
Cosmology in Antiquity. – (Sciences of
Antiquity Series)
I. Title   II. Series
523.1093

Library of Congress Cataloging in Publication Data
A catalogue record for this book has been requested

ISBN 0–415–08372–9 (hbk)
ISBN 0–415–12183–3 (pbk)

for M.W.
amicissime scripsi

CONTENTS

FIGURES

GENERAL SERIES INTRODUCTION

The purpose of the series *Sciences of Antiquity* is to present that part of ancient philosophy that dealt with the natural world. This formed a resource and a model for people of later ages who also had reason to think and write about the natural world, including scientists. Most readers will be aware of the importance of classical learning of this kind to later cultures and the series aims to cover the most important fields of classical enquiry into the natural world. These fields are defined by the interests and activities of the ancients and not by modern science. In some cases the boundary of an ancient and modern topic coincide. One such case is cosmology, and there are parallels too in the limitations placed on the observer by the nature of the subject-matter. To the extent that cosmology includes cosmogony it must be speculative, both for the Greeks and the moderns, and both had conclusions as widely different as 'big bang' and 'steady state', as Rosemary Wright shows. As a 'science' it cannot be experimental and must rely on observations of greater or lesser sophistication, and on calculations based on them. Nor is cosmology (unlike astronomy) in any practical way predictive. Most 'cosmologists' would probably call themselves astronomers, drawn to the big questions of cosmology because of their great interest. Aristotle expressed this interest in a well-known passage where he remarked that the charm and importance of a study of the heavens was matched only by the uncertainty of the knowledge produced; conversely, the insides of animals had no charm whatever but generated knowledge (partly experimental and empirical) that Aristotle valued for its certainty. We should not on any of these grounds of course deny that cosmology is a science, but historical studies like this one help us to think carefully about what 'science' is both now and in the past.

Roger French

ix

ACKNOWLEDGEMENTS

I am happy to acknowledge the receipt of a personal research grant from the British Academy in 1993 which came at a critical time in the writing of this volume. It enabled me to make use of the expertise of Dr Stuart Leggatt, who helped considerably with the Aristotelian passages throughout, and especially with problems arising from the crucial *De Caelo*. Parts of the sections on elements and time, and almost the whole of the ninth chapter (on the mathematical principles involved), derive from draft material which he provided; I am very grateful to this fine scholar for his advice and assistance on these and other topics related to the history of science. I am also indebted to my physicist son, Tom, who produced the computer graphics for the illustrations, and dealt patiently with a stream of queries on the latest answers to questions which the Greeks first raised. My husband sifted through the complete manuscript with a critical eye; the breadth of reading that he and Tom foster, and the interest in the philosophy underpinning their own research, gave this work on ancient cosmology a wider perspective.

M.R. Wright
The University of Reading
September 1994

1

INTRODUCTION

I have written in the belief that the universe is governed by an order
that we can perceive partially now, and that we may understand fully
in the not-too-distant future.

(Stephen Hawking 1993: ix)

The last thirty years have been called 'the golden age of cosmology'.
With the discovery of the microwave background, the launching of
the 'Cosmic Background Explorer' (COBE), the general advances in
astrophysics and the increased sophistication of radio-telescopes,
particle accelerators and computer modelling, it would seem that we
are on the brink of solving the enigma of the origins of the universe,
yet the paradoxes inherent in the subject, the continuing controversies and the difficulties of verification make that solution still
elusive. Many of today's problems awaiting solution are more
sophisticated versions of issues which engaged the interest of ancient
cosmologists. The Aristotelian 'perfect cosmological principle', for
example, of a universe maintained indefinitely by natural laws
foreshadows the 'steady state' concept, whereas the opposed view of
a 'big bang' theory of the universe starting from a single point and
erupting out from there had its adherents then as now.

Ongoing arguments even among the theorists who are in general
agreement on the 'big bang' and the events immediately following
the crucial first moment come up against a need to assume either 'god-
given' initial conditions or some kind of cosmic organising basis in
addition to the recognised laws of physics; to affirm that an initial
condition or an increase in complexity is a fundamental property of
nature is an answer that received short shrift from Plato and his
followers. Once the events are in train 'inflationists' who expect
expansion to continue indefinitely are in the tradition of Anaxagoras,

1

whereas others are closer to Epicurus in assuming a self-regulating world in which the expansion is halted once an appropriate density is reached. The question of whether the advance in development is to be taken as linear or repeating in cycles is another old question, as is the related one of whether the universe, or at least our immediate galaxy, will continue or disintegrate in some way, following the pattern of birth, maturity, decrease and death of the forms of life it contains. Will there be continual regeneration as Empedocles supposed or, in line with the ancient atomists, a 'big crunch' for our world, complementing at its end the vortex-generation of its beginning? The Stoic theory of the ascendancy of fire and a repeating *ekpyrōsis* also appears to be enjoying a revival in the assumption of the incredible initial heat of the 'big bang', in the observed present increase in the earth's temperature and in the view that the universe may in the future fall back on itself 'with stars and galaxies being consumed in a mighty fireball, possibly to re-explode in a second big bang' (as reported by N. Booth in the *Observer* of 5 August 1994).

The model of the anthropocentric enclosed spherical cosmos that was developed in detail from Plato to Ptolemy and continued through the Middle Ages has long been discarded, yet the discovery of the curvature of space restores some interest to old arguments concerned with the outermost 'edge' of the universe. And what of the anthropocentric perspective? Is the human race fundamental or incidental to the whole? A question that was once shunted to theology becomes increasingly relevant as we are made more aware that cosmology itself, like all arts and sciences, is a construct of human intelligence, subject to social and linguistic conditioning and dubious means of communication.

A further relevance of the old to the new comes with the kind of language with which the most up-to-date cosmogonies are presented by experts to a non-professional readership; there is the constant surprise of the reappearance of Presocratic terminology in such works, an excellent example of which is Paul Davies' *The Cosmic Blueprint* (1987). Talk of cold dark matter and hot dark matter, and of processes of heating and cooling, recalls the primary opposites of the Milesians, as does that of dense regions being brought together while the 'rarefied' is thrust outwards. An account of an initial 'soup' of cosmological material in a uniform mixture reads like Anaxagoras' first fragment that 'all things were together', and a 'thermodynamic equilibrium' could pass as a description of Empedocles' pre-cosmic sphere, itself influencing the later physics of the Stoics. There are common grounds in the assumption of orderly arrangements emerging from the outward rippling of featureless swirling 'stuff', and especially in the crucial realisation that cosmological theorising rests on some understanding of the essential linkage of the minutely small with the immensely large.

The name of the science of cosmology is derived from ancient Greek, and has an interesting history. In the earliest Greek texts, the Homeric epic poems of the *Iliad* and *Odyssey*, the word *kosmos* had primarily the sense of 'order', used, for example, of rowers at their place by the oars (*Odyssey* 13.77) or of soldiers sleeping with their equipment properly set out around them (*Iliad* 10.472), whereas the absence of *kosmos* would characterise the ragged rout of an army (*Iliad* 2.214). The Greek aesthetic sense of style saw beauty in arrangement and proportion, so that *kosmos* could be used for geometric decoration on a vase, as well as for the array of dress, perfume, jewellery and sandals put on by the goddess Hera in her glamorous preparations for seduction (*Iliad* 14.187); this meaning of 'adornment' still lingers in the derivation 'cosmetics'. A song or story with the parts well arranged was also a *kosmos*, and to show the courtesy of good manners, adapting to the needs of others was to be *kosmic*. The historians extended this use to cover well-regulated states such as Sparta (so Herodotus at 1.65), officials who maintained political order, and harmonious relationships generally.

By the end of the sixth century BC the combination of these senses of a continuing orderly arrangement of parts showing beauty and adornment was appropriated for the grand structure of earth, sea and the sky above, encompassing by day the sun, clouds and rainbow, and by night the bright patterns of moon, stars and planets. Xenophanes, a refugee from the expansion of the Middle Eastern empire of the Medes in the sixth century BC, is said to have been the first 'who looked up at the sky and had a theory of everything' (reported by Aristotle *Metaphysics* 986b). The move towards calling this whole world-system 'the *kosmos*,' on the other hand, was attributed to his near contemporary Pythagoras in the notice that:

> He was the first to call the sum of the whole by the name of *kosmos*, because of the order which it displayed.
>
> (Aetius 2.1.1)

To this word, still ambiguous between the beautiful arrangement of parts in the whole and the whole itself, was added *logos*, meaning 'a reasoned and rational account', to give the compound noun *cosmology*, the term that was used from then onwards to cover analyses, theories and and explanations of the phenomena of the universe.

The first recorded use of *kosmos* in the sense of 'world order' is from the one quotation extant from the work of Anaximenes:

> As our soul, which is air, maintains us, so breath (*pneuma*) and air surround the whole *kosmos*.

The 'whole *kosmos*', the encircling sky and all that it contains, is presented here as alive and breathing, held and controlled as humans are by the life-support system called air (*aēr*).

Other early uses of *kosmos* show the word in the process of becoming established as an appropriate general term for the universe, 'the whole', 'the all' or 'the sum of things' (the Latin *summa rerum*). Heraclitus, writing soon after Anaximenes, found the vital principle in fire rather than air:

> This *kosmos* no one of men or gods has made, but it ever was and will be – ever-living fire, kindling in measures and quenching in measures.

> (fr. 30)

Melissus, a generation later than Heraclitus, made the same point, but more prosaically:

> It is impossible for there to be change of *kosmos*, for the *kosmos* that previously exists is not destroyed, and the one that does not exist has not come into being.

> (fr. 7)

Empedocles, a near contemporary of Melissus, said that the four elements of earth, air, fire and water were brought together 'into one *kosmos*' by the force of attraction (fr. 26.5), and he described the universal intelligence pervading the whole as:

> Mind alone, holy and inexpressible, sweeping across the whole *kosmos* with swift thoughts.

> (fr. 134)

And this sense of the united arrangement of the universe was the standard use soon after in Anaxagoras, as in the quotation

> All things in the one *kosmos* have not been separated one from another or sliced off by an axe, not hot from cold or cold from hot.

> (fr. 8)

4

Two fragments of the Pythagorean Philolaus probably come from about the same period and continue the theme on similar lines to the previous quotations, as they emphasise the sense of orderly connection and arrangement of like and unlike in one whole:

> Things unlike each other and of different kinds and unequally matched must all have connecting links to be part of one *kosmos*.
>
> (fr. 6)

> What limits and what is unlimited together make a harmony of the *kosmos* and the things in it.
>
> (fr. 2)

Among the later Presocratics, Diogenes of Apollonia spoke with familiarity of 'this *kosmos*' and all that exists in it (fr. 2). The sense came full circle when the the word *kosmos*, which in Homer had described personal adornment and was then transferred to the fair arrangement of the universe, returned with Democritus to the individual, portrayed now as the whole in miniature, the 'microcosm' (*mikros kosmos*, fr. 34).

The medical writers at about the same time were also conscious of the relationship between the order of parts in the individual and in the external world. It was thought that the doctor had to be familiar with the constellations, and to watch out for

> changes and excesses in food and drink, in winds and weather and the *kosmos* as a whole, since from these arise the illnesses that occur in people.
>
> (*Regimen* 1.2)

And the author of the early Hippocratic work, *On Human Nature*, claimed that a person would die if any of the mutually dependent components that made up his or her constitution failed, just as the *kosmos* would disappear if any one of its connected opposites, the same ingredients on a large scale, were to break loose, for, in both, 'from a single necessity, they maintain and nourish each other' (*On Human Nature* 7.58–60).

These early thinkers set out to discard mythical and theological traditions and to forge a new language of nature and necessity to account for the structure and functioning of phenomena. Their great advance came in the recognition of balance and proportion in apparent disorder, and of continuity through the variations; they were sustained by the confidence that the explanation of these was ultimately accessible to human reasoning, however great the intellectual effort involved. *Kosmos* was the name given to the well-arranged, all-containing whole, and *logos* the rational analysis and account of it. From the struggles of these pioneering Greeks to come to terms with and explain the totality of their surroundings was born the science of cosmology.

The new science soon began to develop its own subject-matter and to find its own experts, who transferred the language of human relationships to that of the physical world. So Socrates, with his usual ironic touch, told his respondent that

> clever men, Callicles, say that sky and earth, and men and gods, are bound in friendly community, orderliness (*kosmiotēs*), restraint and law, and so that's why they call this whole thing *kosmos*.
>
> (*Gorgias* 508a)

Socrates himself however declined to join these experts, finding the study irrelevant to questions of human values, aims and happiness, where his own interests lay. Xenophon, who knew Socrates in his lifetime, and wrote biographical notes of him in his *Memorabilia*, reported that:

> Socrates didn't spend his time discussing the nature of everything as most others did, wondering about what the experts call the *kosmos* and the reasons for all the things in the sky necessarily coming about as they do; on the contrary he pointed out the foolishness of those who were concerned with such matters.
>
> (*Memorabilia* 1.1.11; cf. Plato *Phaedo* 98a)

Although *kosmos* still kept connotations of orderly arrangement – for states, groups of people, speeches, personal adornments – as well as for the sky (the *ouranos*) in its night beauty, by Socrates' time in the fifth century BC it had become in particular a technical term for the universe, for what had been called more informally 'the whole' or 'all things', and those who investigated it were recognised as professionals, grouped together as philosophers and in particular as 'physicists', i.e., students of *physis* – 'nature' or 'the natural world'.

The list of 'physicists' starts with the three Ionians, Thales, Anaximander and Anaximenes, from the coastal town of Miletus. They are followed soon after by Heraclitus of Ephesus and Pythagoras, who migrated from the island of Samos to south Italy; his immediate successors were Parmenides and Zeno of Elea, also in south Italy. Empedocles in Sicily from the west of the Greek world and Melissus of Samos from the east side belonged in the next generation, as well as Anaxagoras from the Ionian town of Clazomenae and Democritus of Abdera, the main founder of the atomic theory, who both migrated to Athens. Only then, in the fifth century, did Athens become the centre for philosophy, dominated by the native Athenians Socrates and Plato. Aristotle first studied with Plato in his Academy, and then set up his own school, the Lyceum, nearby. In the post-Aristotelian Hellenistic era the rival schools of Epicurus and the Stoic Zeno of Citium were founded, and over the next centuries both Epicureanism and a modified form of Stoicism became influential in the intellectual life of the increasingly powerful city of Rome. During the same period from the third century BC a great centre of scholarship had been founded in the Museum and Library of Alexandria where some of the brightest and most influential astro-cosmologists worked over a number of centuries, culminating in the great Ptolemy.

While it is necessary to recognise the early background to cosmological thought in the achievements of the ancient Near East in Mesopotamia, Egypt and the Semitic cultures, the innovations and theoretical advances belong with the early Greek philosophers, the Presocratics. They first faced many of the key questions and introduced most of the major themes. Among their achievements were the use of models as a method of approaching an understanding of the unknown from the known, and the related concept of cosmobiology, the view of the cosmos as an organic entity, with the associated comparison between the whole as macrocosm and the individual as microcosm. In addition, the Presocratics initiated the study of the elements of which the whole would be composed, the sources of its life and movement, the explanations of time and change and the underlying mathematical principles. They were particularly interested in the emergence of orderly arrangement from disorder at the generation of the cosmos, and in the analysis of the resulting construct in so far as it was open to human observation and reason. They were the first to tackle problems at the limits of time and space that are still with us, as they laid out the lines of debate between a temporal starting-point in a particular location and a continuous 'steady state' hypothesis. They wondered whether the outer boundaries might be fixed, expanding or collapsing, and whether cosmic patterns and events are random or meaningful and amenable to formulisation. They questioned if and how the end of the cosmos may come, what place humanity had in the whole, whether life and reason may exist elsewhere, and overall how to find the simplest explanations for the diversity of phenomena, for order emerging from obscurity and for permanence underlying cosmic change.

These debates were carried forward and tackled with greater sophistication, combined with creative imagination and ruthless logic, by Plato and Aristotle, and their world picture was refined and elaborated in the mathematical astronomy of the Alexandrians; at the same time the basic principles were being challenged by the Epicureans and reworked by the Stoics. On the sidelines the continual interest in these debates was reflected in popular literature, in epic, tragedy, comedy and satire, and engaged the minds of a range of social classes, from the slave Epictetus to the Emperor Marcus Aurelius.

After the necessary orientation provided by a survey of the most important evidence to survive, the present study lays out some of the main themes that are still seen as fundamental to the study of cosmology. Because of the wealth of material available covering such an extensive time span the selection is difficult. The result therefore tends to be a personal anthology of topics and texts, although it is hoped that it is one which will highlight their enduring interest and value. The first of these themes looks at ways in which the inaccessible is made intelligible by bringing it within the scope of what can be grasped as mythical narrative, formulae and models, and using the linguistic devices of metaphor and analogy. The most important of these, the subject of the fourth chapter, is the view that the whole is a living creature, animate and possibly also sentient and intelligent, while the individual is a small-scale version of the whole, a 'microcosm'. Various human institutions mediate between the two as 'minicosmoi' in such forms as the household, the theatre, the *polis* and in particular the cosmopolis.

In Chapter 5 the problems of chaos and cosmogony are studied in their ancient context. In opposition to the 'steady state' supporters, a range of solutions was tried in myth, science and philosophy to provide for an explanation for the emergence and growth of the present ordered world-system according to recognised natural laws from a state of random or formless disorder. Complementary to this was the question of a possible death or destruction of this system following maturity and decline, as in the parameters of all known forms of life, or the alternative version of an expansion that might be continuous and 'inflationary'. In addition, a plurality of systems was envisaged by some, either simultaneously in a limitless spatial location, or succeeding each other in a temporal series without beginning and end.

In Chapter 6 comes an investigation into the underlying nature of reality. The results will inevitably be relative to one's orientation: as a physicist may talk in terms of energy, a chemist of gases and a biologist of DNA strings, so the ancient philosophers of nature worked on the concept of element. They reached the conclusion that the wide variety of phenomena could be explained by the arrangements and rearrangements of basic materials according to certain formulae, or to natural processes that take place in connection with them or to their fundamental mathematical structure. The most extreme form of elemental materialism was adopted by the ancient atomists, who assumed that in truth everything was ultimately reducible to innumerable multitudes of atoms moving through limitless void.

The most influential theory posited the four elements of earth, water, air and fire (of which the four-letter alphabet of DNA strings and the four-colour map theory are distant descendants). There were however those led by Aristotle who suggested a fifth element called *aithēr* for the high area above the moon, immutable, divine, eternally rotating, far removed from the generation and decay of life on earth. This theory supported old myths of favoured animals or humans immortalised as constellations, and traditions of the stars as the homes of the souls of the good, but was countered by the Stoics. They envisaged divine breath as *pneuma* transversing the gulf between earth and sky in a dynamic continuum which ensured a sympathy of the whole with its parts.

The eighth chapter examines the theme of time and cosmology. It begins with the temporal measurements of the solar, lunar and stellar calendars that were first established in Mesopotamia and Egypt, and continues with philosophical puzzles about the beginning and end of time, and the meaning of Plato's definition of it as 'a moving image of eternity'. The theme connects with three cosmological topics that have been of perennial interest: the Harmony of the Spheres, the Great Year (when all the planets return to the same configuration) and the exact repetition of a cycle of events in Eternal Recurrence. Chapter 9 is more restricted; it deals with the mathematical bases of cosmology, a subject that is particularly important for the advances made in the theoretical development and the elegant sophistication of the models used. The different reactions to Plato's work by Aristotle and others in the Academy created an interest in the links between physics, mathematics and astronomy that stimulated the great research programmes carried out at Alexandria, including the heliocentric theory of Aristarchus, and Ptolemy's *Amalgest*.

Finally, Chapter 10 explores the role of the divine in the workings of the universe, a theme which spans all ages and cultures, and finds expression in both myth and ritual. The 'physicists' were more interested in 'natural theology' where the immanence of divinity is shown in the working of natural law, in the inherent designs and mechanisms of natural processes and in the tendencies towards certain 'ends'. Various interpretations emerged in the Presocratic inclination to find some kind of intelligent control in the universe as a whole, and continue in such concepts as Plato's craftsman-god, Aristotle's prime mover and Stoic pantheism. Against these was ranged the atomists' denial of any involvement of the divine in the formation or maintenance of world-systems. The arguments continue, and even now a place is found for natural or 'creation' theology, between atheism and formal religion, which is not incompatible with the latest developments in cosmology. A crucial common feature is that there is an intelligible order to the universe spanning the range from the smallest and least to the enormity of the whole, which is accessible to human reason and an appropriate study for it.

2

A SURVEY OF COSMOLOGICAL TEXTS

Cosmology is unique among ancient sciences in being based on a wide variety of texts. Where writers on topics concerned with medicine or geography, for example, used the medium of the straightforward prose treatise, an overview of works dealing with the structure of the universe and the celestial bodies, and the relationship of the human race to the whole, needs to take into account verse and prose writings in a broad range of literary genres. In some cases there are only fragments of the original works, and two of the most influential philosophers, Pythagoras and Socrates, wrote nothing; their theories have to be compiled from a range of evidence, often conflicting or untrustworthy.

The most interesting work was carried out mainly by the Presocratic Greeks in the sixth and fifth centuries BC, by Plato and Aristotle in the fourth and then by followers of the Stoic and Epicurean schools in Greece and later in Rome, and it is on these figures that the emphasis lies. But their cosmology needs to be seen in context, from its beginnings on the seaboard of Asia Minor, where roads were open to Egypt and the Middle East, to its most significant discoveries by the scholars in Alexandria. The transfer to Rome gave rise to the philosophical works of Cicero and Lucretius in the last century of the Republic, to Seneca in the early empire and then to the writings in Greek from the two ends of the spectrum in Roman society in the second century AD: the *Handbook* of the slave Epictetus, and the *Meditations* of the Emperor Marcus Aurelius. Alongside these developments, advances in mathematics, medicine and even architecture were sometimes relevant, as were the comic sketches by Lucian and Plutarch's serious moral essays; political theory also had its input in the concept of world-citizenship – cosmopolitanism in its literal sense.

11

There has been much controversy recently over the contribution of Asian, African and Semitic races to Greek culture. Any study of Greek science, including cosmology, must begin with them, and some estimate made of their achievements in their own right and their contribution to Hellenic thought. The oldest surviving pieces of written texts are the cuneiform tablets from the region of Mesopotamia, dating back to about 3500 BC, and to the first settlers in the region, the Sumerians. Signs were scratched with the tip of a reed on to a small flat rectangle of soft clay which was then baked dry by the sun or in an oven to give a permanent record (there are also versions on cylinders and stone). Pictograms drawn in wedge-shaped lines were used first, then later replaced by symbols for words, numbers, syllables and phonetic elements. About 2500 BC, Sumerian supremacy in the city-kingdoms, the chief of which was at Ur, was challenged by the Semitic Akkadian nomads under Sargon, who, like the Hittites in the Syrian area, took over their writing and their calendar along with other arts and skills. Then a second wave of Semitic invaders, the Amorites, settled in the region, with their headquarters in the town of Babylon; their sixth king was the great Hammurabi. Writing by this time covered astronomical records and measurements based on geometrical proofs as well as the king's laws and general accounting (which used arithmetic according to a sexagesimal system, i.e., on a scale of sixty). Two libraries were built to house the tablets, which were arranged on shelves with indexes and cross-references. For over two millennia these libraries stored observations of celestial phenomena, which with increasing accuracy developed to cover the path of the sun through the zodiac, the phases of the moon, the positions of Venus and the irregularities and periodic revolutions of the other planets, Mercury, Mars, Jupiter and Saturn. Astronomers from 747 BC organised this material into a uniform system, and used it to date the regularity of eclipses of the sun and moon, and to calculate the solar year to within twenty-seven minutes of its actual length. The calendar had first been based on the moon, and, to bring lunar months into alignment with the solar year, they first posited a solar cycle of eight and later of nineteen years, which is the equivalent of nearly 235 lunar months. It was this which was adopted in Athens by Meton in 433–432 BC (although the precise date is in dispute). Herodotus (2.119) said that the Greeks also learned the use of two types of sundial from the Babylonians: the *gnōmon* (the familiar

12

pointer on a plane base to mark the hours of daylight) and the more complex *polos*, which had a pointer fixed in a hemispherical bowl.

The Babylonians (known to the Romans as 'Chaldaeans') also developed the seven-day week which, with its Semitic connections, eventually prevailed over the ten-day Egyptian week and the eight days of the Roman one. Light and dark from dawn to dawn were divided into twelve hours each (of varying length according to the season); each twenty-four hour period was marked by ritual and praise for the seven planetary gods in turn, and the days were named after them. (Even the Norse elements retained in some of the English names go back to these gods.) In addition, the Babylonians divided

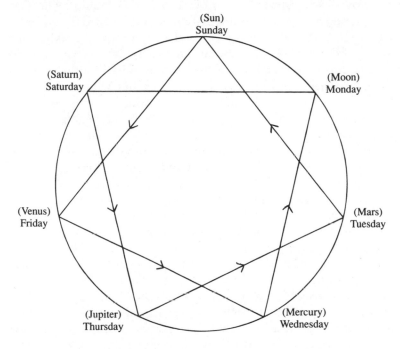

Figure 1 The days of the week derived from the planets.
The chords marked Saturn–Jupiter–Mars–Sun–Venus–Mercury–Moon are in order of decreasing distance of the planets from earth.

the zodiac circle remarkably accurately into degrees (with minutes and seconds), and then went on to relate the zodiac constellations to the birth date and life events of individuals. Such astrological mapping emphasised the concept of humanity's affinity with the

13

cosmos, but it became the source of continuing superstition, some-times trivial but often dangerous.

Among the earliest known continuous pieces of literature are the Mesopotamian epics of creation and of Gilgamesh. Fragments of texts of these poems are found in a variety of forms and cuneiform languages throughout the ancient Near East, but especially in Babylon, in Nineveh (in the palace of the Assyrian kings in the seventh century BC), and in the collection from Boghazköy on the river Halys. The *Epic of Creation* from Babylon is preserved in its most complete form on six tablets each of 130–60 lines. It tells of the gods of heaven and earth arising from a union of fresh water and a 'chaos' of sea waters. The hero is the sun-god Marduk who slew the dragon representing the original chaos, and fastened the monsters who were its children (such as Leo and Scorpio) into the zodiac, and arranged the movements of moon and planets. The human race was then said to have been born of the earth, fertilised by the blood of the slain. There are a number of variations, but with the common theme of a god of light and order defeating representations of darkness, turmoil and evil. The widespread and popular *Epic of Gilgamesh* similarly shows the triumph of a youthful sun-god. The extant remains are a jigsaw of cuneiform fragments, versions and translations, but a consecutive narrative from an original twelve-tablet form survives. The heroic adventures of Gilgamesh with his human companion Enkidu can be interpreted as an account of the cycle of the twelve-month year, commencing with a spring birth, ending with the world of the dead, and including a great flood.

Egypt rivalled Mesopotamia in its interests in mathematics and astronomy, its myths of the world's origins and in having a very early writing system, that of hieroglyphs. This system, like cuneiform, originally consisted of pictograms, which then became word-signs, over 800 in total. The hieroglyphs were carved on stone for monu-ments, tombs or stelae or on wood or written in a more abbreviated form by scribes with reed-pen and ink on papyrus rolls. Scientific papyri dealt with geography, medicine, astronomy and mathematics, especially in practical examples of geometric measurements. Cos-mogonies are found in pyramid and papyrus texts, and mainly at four locations: at Heliopolis (honouring the sun-god Re'), at Hermopolis where the narrative involves creation from a cosmic egg and an Octet of gods concerned with the sun and the Nile, at Memphis with Ptah as the creative principle and all-knowing reason, and at Thebes where the origin is with the sky-god, the self-creating Amon, 'Greatest of

Heaven, Eldest of Earth'. Amon, Re', Ptah and the unique god Aten honoured by Akhenaton represent in different ways the divinity and creative power of the sun, which was symbolised by the lotus-flower, and celebrated in hymns and litanies.

For three millennia the Egyptians showed a particular interest in astronomy, fostered by the sightings in the clear night sky above their land. Farmers, shepherds and sailors from earliest times were familiar with the interchanges of day and night and the variations in the length of each; they knew of the lunar months and the cycles of the seasons, and enough about the constellations to plot their way and to deduce from it the times of year suitable for specific tasks. The first positive result of this interest was to have an organised calendar, based on the sun rather than the lunar months of Mesopotamia. The Egyptian year started in July with the solar rising of the bright star Sothis (i.e., Sirius), which coincided with the annual flooding of the river Nile, and it was measured by twelve months of thirty days each, with an intercalary five days. There were three seasons of four months (each month with three 'weeks' of ten days) characterised by Nile flooding, planting and harvesting. Days and nights had twelve hours each, varying according to the season, and the sexagesimal system for minutes and seconds of each hour was also known, perhaps from Babylonia. Calculations of the hours were established by various devices, at night by a star clock (replaced about 1500 BC by a water clock), and by day by a shadow clock, another version of the *gnōmon*, with divisions for morning, evening and twilight hours.

From about the thirteenth century BC the Egyptians had distinguished over forty constellations, including the zodiac signs, as well as the five planets of Saturn, Jupiter, Mars, Venus and Mercury. The familiarity with the timing of the solstices and equinoxes was shown most dramatically by the building of the great temple of Amon-Re' at Karnak, which was aligned with the rising of the sun in mid-winter. The origins of sky, air and earth, from a primeval 'abyss' (Nun), followed by the emergence of the sun (Re') and moon were told by the Egyptians in the form of cosmogonical myths which had clear affinities with those found in the *Theogony* of the Greek Hesiod. There was also the sophisticated theology connected with Ptah at Memphis. According to the Memphite teaching, for which there is some direct evidence, Ptah was the one god, Lord of Truth and creator of all, both divine and human, and was also regarded as a cosmic intelligence, bringing life into being by word alone, and responsible for moral as well as physical order; his representation

15

was not, like most Egyptian deities, with animal attributes, but as a deity incorporated into a pillar, the symbol of justice.

An important contribution from the Phoenicians came with the movement of their phonetic alphabet to the Aegean in the ninth and eighth centuries BC. This move was connected with the myth of Cadmus travelling from the East in search of his sister Europa, and settling eventually at Thebes in Boeotia. But from a much earlier time there were various transcriptions of different Greek dialects including Linear A and B, following the routes of trade and conquest. Eventually one version, the eastern Ionic, predominated, and this Indo-European language was written down in the Semitic script. Some of the Phoenician letters were dropped and others adapted, but the critical change was to add vowels to what was a consonant only alphabet system (as are all Semitic and Arabic writings). The result was finally to break free of pictured and syllabic signs, and to develop an alphabet that could express in letter form all the nuances of the spoken word.

A second advance that came with the superior eastern Greek alphabet was a more elaborate method of numeration. The Egyptians had had a primitive method of decimal numbering marked by repeating simple line forms, and the Babylonians a sexagesimal system marked by circles. The Phoenicians used letters for numbers, but the Greeks made vast improvements on their system. They developed a decimal system with letters up to ten, and another set of letters for the tens and hundreds with an adjacent mark to show that the letters were being used as numbers; a different mark indicated that alpha was being used for 1,000, and so on. The result was that sophisticated calculations could easily be made with very high numbers, as, for example, Archimedes' reckoning of the number of grains of sand that could possibly be contained in the cosmos. The Roman system, which used only seven letters (C, D, I, L, M, V and X) that needed complex additions and subtractions to cover a wider range, was much harder to manage.

Ancient Greek literature starts with the Homeric epic poems, the *Iliad* and *Odyssey*, collected as oral continuous narratives in the ninth and eighth centuries BC, and edited as written texts in the Athens of the tyrant Peisistratus about 540 BC. The cosmic structure assumed in these poems was a simple one of earth as a circular disk around which flowed the freshwater river Ocean; the hemisphere of the vault of the sky was above, and the matching realm of Tartarus below. In a threefold partition among the oldest Olympian male deities, Zeus had control of the sky and acted as a god of thunder and the weather generally, Poseidon ruled the seas and Hades the nether region. Iris, goddess of the rainbow, bridged sky and earth in her role of messenger of the gods. Dawn, sun, moon and stars were thought to rise from Ocean in the east, cross the sky in an arc and set in the west; then presumably they went round the disc northwards to rise again. Some basic astronomy was shown incidentally in the narratives: Arcturus, Orion, morning and evening star, the Hyades and Pleiades were recognised, and also the Great Bear, which turns round on itself, and is the only constellation not to set in the west in the waters of Ocean (*Iliad* 18.487). The rising of Sirius, the 'dog-star', was

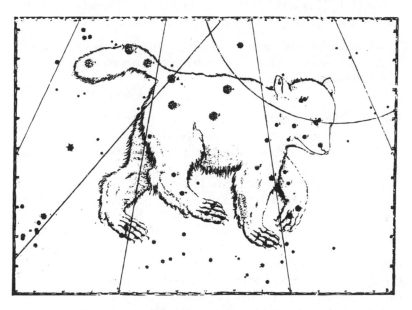

Figure 2 The constellation of the Great Bear.
One of the first constellations to be recognised, it was pictured on
Achilles' shield in *Iliad* 18.

particularly important, welcome to the Egyptians because it signalled the time of the annual flooding of the Nile, but dreaded by the other Mediterranean peoples as a warning of fiery heat to come.

Hesiod, from Ascra in Boeotia, is the first named European author, with two poems attributed to him, dating approximately from the beginning of the seventh century BC, a little later than the Homeric epics and similar to them in language and metre. The main part of one, the *Works and Days*, gives advice on farming, and in this the times of year for the different agricultural tasks are marked by solstices and star risings which had once had mythical connotations. Events in the sky – winds, weather changes, the dawn, the shapes of constellations – show traces of these anthropomorphic narratives, although they are often little more than time formulae in the absence of any other means of marking a calendar. For example, the lines

> when the Pleiades, Atlas' daughters, start to rise, begin the harvest, and plough when they set
>
> (*Works and Days* 383–4)

indicated 19 May and 3 November respectively. Pruning should be done at the beginning of spring, on 24 February:

> when 60 days of winter have passed after the solstice, then Arcturus leaves Ocean's holy stream, the first to shine out in the twilight.
>
> (*Works and Days* 564–7)

Similarly the constellations mentioned in Homer – the Pleiades, Hyades and Orion – mark the onset of winter. The farmer finds his work tied to the earth, yet dependent on the movement of distant constellations.

The second poem attributed to Hesiod is the *Theogony*, about a thousand lines long and also in the epic style. Its composition is roughly contemporaneous with that of the Book of Genesis, and relates the comparable theme of the initial division of dark and light, and the emergence of the cosmic masses of earth and sky. Hesiod uses a genealogical model (rather than that of a creator-god) to explain the arrangement of the world-system, the articulation of the earth's surface into its natural features and the appearance of meteorological phenomena. The succession myths and the great battle with the Titans that led to the final supremacy of the Olympian gods were woven into this material, as well as an aetiology for the discovery of fire, the sufferings that are part of human history and for the advances in law and culture. The poem is important not for either historical or scientific veracity, but because it bridges the ideas of the ancient Near East and the new lands of Hellas, mediating the myth-making of the past with the methods of reasoning to come. It also put the form of the Homeric epic to a new use in didactic explanation, and this was the medium adopted by the Presocratics Parmenides and Empedocles, and later in Rome by Lucretius.

Between Hesiod and the Milesians lurk the shadowy figures of

Orpheus, Musaeus and Epimenides. They are credited with cosmogonies usually starting from such vague Hesiodic entities as Chaos, Night, Aither and Erebus, and relate a mating and the subsequent production of an egg, from which emerges a significant personage or personification. Another early mythographer, Pherecydes of Syros, narrated a different genealogy starting from Zas (i.e., Zeus) and Chronos ('Time'), which involved the biological model of a tree rather than an egg, and also the artefact of an embroidered cloth which portrayed the natural features of Earth and Ocean.

Pherecydes' fragmentary mythology is sometimes said to be the first European work in prose, but the claim is more justified for the philosophical books, later given the title *On Nature*, by Anaximander and Anaximenes, dating from the sixth century BC. These two, together with their predecessor Thales, came from Miletus, the most important Ionian city and a leading trading centre, with the Persian empire as its hinterland. Thales was the first named 'stargazer', laughed at for falling down a well while staring upwards. What is significant about these Milesians (or Ionians as they are also termed) is a new approach to the external world which earned them the title of 'physicists'. For all the accuracy, expertise and professional dedication of the Babylonians in their calculations and observations, for them the record of the repetition of celestial movements appears to have been an end in itself, with little curiosity revealed, or attempt made to investigate or explain general laws underlying the phenomena. The Greek Ionians in contrast expected that the complexities of the natural world were reducible to simple principles and could thence become the subject of human reasoning; this road to discovery was open-ended for them, with each generation of students ready to criticise, adapt and improve on the results of those who preceded them. At the same time the spread of literacy meant that the different theories were permanently available for dissemination and discussion.

Only one sentence each is preserved in the original wording from the two main Ionians. Simplicius, the Aristotelian commentator, quotes Anaximander:

> From the source from which [opposites] arise, to that they return of necessity when they are destroyed, 'for they suffer punishment and make reparation to one another for their injustice according to the assessment of time', as he says in somewhat poetic terms.

Anaximenes' sentence is from the collection of Aetius:

> As our soul which is air maintains us, so breath and air surround the whole cosmos.

These are enigmatic statements and riddled with controversy, but of great significance for a number of themes connected with cosmology. We also learn from secondary sources that Anaximander posited the earth as drum-shaped with an upper and lower surface, held in place by free suspension. He had a detailed explanation for the movements and distances of sun, moon and stars, and a theory of cosmic 'justice' and equilibrium maintained between opposite forces. Anaximenes replaced his predecessor's 'indefinite' first principle for one which had the specific quality of air, which by its quantitative variations could account for phenomena as well as being the essential life support for man and cosmos alike.

Also from Ionia came the major figure of Heraclitus of Ephesus, who deposited his one book in the temple of Artemis as a city treasure. The key to his theory was *logos*, the true analysis and description of the way things are, which is unnoticed by most people as they drift along in a day-dream. They need to be woken up and made aware of the true nature of the cosmos: that it is maintained by the tension of opposites, permeated and controlled by the energy of 'ever-living fire', and that one's own life is involved in it. Apart from the elaborate first sentence on *logos*, Heraclitus' book is a collection of short 'sound-bites' – striking, ambiguous and deliberately puzzling after the fashion of the Delphic oracles; even in antiquity Heraclitus was called 'dark and obscure'.

Heraclitus despised *polymathia*, the straightforward amassing of facts, and censured Xenophanes and Pythagoras in particular. Xenophanes in his verses had initiated the attack on the traditional anthropomorphic attributes and immoral behaviour of the Homeric gods, and in their place suggested one god, motionless and intelligent, who activates the whole by the workings of his mind. Xenophanes was linked with Pythagoras in his reported wisdom (the first to have a theory of everything, according to Aristotle), and like him travelled from the eastern side of the Greek world to the western colonies in south Italy.

Pythagoras wrote nothing but was credited with extremely influential theories in mathematics, music, psychology and psychotherapy. His followers were apt to put his name to their own work so that it is difficult to trace the chronology of Pythagorean thought, but one of his immediate successors in Italy, Philolaus of Croton, is known to have made important contributions to cosmology, including substituting a 'central fire' for the geocentric theory, and supposing the existence of dark 'counter-earths'.

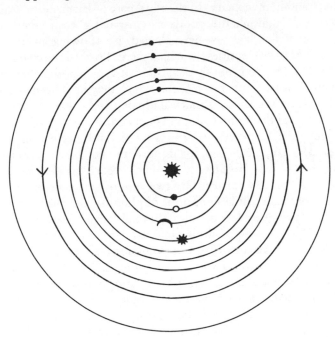

Figure 3 The cosmos of Philolaus.
Around the central fire there rotate in order: Counter-earth, Earth, Moon, Sun, Mercury, Venus, Mars, Jupiter, Saturn.

The Ionians in Asia Minor had a small colony in south Italy called Elea. Parmenides came there soon after its foundation, and his brand of philosophy was therefore subsequently known as 'Eleatic'. It was formulated in a poem in epic hexameters in three parts. The prologue narrates the chariot journey undertaken by a young man which tracked the path of the sun and descended into the west; he then passed through gates and along a broad road to meet a goddess who gave a revelation. The next section of the poem consists of the 'Way of Truth', the first recorded stretch of sustained philosophical argument. The goddess who presented it stated that if the argument were judged by *logos* ('reason'), and not by what appears to the senses to be the case, only *esti* ('is') could be allowed as an object of thought

21

or speech, and its opposite *ouk esti* ('is not') had to be rejected outright. This premise struck at the foundations of any cosmogony, for it allowed to the whole no temporal beginning or end, no movement or change, no temporal or spatial gaps to interrupt continuity and homogeneity. In the third part of Parmenides' poem, the 'Way of Opinion', the goddess reinstated a cosmology (the principles of which had just been denied) by allowing an initial – wrong – move of two entities, to which were allocated the characteristics of fire and night. From these a Milesian-type world-system was constructed with a number of features which may have been original to Parmenides, such as a spherical earth supported by its own equilibrium, and the moon gaining its light from the sun.

Parmenides' basic premises in the 'Way of Truth' were a challenge for those who came after him, for if plurality and change were to be accepted then counter-arguments would be needed to establish them. His own position was bolstered by two supporters. Zeno of Elea set out to demonstrate that assumptions of plurality and change would lead to conclusions no less paradoxical than Parmenides' seemed to be, and to this end proposed his famous puzzles: if there are many things they would have no size and simultaneously be infinitely big, they would be of a definite and an indefinite number, and if moving they would be simultaneously moving and at rest, or unable to traverse a given distance or overtake an object moving more slowly (the problem of 'Achilles and the Tortoise'). The difficulties these puzzles raised about infinity, infinite divisibility and the division of 'now' were to have important effects on the mathematical principles of cosmology. Parmenides' second supporter, Melissus of Samos, came from Pythagoras' homeland, and successfully commanded a fleet there against Athens. He caused further trouble philosophically when he raised questions about the 'emptiness' of space, the outer edge of a limited cosmos, extension involving body and the minimum change which would result in the destruction of the whole.

Empedocles was from Acragas in Sicily, roughly contemporary in the fifth century with Zeno and Melissus. Like Parmenides he wrote in epic hexameters, in which he attempted a compromise between observed cosmic change and his predecessor's denial of it by postulating a limited plurality of four basic elements – earth, water, air and fire – which permanently kept their character, and could not be increased or diminished in any way. Apparent generation, alteration and destruction were to be explained by the arrangements and rearrangements of the four which were initiated by contrary principles of attraction and repulsion working on them. The whole was described as a self-contained sphere passing through cycles of rest and change, with recurring stages of conflict which produced various forms of life. The birth of an individual was merely a combining of elemental parts, and death their disintegration, with the components then being available for further combinations. It seemed that it was possible for some particularly harmonious blends to survive for a time as independent units – perhaps even as rational gods – within the limits of the whole, but eventually they would be drawn once again into a world of conflict.

Anaxagoras was slightly older than Empedocles but wrote later. He came from the Ionian city of Clazomenae, and was the first of the philosophers to find a home in Athens, where his book, in prose, was for sale in the market. Eventually he was prosecuted and exiled on charges of impiety which included his statements that the sun was a hot stone and the moon made of earth. His cosmogony started from a complete and uniform fusion of all the elementary components, infinitely divisible into homogeneous parts; in his language 'all things were together' (fr. 1) and 'everything was in everything' (fr. 2). A vortex arose as a result of the initiation of the working of 'Mind' (*nous*) on this material, which caused heavy parts to come to the centre and the lighter to move outward to encircle it, so that a recognisable world-system then emerged. Anaxagoras was a pioneer in having an indefinitely expanding universe (as the 'ripples' from the vortex ever widen) rather than one which had reached its limits in an enclosed system.

A universe without limit in which an infinite number of atoms were in constant random movement characterised the next and last of these early systems, that of the atomists Leucippus and Democritus. Although they are roughly contemporary with Socrates and the sophists of the fifth century, their ideas belong more to the pluralism of Empedocles and Anaxagoras, and so they are generally classified as Presocratics. Little is known of Leucippus, and even in antiquity he was quoted in conjunction with Democritus. The atoms they postulated as the basic constituents of things (the word *atoma* means units 'unable to be cut') were eternal, immutable, physically if not theoretically indivisible, and with no qualitative differences. Apparent differences were to be attributed to convention (*nomos*), for in reality there were only atoms and void ('empty space' or *kenon*). Since atoms were too small to be seen and void was intangible, the senses could not be a reliable guide to how things really are, but provided only a 'bastard' kind of knowledge tied to the transitory and subjective circumstances of the perceiver. As with Anaxagoras, the atomists supposed that the present world-system arose from a vortex, when a group of atoms were caught in a rotation, with like then attracted to like, the heavier to the centre and the lighter outwards. But since according to their theory material and space were limitless, there would be not only this world-system, but others like it continually arising and disintegrating elsewhere and at other times.

After the atomists the history of cosmology was virtually suspended, and no new ideas emerged until the writings of Plato in the early fourth century BC. Diogenes from Apollonia, a colony on the Black Sea, stitched together a patchwork of previous theories, concentrating in particular on Anaximenes' concept of air as a single substrate. Another writer, similarly interested in amalgamating Anaximenes' theory of air to later views, and said at one time to have taught Socrates, was Archelaus of Athens. Ideas like these, along with some of those put forward by the sophists, were caricatured by Aristophanes in the representation of Socrates in his comedy *The Clouds*. In another relevant comedy, *The Birds*, he combined ridicule of contemporary notions of political utopias with a hotchpotch of cosmogonies in the 'Cloud-cuckoo-land' he invented between sky and earth.

The sophists were teachers or 'professors' who travelled the Greek world in the fifth century BC offering an education in statecraft and public-speaking for young men with a political career ahead of them. They concentrated, like Socrates, on issues concerned with human affairs and the foundations of ethics. Some, such as Hippias of Elis, were polymaths, and would also lecture on science subjects. In three main areas the influence of these sophists had wider implications: in the controversies over natural law and conventional justice, in their interest in the origins of the human race, of language and of societies, and in their moral and epistemological scepticism. In these they were influential in forcing a division between those who could accept a finite universe governed by reason and law, and those favouring one that was unlimited, with no overall purpose, but where everything happens 'by chance'.

The strongest stand against moral relativism and a purposeless cosmos was that taken by Plato (the 'Broad-shouldered'), born about 429 BC into the Athenian aristocracy, and founder of the first European university, the Academy, where (apart from two visits to

Sicily) he taught and wrote for forty years until his death in 347 BC. All Plato's works meant for publication survive, but there is no record of his lectures or communications with the students at the Academy. A tantalising reference to a famous lecture *On the Good* records that it turned out to be mainly on pure mathematics, and reports of 'unwritten doctrines' from Aristotle and others are the source of much controversy. The works that are extant, twenty-five dialogues and the *Apology* (Socrates' defence at his trial), reveal Plato as the greatest master of Greek prose in all its variety; the sharp philosophy is frequently masked by the charm, elegance, clarity and ease of his style. Nowhere is this tension between the philosopher and the poet-craftsman shown more fully than in the myths, and it is in the form of myth, which belongs to the area of opinion and the unverifiable, that Platonic views on cosmology are mainly to be found.

Socrates is the narrator of the three myths of the soul, which come at the end of the *Phaedo* and *Republic* and in the course of the *Phaedrus*. In each dialogue Plato offers different proofs to demonstrate the immortality of the soul, and follows these with a myth which accounts for those features that would not be susceptible to logical treatment – judgement on the individual life and the meting out of punishments and rewards. These events clearly do not take place in the known world, and instead they are given a cosmic setting of power and beauty. The *Phaedo* has a strange geography of the 'true earth', related to our world as this is to the one under the sea, of pure colours and bright jewels; the people there 'see the sun and moon as they really are' and above that are 'habitations even more beautiful'. In the *Phaedrus* myth the gods are represented as encircling the outer heaven in chariots, joined for a greater or less time by the souls of philosophic mortals, 'looking down at what we now say exists, and gazing up to that which truly does' (249c). The myth in *Republic*, known as the Myth of Er from its narrator, includes a model of the cosmos as the 'spindle of necessity' with whorls representing the orbits of the planets, and a Siren on each 'borne around in its revolution and uttering one sound, one note, and from all the eight comes the concord of a single harmony' (617b). This is the first detailed description of 'the harmony of the spheres', although the concept goes back to the Pythagoreans of more than a century earlier.

The most famous narrative of the cosmos however is the myth delivered as a monologue by Timaeus in Plato's dialogue of that name. As with the area of life after death, the origins and structure of the cosmos are subjects that belong with what may be probable rather than what is true, and are to be explored, not with the cut and thrust of dialectical argument, but through the medium of 'a likely tale' – not by *logos* but in myth. The *Timaeus* is so innovative and fertile in ideas, and had such influence on later cosmological thinking, that discussions of the various themes in ancient cosmology need to take account of it continually.

Plato also has an interesting myth involving backward running time which is told in the *Statesman*, and there is a section on planetary movement in his last work, the *Laws*. An essay called *Epinomis* is preserved in the Platonic corpus, but, because some of the cosmological details contained in it are at variance with the *Timaeus*, its authorship is disputed. The *Epinomis* introduces a fifth element, *aithēr*, in addition to earth, water, air and fire, and then gives a vastly increased diameter to the outer sphere of the *aithēr* with the other ratios expanding in proportion, so that, at last the sun was recognised as being larger than the earth.

A number of bright mathematicians were associated with Plato and the Academy. Archytas of Tarentum, a Pythagorean, was said to have been the founder of mechanics, to have worked on musical theory and to have solved the problem of doubling the cube. Theodorus and his pupil Theaetetus advanced the study of these and similar puzzles, and produced a comprehensive theory of irrational numbers. The star scholar however was Eudoxus who came from Cnidos in Asia Minor; he studied under Archytas, and also spent some time in Athens in loose collaboration with the Academy. Eudoxus did research in the mathematics of irrationals and infinitesimals, and in astronomy. On his return home he built his own observatory in Cnidos, made practical observations and produced his famous hypothesis for the retrograde movements of the planets. This included a backward turning movement for them on their path through the zodiac like a figure of eight which he called a *hippopede*, i.e., a 'horse-fetter'. The hypothesis was further developed by Callippus, another great mathematical astronomer, who came from Cyzicus but also studied in Athens. Heraclides travelled from the Black Sea to join the Academy, and there produced theories about the daily rotation of the earth on its axis, and also about the relative positions and paths of the planets, with an especial interest in Mars and Venus. The freedom of movement of these scholars and their pupils as they travelled great distances around the lands of the Mediterranean contributed to the reputation of the fourth century

BC as one of the great eras of European learning for its intellectual excitement, exchange of ideas and advances in mathematics, astronomy and cosmology.

Aristotle was the most famous member of the Academy, a student there for twenty years before he went back to Macedon as tutor to Alexander, and then finally returned to Athens to found his own institute of higher education, the Lyceum. This building had a covered walkway, a *peripatos* in which to stroll up and down, so that Aristotle and his followers were often called 'Peripatetics'.

Aristotle wrote a number of pieces in a literary style for general publication, mostly philosophic dialogues, but these have survived only in fragments. Some of the writings that have come down under his name, especially the collections of basic material, were probably co-authored by researchers in the Lyceum, or derived from classwork. The genuine corpus however covers all areas of learning – logic, physics, metaphysics, cosmology, meteorology, psychology, biology, ethics, rhetoric, politics and literary criticism. The treatises are extraordinary in the form in which they are preserved; they consist of notes, memoranda, catalogues, summaries, commentaries, argument and counter-argument, in which Aristotle wrestles with his predecessors' ideas and the various possibilities opened up by his own theories. But, in the main, on whatever theme Aristotle has in hand, the discussion is deep and subtle; apparent obscurity often arises from the speed of his thought and the need at the same time to forge a new language for what was being expressed. The backtracking, recasting, disregard of formal grammar, rejection of conclusions reached, admissions of doubt, continual awareness of possible objections and the sheer concentration of argument in the Aristotelian treatises provide a unique insight into the actual workings of a great intellect.

The books by Aristotle most relevant to cosmology are parts of the *Physics* for the principles of mathematics, causation, change and movement, *On Generation and Corruption* on elements, the three books of *Meteorology* (the fourth was probably written by his pupil Strato), and in particular the specialist work known as *De Caelo*. Another key text is the twelfth book of the *Metaphysics* (usually referred to by its Greek number as *Metaphysics Lambda*) which deals with primary substance, the rotation of the planets and the divine unmoved mover as first cause. This is written with more care than usual, and is rounded off with a quotation from Homer, so perhaps it was a separate essay or lecture, although even here it is probable that he wrote the eighth chapter (on the fifty-five celestial spheres) some time afterwards. A book with the title *De Mundo – On the Universe –* is preserved in the Aristotelian corpus, but is generally agreed to be by a later author.

Aristotle considered the world-system to be in a 'steady state', abiding by the same basic pattern, without beginning or end. He allowed continual variation and oscillating change on the earth and below the moon, for this was produced by the natural and enforced movement of the four elements and their transformations, but none in the vast and distant upper regions. Here he introduced the concept of the fifth element to account for the eternal and unvarying character of the celestial bodies in their orbits, where even the 'wanderings' of the planets (as Eudoxus had shown) could be explained by regular though complex circular patterns. The stars and planets were not only spherical, eternal and constant in their movement but, because they were made of *aithēr*, they were also to be considered intelligent and divine. Aristotle agreed with Plato in this and in his overall concept of an enclosed geocentric cosmos, rationally ordered and maintained.

Aristotle was succeeded in the Lyceum by his student Theophrastus, whose main extant works deal with the classification and physiology of plants, but there are fragments preserved from his *Metaphysics* which are critical of Aristotle's world-system, and also an interesting monograph *On Fire*. Other Peripatetics of the time were Eudemus, who recorded scientific developments in a series of *Histories*, Euclid, not the mathematician but an astronomer, author of a work called *Phaenomena* of which the Preface is extant, and Strato, head of the Lyceum after Theophrastus, who was responsible for a theory of space which challenged that of Democritus' continuous void.

As well as the Academy and the Lyceum, there was a third great centre of learning in the ancient world known as the Museum, founded in Alexandria in Egypt by Ptolemy Soter around 280 BC in conjunction with the great library there. Its first and perhaps most famous scholar was Strato's pupil Aristarchus of Samos, 'the ancient Copernicus'. His essay *On the Sizes and Distances of the Sun and Moon* is one of the most complex Greek texts extant, applying to astronomy principles of arithmetic, geometry and trigonometry in the calculation of the dimensions of the bodies; he also further refined time-keeping and the calendar. But Aristarchus is most famous for his hypothesis that the earth rotates on its own axis in an oblique circle around the sun within a spherical cosmos vastly greater than any yet envisaged, a hypothesis that was immediately challenged by his contemporary Cleanthes the Stoic as an act of impiety; this brilliant heliocentric theory in the end was followed only in Babylonia, by Seleucus. Another famous Alexandrian, Apollonius of Perga, was also a mathematician, remembered for his work in seven books *On Cones*, which derived the three types of cone from a common model, and provided the principles of stereographic representation used in armillary spheres. He also wrote on planetary motion in epicycles and on 'eccentric' circles (i.e., off from the earth as centre) for solar variations and differences in the seasons.

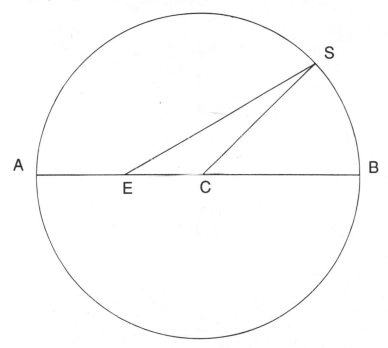

Figure 4 The eccentric circle.
The eccentric circle (i.e., off centre from the earth E on the diameter AB) gives the path of the sun around the hypothetical centre C, calculated from the 'angle of equation' ESC.

Eratosthenes of Cyrene was a further notable mathematician–astronomer who studied at Alexandria in the third century BC, where he was in charge of the library there, and was known as the 'pentathlete' of science. He was the first to produce a *Chronology* of historical events, and another of philosophers; he wrote on arithmetic (including the 'sieve' for prime numbers), on geometry, geography (including ethnography) as well as on literary criticism; the work called *Katasterismoi* (*Transformations into Stars*) describes the mythology of the constellations. His study of the earth was particularly important, for he applied mathematical principles to the sphere of the earth, dividing the five zones further into longitudes and latitudes, and used the principle of similar triangles to calculate (with surprising accuracy) the circumference of the earth, and from this calculation, along with the work of Aristarchus, the approximate distances of the sun and moon from the earth were inferred.

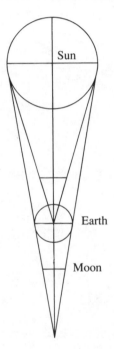

Figure 5 Distances of sun and moon from earth.
Calculated by Hipparchus at the moon's eclipse, from the similar triangles on the radii of the aligned spheres of sun, earth and moon, using the earth's radius and the angle of the shadow cone.

Last in this group was the most famous mathematician of all, Archimedes of Syracuse. He came from the West to Alexandria, but eventually returned to his home-town, where he terrified the Romans who were besieging it by inventing a series of powerful war machines against them. The Romans however were eventually successful, and Archimedes, engrossed in his diagrams, was killed by one of the soldiers for not showing sufficient respect. The memorial on his tomb was of a sphere circumscribed by a cylinder with the related ratios, the discovery that pleased him the most. His particular importance in the history of cosmology was the construction of an armillary sphere (which Cicero saw and admired) and an essay explaining the principles of its construction. Also of interest is his *Sand-Reckoner*, a system for calculating very large numbers (in this case the number of grains of sand that could be contained in a finite cosmos), and his understanding of the leverage of weights which led to the boast that, given a place to stand, he could move the whole earth.

Among the immediate successors of Socrates had been the Cynics (or 'dog' philosophers) who first advocated the concept of the 'cosmopolitan'. This viewed the individual not as a citizen of a particular state but of the whole world, and in turn the cosmos was the individual *polis* writ large – the city 'of gods and humans'. The Cynics' ethical and political views were taken over and expanded by the Stoics, who grafted them on to their physics (based on an adapted form of the fire and *logos* of the Presocratic Heraclitus) and the advances made in logic and dialectical skills by other Socratics, notably the Megarians.

The founder of Stoicism was Zeno of Citium in Cyprus, who came to Athens in 313 BC and set up a school in the Painted Colonnade ('Stoa Poikilē', hence the name 'Stoic'). He worked out a complete philosophy in which logic and physics were the foundation studies for a system of ethics which had virtue as the only good, vice the only evil and all else a matter of indifference. His successor was Cleanthes, who emphasised the life, intelligence and divinity of the cosmos; it was he who was quick to attack Aristarchus for his impiety in making the earth a minor satellite of the sun. Stoic philosophy was then systemised and expounded in the voluminous writings of Chrysippus from Cilicia, the third head of the school. Unfortunately, as with the Presocratics, the work of the early Stoics is preserved mainly in fragments, quotations and summaries, and additionally in later Latin versions. This material, despite its inadequacies, is extensive enough for an understanding of the main concepts and arguments of Stoicism.

The Stoics kept to the tradition of a spherical world-system, the

31

earth at the centre and the celestial bodies in circular movement around it. The whole was thought to be corporeal, but surrounded by void which was regularly drawn in to it and then exhaled. Two concepts in their cosmology were of particular significance. The first was the doctrine of *pneuma* (basically meaning 'warm breath') which involved a pioneer version of the continuum theory of matter, and countered the atomists' hypothesis of discrete units. *Pneuma* was understood to be a force totally informing matter and making of any particular body a dynamic entity with constant interaction between 'tensions' in its structure. This resulted in the concept of 'sympathy' through the whole of nature, in which any change however slight in any part of the whole affected all the other parts, so that the internal dynamism of the cosmic structure was thought to be continually shifting, while the whole remained ordered and coherent. The second important feature of Stoic physics was the temporal application of this spatial continuum, with a consequent ordered cycle of trans-mutations. These took the form of the shorter circuits of sun and moon to give day, month and year, and the larger rotation of the planets for the 'great year', the summer of which was marked by the ascendancy of fire. At this time the transitions through the cosmic seasons brought the state of *pneuma* to its hottest and driest when it absorbed the material of the universe into a periodic, universal 'burn-up', the *ekpyrōsis*, after which the tension was reduced, and the cycle began anew in a series of endless repetitions.

A strong motivation for the development of Stoic physics was the reinterpretation of its rival theory, the atomism of Democritus, by Epicurus, who was born in Samos in 341 BC. After various travels Epicurus installed himself in Athens in a house with a Garden, which became a permanent school of philosophers, in competition with the Academy, the Lyceum and the Stoa, and the first to admit women. Epicurus produced his own 'theory of everything', which covered the three main areas of the criteria of perception, physics and ethics. In his revision of atomism, which is relevant for his cosmology, he recognised that, since atoms have to be characterised by weight (as well as shape and size), their movement would be linear through the void. To allow for an initial move to start the formation of world-systems, Epicurus supposed that an atom could 'swerve', i.e., make an instantaneous, random minimum deviation in its free-fall. This would then have knock-on effects on the surrounding atoms and start a vortex of complementary rotations, which could lead to the main divisions of a cosmos. In other respects the earlier atomism was reaffirmed: atoms were infinite in number, and moved through an infinite extent of void in an eternity of time, *kosmoi* were continually being formed, increasing and then degenerating in the extent of boundless space, and within any particular system atoms and void were the sole constituents of everything. Two implications of the theory that were emphasised by Epicurus and his followers were, first, that soul also was assumed to have an atomic structure which disintegrated with the body at death, and, second, that there could be no divine creation, care or governance of the universe or any of its parts.

The Hellenistic philosophies became known in Rome from the third century BC onwards as the result of various movements. Ideas from the Greek colonies in south Italy started to spread northwards, conquests in the mainland brought back Greeks to be schoolmasters and private tutors, and adolescents from the wealthier Roman families travelled to the centres of learning in the Greek world, touring the schools at Athens, Alexandria, Pergamum and Rhodes. The two philosophies that had most impact on Rome were Epicureanism and Stoicism, and these were made widely available through their presentation in Latin in the last decades of the Republic by Lucretius and Cicero.

Epicureanism was a complete and comprehensive system passed on more or less intact over the centuries. Lucretius, in other respects an unknown figure, was its great Roman advocate, and his unfinished poem is one of the main sources for ancient atomism; otherwise all that survives from Epicurus himself are three letters containing a summary of his theories on atomism, meteorology and ethics, a list of *Key Doctrines* and various aphorisms and fragments. Lucretius used his poetic gifts to popularise the complexities of Epicurus' scientific achievements and so to drive home the fundamental message of the possibility of a happy life for all, free of the fears of divine interference during life and of suffering after death. His task however was doubly difficult, for the Latin had to be forcibly adapted to the Greek hexameter, and the technical terms were hard to translate. But he saw the task as a joyful one, and compared his poetry to 'the pleasant honey of the Muses', which sweetens the sometimes harsh truths of an atomic universe. The relevant books of his *De rerum natura* (*On the Nature of Things*) are the first, which establishes the basic axioms that only atoms and void exist, the second dealing with the nature and movements of atoms (including the 'swerve'), the fourth on the formation of this particular world-system and the threat of its eventual collapse, and some of the meteorological phenomena in the sixth.

Stoicism, in contrast to the 'package deal' of Epicureanism, was continually being modified and adapted. Two Greeks were key figures in its introduction to Rome and its Romanisation: Panaetius, who introduced the philosophy to the intellectuals who gathered round the younger Scipio, and his pupil, the great Posidonius of Rhodes, but again the writings of neither are extant. The main emphasis shifted to practical achievements, especially to the life of political service and physical endurance which appealed to the Roman character. It is these aspects on which Cicero concentrated in a series of philosophical essays which he produced during his enforced retirement from Rome in 45 and 44 BC, and which have survived. One of these (known as *On the Ends of Good and Evil*) contains in its third book the famous Stoic argument for the cosmos being 'a city of gods and men' (3.64), in which all human beings are literally cosmopolitans, and as such have duties to one another as to fellow citizens. Cicero also translated parts of Plato's dialogues into Latin, including a large section of the *Timaeus*, and these translations contributed to Plato's influence on medieval cosmology. Cicero's most relevant original text however is the mythic account of the geography of the earth and the structure of the cosmos given in the 'Dream of Scipio', which concludes *On the Republic* (in imitation of Plato's 'Myth of Er' at the end of his *Republic*) and which survived as a separate work. Scipio relates that in his dream he was taken by his older relative, Africanus, to a position in the sky where he could look up to the larger spheres of the stars and down to the earth; the Roman Empire as it appears from this standpoint is put into perspective, being seen as only a small transient part of a minor planet. The Dream also incorporates the explanation of the harmony of the spheres and an astral eschatology.

Cosmogonies of a reputable nature (i.e., along Platonic and Stoic lines) were popular with Roman poets, a fashion that went back to such Hellenistic writings as the opening book of the *Argonautica* by Apollonius of Rhodes. There is a full-scale version by Ovid at the beginning of his *Metamorphoses*, since the imposition of order on chaos by god and nature is the first and greatest 'metamorphosis' of those which the poem recounts. Vergil narrates a minstrel song on the beginning of the world in his sixth *Eclogue* and in the first book of the *Aeneid*; the ghost of Anchises gives a more detailed account to his son Aeneas in the sixth book of the epic as a preliminary to the patriotic theme of the Pageant of Roman Heroes awaiting birth. In his earlier work, the four books of *Georgics*, Vergil had reverted to the form of a farming manual after the style of Hesiod's *Works and Days*, and, as with Hesiod, the times of year for the various tasks were given by constellations in formulaic phrases. Vergil writes, for example, of when 'the shining-white bull with gilded horns opens the year and the setting Dog-star sinks opposite him' (1.217–18) for a date that was by then generally known as the Ides of April. Of more interest is the passage later in the first book (1.231–51) which is an adaptation of the cosmic structure of Eratosthenes (and incorporates the line from Homer on the constellations of the Bear). It describes the heavens encircling a fixed, spherical earth of five zones from the north to the south poles, with people in the antipodes:

> when the panting horses of the rising sun first breathe on us,
> there, in the red of evening, Vesper kindles his late light

but the effect is ruined by the attempt to find a place as well for the river Styx and the world of the dead.

A Greek poem from the third century on astronomy, the *Phaenomena* by Aratus of Cilicia, enjoyed a vogue in Rome; parts of it were also translated by Cicero, and later (surprisingly perhaps) by Augustus' heir Germanicus while he was on military service, who corrected some of the factual errors in the original. At about the same time the senator Marcus Manilius was writing his poem the *Astronomica*, more astrology than cosmology, in five books of Latin hexameters. A generation later came the writings of Nero's tutor, the younger Seneca, which include *Natural Questions* and the philosophic letters to Lucilius, and the extensive *Natural History* of the elder Pliny, the second book of which is concerned with cosmology.

The remaining writers to be considered were all Greek or writing in Greek. Astronomy had been one of the many interests of Posidonius, and he had achieved the most accurate calculation yet for the diameter of the sun and its distance from the earth. Two of his successors continued these interests: Geminus who produced a compendium on the calendar, the celestial sphere and the planetary orbits, called *Introduction to Phaenomena*, and Cleomedes who some time later wrote a work called *On the Circular Movement of Celestial Bodies*. The widely travelled polymath Plutarch, born about AD 46, crossed between the Greek and Roman worlds, being both an Athenian citizen and holding Roman office. From his encyclopaedic output one essay is particularly important, an anti-Stoic cosmology known as *On the Face Appearing on the Orb of the Moon*. A generation later came Theon of Smyrna with a commentary on Plato involving arithmetic, harmonics and astronomy. His contemporary was the great Ptolemy of Alexandria, whose works are still extant in Greek, and in translations into Arabic and Latin.

Ptolemy's longest work, the *Amalgest* (or 'Great Collection'), survived as the accepted description of the cosmos until it was challenged in the sixteenth century by Copernicus and Galileo. It rejected the startling heliocentrism of Aristarchus and went back to the description by the earlier Hipparchus, itself still substantially that of Plato and Aristotle. In this the human race was centrally placed, on a static earth at the mid-point of the cosmos, the planets revolved around it in sequence, and at the circumference was the *empyrean* with the fixed stars encircling and containing the whole in a system of elegant order. An account survives for a working model – the *Planispherium* or armillary sphere – based on Ptolemy's own refinements of the complex trigonometrical calculations which were involved in the theory of the planetary movements. Ptolemy also worked on optics, produced an eight-book *Geography* with maps and, in addition, a *Catalogue* of nearly 2,000 stars which he had personally observed and identified.

This summary finishes with two other quite disparate figures from the second century AD. The first was Lucian, a travelling sophist and profusive writer, who, in his *True History*, described a fantasy journey to the moon in the most famous piece of space fiction from antiquity. The second, the Roman Emperor Marcus Aurelius, composed a work, *To Himself* (also known as *Meditations*), during his long military campaigns. In this book he reflected from a mainly Stoic standpoint on human life and fortune, and, when he touched on questions of natural science, he was inclined to interpret cosmology in theological terms. This was also the tendency of Plotinus, the Neoplatonists and some of the great commentators on Aristotle, but these lie outside the period, from the eighth century BC to the second AD, on which this work focuses.

3

MODELS, MYTHS AND METAPHORS

Cosmology is neither a science of description nor of explanation. Observational astronomy maps and describes what can be seen in the sky by the most powerful radio-telescopes or recorded by man-made satellites and microwave detectors, but these are ultimately subject to the limitations of human perception and calculation. Galaxy formations 300 million light-years in diameter have been noted, as have quasars so distant that their age goes into billions of years, yet the spatial and temporal 'whole of things' remains elusive. Explanations by principles of physics, for example, or probability predictions or chaos and catastrophe theories are similarly inadequate; they may help with constituents or patterns, but the whole, while it needs to be made intelligible, cannot be brought under general laws because it is by definition unique. The best approach is by means of models of various kinds, which can assist in the simplification and interpretation of the complexities of the observed data. As Milton Munitz (in the article on Cosmology in *The Encyclopedia of Philosophy*) concludes: 'What is to be understood by "the universe" can only be approached and identified through the use of models, not independently of them.'

The complex formulae of the models of contemporary astrophysicists are a far cry from anything in ancient Greece, but even so Helene Tuzet (in the *Dictionary of the History of Ideas* s.v. Cosmology) finds it enlightening today to adopt the dichotomy set up by two early Greek philosophers when she analyses cosmic images as Parmenidean or Heraclitean. She concludes that, 'despite constant progress, our knowledge will probably remain, even in our time, indirect and limited; speculation and imagination will both probably continue to enjoy more or less an open field'. Speculation and imagination the Greek cosmologists had in abundance, and this is shown particularly in the wide variety of models and illustrations which they used in a cosmological context.

First is the basic Homeric model of the universe as a round house with the earth as its circular floor, the sky as a disc of comparable size above it, and the two held apart by pillars situated at the Straits of Gibraltar. In mythology they were kept in place by the Titan Atlas:

> who knows the depths of every sea, and himself holds the high columns which keep earth and sky apart.
>
> (Odyssey 1.52–4)

In other versions he supported the sky on his 'brazen back' (Euripides *Ion* 1–2), or as in Hesiod:

> Atlas, forced by harsh necessity, at the ends of the earth keeps up the broad sky, which rests on his head and tireless hands.
>
> (Theogony 519–21)

Because the hero Herakles briefly took over the burden, with one foot in Africa and the other in Europe, the Straits of Gibraltar were known as 'the pillars of Hercules', and the ocean beyond was named after Atlas as the 'Atlantic Sea'.

Another part of the Homeric picture showed the freshwater river Oceanos encircling the disk of earth, and then sky as a hemisphere of bronze or iron covering it; the sun, moon and stars (except for the Bears) were thought to rise from Ocean in the east, set in the west and then move round or under the river to rise the next day. A more literal 'sun boat' featured in Egyptian myth: the sun-god Re' traversed the sky standing in a boat with gods or stars behind him; at night he rowed the boat back round by the waters, or it was pulled by the spirits of the dead. The sun could also be envisaged as climbing to the zenith and descending in a chariot, driven by the god Helios himself, or by his daughters ('with axles blazing' in Parmenides' *Proem*), and once, disastrously, by his son Phaethon.

The distances involved were first calculated by timing free-falling objects. In the *Iliad* Hephaestus was said to have been thrown by Zeus out of Olympus (the main home of the gods which even in Homer was more often in some indefinite area of the sky than on the mountain in Thrace), and he kept falling from sunrise to sunset before he landed on the island of Lemnos (*Iliad* 1.590–4). In Hesiod, Olympus was as far above the earth as Tartarus below it, with the distances given:

An anvil of bronze, falling from the sky, would fall nine nights and days, and reach the earth on the tenth; and if the anvil fell from earth, would fall another nine nights and days, and come to Tartarus on the tenth.

(Theogony 721–5)

Lucretius the Epicurean, on the other hand, used the movement of lightning, the fastest travelling object, to help the reader to try to comprehend what limitless space would mean:

The nature of space and the extent of void is such that bright lightning could not cross it in its course if its path went on continually through time nor even diminish the distance still to cover – so far extends in every direction without end the inexhaustible resource of the universe.

(1.1002–7)

But why does the earth itself not fall downwards? A variety of models and simulations were used to solve this basic problem. Heavy objects can rest on water but not air, so Thales, according to Aristotle, thought that the earth stays as it is because it floats on water 'like a log or something like that' (*De Caelo* 294a28–34), but without asking the further question of what then supports the water. Xenophanes supposed that the earth just goes down indefinitely. A breakthrough came with Anaximander, the second Milesian, who put forward the idea that the earth was like a cylinder in shape, with a depth three times its breadth, describing it as 'rounded, like the drum of a column; we stand on one of its surfaces, and there is another opposite' ([Plutarch] *Stromata* 2). The Greeks built their columns upwards in drum-shaped sections one above the other; each section or 'drum' would therefore have a plane round surface top and bottom. Such a shape also suggested to Anaximander the concept of antipodes (the word means literally 'feet opposite') with people living on the underside 'upside down'. Furthermore:

the earth stays aloft, not supported by anything but staying where it is because it is the same distance from everything.

(Hippolytus *Refutations* 1.6.3)

The model here is of a spherical container with the drum-shaped earth at rest in the centre, held there according to what is known as 'the principle of sufficient reason', i.e., if there is no cause for an object to move in one direction rather than another, it stays where it is.

Anaximander's ideas were unacceptable to his successor Anaximenes, who returned to a disc-shaped earth, now compared to a table, with the hemispherical vault of the sky fitting over it. The justification for this, which was sufficient to convince Anaxagoras and Democritus as well, is given by Aristotle:

the flatness of the earth is the reason for it staying where it is, because it does not cut the air underneath but covers it like a lid, as flat bodies are seen to do; they are not easily moved even by wind because of their resistance.

(*De Caelo* 294b13–21)

If the air was thus enclosed and compressed beneath the flat earth Anaximenes thought that the air could then 'ride on it' ([Plutarch] *Stromata* 3). Anaxagoras developed the idea further by suggesting that the air could bear the weight of earth 'like water in a clepsydra' ([Aristotle] *Problems* 914b10), for the air would press against the earth in the enclosed cosmos and stop it falling, in much the same way as it could press against the perforations of the clepsydra and prevent the water flowing out. (The clepsydra had a narrow opening at the top and a perforated base; when filled with liquid and the opening plugged, it could transfer the liquid from one container to another. Empedocles adopted its mechanism to explain the reciprocal movements of blood and air in respiration.) Another illustration Anaximenes used to show that compressed air could bear weight was that of felting, whereby layers of wool were strengthened by being pressed together, soaked and heated, i.e., 'steamed'.

However the mathematically-minded Pythagoras preferred to return to Anaximander's scheme. He realised that a body 'held aloft' and equidistant from every part of the circumference of a surrounding sphere would itself have to be spherical, and this then would be the shape of the earth. A spherical earth is also attributed to Parmenides and Empedocles, but Pythagoras may have been the pioneer. Later Pythagoreans posited a central fire, but the model at first is geocentric, with sun, moon and probably stars also spherical, and rotating beneath a fixed heaven around the stationary earth. It is reported as such by Plato in the *Phaedo*:

If the earth is a sphere in the middle of the heaven, it does not need air or anything else like that to stop it falling, but the uniformity of the heaven (the *ouranos*) in every direction and the equilibrium of the earth is reason enough to hold it in place;

for anything in a state of equilibrium placed in the centre of what is uniform will not incline in one direction rather than another but stay as it is without inclining.

(108e–109a)

Thus if one could look at the earth from above it would appear as a ball made from twelve pieces of different colours. But this account in the *Phaedo* is in a myth, and comes with a warning that it cannot be true, only probable at best. Even so we are misled by appearances, Plato continues, for we actually live in a hollow of the earth, sitting round the Mediterranean like frogs round a pond, and there are other hollows like this where water, clouds and air collect. The real surface is above, and would be seen as 'purer and more beautiful' if only we could push our heads into that bright air, as fishes look up at our world from the sea. This whole setting is a mythical attempt to reconcile the appearance of the whole Mediterranean basin as a depressed region partly surrounded by mountains (and similar depressions were likely to be elsewhere) with the general requirement of a spherical earth.

Not only did it become standard to acknowledge a spherical earth, but in the third century BC Eratosthenes worked out its circumference. The calculation was based on the distance from Syene to Alexandria, on the same meridian in Egypt, as 5,000 stades. When the sun was directly overhead at Syene, the angle on the sundial at Alexandria subtended an arc one-fiftieth of the circle. The exact figure depends on the length of his unit of measurement, the stade, but if the benefit of the doubt is allowed the result is fairly accurate at approximately 40,000 kilometres.

Cicero, in the 'Dream of Scipio', gave the view of the earth generally accepted by educated Romans in the first century BC. In this the earth is spherical, in the centre of the cosmos, but quite small compared to the celestial bodies. It is divided into five zones: the two most widely separated are icy, the central and broadest zone scorched by the sun's heat, the two temperate zones north and south each have their antipodes. The lands surrounding the Mediterranean Sea can therefore be no more than a quarter of the habitable part, so that the Roman Empire covers only an insignificant area of a small planet, and, given periodic natural disasters, it is unlikely to survive for any length of time.

What of the celestial bodies? Models for their shape, size and movements varied from the simplest to the complexities of Ptolemy's armillary sphere. Most obviously the night sky is 'spangled', so that, as Plato said, it is like a painted ceiling, and the intricate designs (*poikilmata*, literally 'embroideries') in the sky the fairest to be seen (*Republic* 529b–c). Pherecydes told a myth of a cloth or veil embroidered with the features of the world and stretched out on the branches of an oak tree to represent sky and earth. Anaximander, the first philosopher to try to give a more rational account, described sun, moon and stars as the rims or felloes of chariot wheels encircling the drum of the earth obliquely; the sizes and distances of the wheels of sun, moon and stars from the earth are given in mathematical proportion, albeit the simple one of 27, 18 and 9 (and with the wheel of stars wrongly given as the closest). The wheels were thought to be made of fire and surrounded by air which concealed the fire (as in Homer, a god can make a hero invisible by enveloping him in mist), except for an opening 'like the nozzle in a pair of bellows', one opening for the sun and moon rings, and a number of openings for that of the stars (Hippolytus 1.6.4–5; Aetius 2.20.1 and 21.1). Eclipses and phases of the moon could then be explained by the opening being partially or fully closed.

This pattern of wheels and 'nozzles' was immediately rejected by Anaximander's successor, Anaximenes. In Homer the vault of the sky had been given as metallic, of iron or bronze, whereas Anaximenes called it 'crystalline' (*krystalloeidēs*, i.e., 'like ice'), being hard, clear and colourless. He supposed that the fixed stars were fastened on to it 'like nails', and that the whole hemisphere with the stars revolved 'like a skull-cap around the head'. The sun, moon and planets, being broad and flat, floated on the air 'like leaves', but they too were taken round in the skull-cap's rotation; they did not sink beneath the earth but behind mountains in the north, which hid them from view. When Anaximenes speaks of nails, leaves and skull-cap, in some ways he advances on Anaximander's wheels and nozzles in that the celestial bodies are now in the right order and have more intelligible movements, but his concept of a flat earth 'like a lid' is disappointing after Anaximander's 'the drum of a column'. In any case the language of both is naive, but it started cosmology off on its long history of using models in the representation and investigation of phenomena.

Accounts of the sun are particularly interesting in this respect, because of the additional factor of its supposed divinity. In fifth-century Athens Anaxagoras was actually indicted on a charge of impiety for saying that the sun was a hot stone bigger than the

Peloponnese. Even when the cause of eclipses was widely known, Nicias lost the Athenian fleet that he was commanding in Sicily because he saw a lunar eclipse not as a natural event but as an ill omen, sent to delay a strategic withdrawal. Plato gave a complex analysis of the sun in the sixth book of the *Republic* as essential for the nourishment of organisms, as the source of light and the necessary medium for the functioning of the eye, but the purpose of the analysis was to show the sun as child and model of the Form of the Good. In the *Laws* he made it a serious offence to deny the sun's divinity.

Xenophanes was in the Milesian tradition when he said that the sun was made of clouds that are set on fire. Heraclitus saw it as a bowl of fire that burnt out every night, and was then kindled and fuelled again in the east to bring in the next day. Empedocles with more insight spoke of the sun as 'lentiform' (Plutarch *Roman Questions* 288b), both in its lentil-seed shape (i.e., disc-shaped from the front view but an elongated double convex from the side) and in acting as a lens. He explained how the convex surface of the sun facing the *ouranos* attracted its fire and drew it towards itself in a concentrated form; this was then transmitted through the opposite surface of the sun as light and heat to the earth below. At night, when the sun travelled under the earth, the bulk of the earth itself blocked off the light from part of its surface.

As with the sun, there were many ways of representing the moon. In myth the moon was feminine – sister, consort or daughter of the sun – and connected to a great deal of superstition, especially witchcraft and sorcery. The twenty-eight days of its waxing and waning constituted a basic calendar unit, and, in its time-keeping, was obviously connected with the human reproductive cycle. Artemis (later adapted to the Roman Diana) was known as sister to the sun-god Apollo, patroness on earth of childbirth and young girls, in the sky of the moon, and beneath the earth identified with Hecate, goddess of the dead, and honoured at cross-roads. But the physicists put all this aside as they grappled with two particular problems – the moon's reflected light and the cause of eclipses.

Anaximander's model of the moon-wheel allowed for the waxing and waning of the moon when more and less of it was being revealed through the aperture; an eclipse was the total closure. Parmenides similarly (in his *Way of Opinion*) described the moon as made of air and fire, which had separated off from the denser part of the Milky Way and was now encircling the earth like a wreath or headband (*stephanos*). He also realised that the moon obtains its light from the sun, adapting Homer's phrase of a stranger, 'a man from somewhere else' (*allotrion phōs*) for 'a light from somewhere else' (fr. 14). Empedocles used the same phrase, and explained how a lentiform moon collected the sun's light on its upper convex surface, but, since it was made of compressed air, did not refract it, so only a pale reflection of the sun was cast, without its heat or brightness. It moved round the earth and was estimated to be half its size, so that lunar phases and eclipses could be accounted for by the extent to which the moon was overshadowed by the earth, and solar eclipses by the moon coming directly between earth and sun. Anaxagoras said that the moon, like the sun and stars, was a stone torn from the surface of the earth in the initial rotation. Democritus, also starting from a vortex, understood the sun and moon to be earthy lumps initially moving off on independent courses (and perhaps about to start separate systems), but then the sun was ignited and brought into orbit with the moon beneath it. The eventual arrangement for this world-system of earth, water, air and fire he explained as due to the natural tendency of like to move towards like, as birds of a feather flock together, grains are sorted into kinds by riddling and pebbles on a beach are found arranged with all those of similar size and shape together (fr. 164).

The Pythagoreans, on a quite different tack, used formulae as models, or, as Aristotle puts it, 'they believed the principles of mathematics to be the principles of everything'. Aristotle explains at length that:

> since they saw that the attributes and ratios of a musical scale (*harmonia*) can be given in numbers and the complete nature of everything else seems to resemble numbers and they take numbers to be primary in nature as a whole, they supposed that the elements of numbers were the elements of all things and that the whole heaven (*ouranos*) was harmony and number. And in numbers and harmonies they collected and fitted all that they were able to show agreed with the attributes and parts of the *ouranos* and with the whole cosmic arrangement; if there was a gap anywhere, they added something, to make it all cohere, for example the number ten is apparently perfect and contains the whole nature of numbers, so they say that the celestial bodies are ten, but, as we can only see nine, they invent a tenth – the counter-earth.
>
> (*Metaphysics* 985b31–986a11)

The discovery that the primary intervals of Greek music, namely the octave (1:2), the fifth (3:2) and the fourth (4:3), depended on fixed numerical ratios was likely to have been made by Pythagoras himself. The rate of vibration to produce the intervals varies with the length of the string, so that a string twice as long as another vibrates at half the speed to give the bottom note of the octave, and the shorter the top note. The same effect is produced by stopping one string halfway down, and the other ratios can be similarly reproduced on the string's length. We know from Plato that experts in harmonics would 'vex and torture strings and rack them on the pegs' as they tried to distinguish ever finer intervals (*Republic* 531b). Since music depended on such exact proportions two results were thought to follow: first, that mathematical principles were likely to be fundamental in other areas too, where they had not previously been noticed, and, second, that if celestial bodies moved in orbits at fixed intervals it was likely that they would emit concordant notes as they did so – the basis of 'the harmony of the spheres'. For this the eight notes of the octave would be involved, one each for the outer sphere, the five planets (Saturn, Jupiter, Mars, Venus, Mercury) and sun and moon. So it is described in Plato's Myth of Er and at the end of the *Republic*, and in Cicero's adaptation of the myth at the end of his *On the Republic* – the Dream of Scipio.

Further, the influence of number in the model used required ten celestial bodies, since ten was a perfect number and a sacred symbol for the Pythagoreans; it was the sum of 1, 2, 3 and 4, and could be represented geometrically as an equilateral triangle of four units for each side, with the four integers counted from each point as:

In this representation it was called the 'tetractys' and at an early stage was thought to contain within itself 'the whole of number', and as such was particularly honoured. Ten celestial bodies were therefore expected, and because there were only nine (the sphere of the fixed stars, sun, moon, five planets and earth) a tenth, the 'counter-earth', was added. This was Aristotle's slightly flippant reason for their introduction of a tenth body. It is more likely however that the 'counter-earth', an early version of 'dark matter', was introduced to account for eclipses, and something like this was already in Anaximenes' theory, as dark, earthy bodies carried along with the stars (Hippolytus 1.7.5). The Pythagorean system was finally re-organised by Philolaus, who took the momentous step of moving the earth from its position in the middle, and replacing it by a central fire, the 'hearth of the cosmos', with the counter-earth revolving round it, the earth beyond that, then moon, sun, planets and the fixed stars at the periphery.

Plato understood the limitations of models. He says, for example, that a geometer might use diagrams of exquisite elegance, but would think it ridiculous to study them seriously as a way of understanding true mathematical relationships. Even more surprisingly the structures and movements in the visible heavens were said to be irrelevant to theoretical astronomy:

> we shall treat astronomy like geometry, as setting us problems for solution, and ignore the things in the sky if we are going to study astronomy properly, and do something useful with our natural intelligence.
>
> (*Republic* 530b–c)

But at the end of the *Republic*, in the Myth of Er, Plato needed to give some representation of the cosmos as the setting for the journey of the soul after the death of the body, and he used man-made objects for this purpose – a column, a trireme and a spindle. In the myth Er explains how the souls come to a place of judgement in a meadow on the earth's surface, and after a thousand years' journeying, for the good souls through the sky and for the wicked beneath the earth, they move on again:

> and on the fourth day they arrived at a place from which they could see, extending from above through the whole sky and earth a straight light, like a column, very similar to the rainbow, but brighter and purer; and they reached this light when they had travelled for a further day. There, in the middle of the light, they could see the limits of its fastenings stretching from the sky – for it is this light which fastens the sky together, holding together the whole circumference like the main undergirth of a trireme – and from the limits extend the spindle of necessity which keeps the orbits turning; the shaft and hook are made of adamant, and the whorl is of this and other material.
>
> (*Republic* 616b–c)

The meaning of this passage is highly controversial, and the language of simile, metaphor and model is strained to the limit. The place first mentioned is obviously still within walking distance on the earth, and the column of light passes along its surface here. The souls can look up and down the light (as if they had come to the rainbow's end) and see the poles of the outer sphere of the universe, and understand how this is held taut by the column of light acting as the main undergirth of a trireme, fastened at each end and keeping the transverse timbers together. But the column of light then becomes the spindle of Necessity, and what was at first a full-scale representation becomes a small-scale model, small enough to be held on the lap of Necessity and given an occasional turn by the three fates to keep it all in motion. Necessity and the fates here represent the inevitable state of affairs, within the constraints of the mythical narrative.

The whorl of the spindle was more complex than at first appeared as it had eight parts, one fitting into the other around the shaft like hemispherical bowls; the result was to give a cross-section of the cosmos. The outer whorl represents the sphere of the fixed stars, then, moving contrary to it, come the five planets, then the sun and moon and finally the earth stationary at the centre. The eight each have a siren carried round in the orbit and emitting a note, together making 'the harmony of the spheres'.

The *Timaeus* is Plato's great cosmic myth, and many of its details, like those of the spindle of Necessity in the Myth of Er, will be relevant later; here a few general points may be made. Despite being so dismissive of the use of models in the *Republic*, Plato in the *Timaeus* found it impossible to embark on an explanation of the revolutions and counter-revolutions, conjunctions, eclipses and the whole 'dance' of the celestial bodies without one: 'to attempt to tell of all this without a visible representation of the celestial system would be labour in vain' (40d). The 'visible representation' in the *Timaeus* was, first, of an artefact produced according to a model by a craftsman working on formless material, and, second, of a child born of the mother's constituent matter following the form contributed by the father. With the emphasis on divine reason and purpose throughout, Plato's cosmology became subsumed under philosophy, and even, as with Aristotle's *Metaphysics Lambda*, under theology. Furthermore, the insistence on circle and sphere being the most beautiful and most perfect shapes gave undue importance to aesthetics.

The maker of the cosmos in the myth of the *Timaeus* was called a craftsman, a *dēmiourgos*, meaning literally 'worker of the people';

the aristocratic Plato represented the divine maker of the cosmos in terms of an ordinary workman. There is a description at the beginning of the *Cratylus* (389a–d) of how such a workman (a carpenter or a potter) produces his artefact, where the particular point is made that he fashions the material not in imitation of broken or imperfect instances of the required object perceived around him, but following the 'form' in his head and taking into account the use required of the end-product. In a similar way in the *Timaeus* 'since the cosmos is beautiful and the *dēmiourgos* good, he was looking at the eternal', and so the cosmos is a likeness (an *eikōn*) of what is accessible to reason and unchanging, and an account of it correspondingly can be no more than 'likely'.

In the narrative the *dēmiourgos* first made the 'soul' of the cosmos, and in this he acted like a metallurgist. He took a deep bowl (a *kratēr* – used most commonly for mixing water with wine) into which he poured three composite ingredients, named as intermediate existence, sameness and difference (made in each case from a combination of the indivisible and divisible). These were thoroughly mixed so that every part contained all three ingredients. Then, as a metallurgist might do with his alloy, the divine craftsman hammered out a strip, and marked it in proportions corresponding to the squares and cubes of the first three numbers (i.e., 1, 2, 3, 4, 8, 9); these were then filled in with the intervals of the harmonic scales. After this the *dēmiourgos* cut the strip down the middle to make two bands, turned each band on itself, put one inside the other and fastened the ends. The outer band was made the circle of the same, and set moving in one direction to give the orbit of the fixed stars, the other was slit into seven sections, and put into motion in the opposite direction to give the orbits of sun, moon and planets. The soul of the cosmos, thus constituted and divided, was 'invisible, endowed with reason and harmony, the best product of the best craftsman'. The visible body of the world was put within it, and the two fitted together at their centres. Within this compound the soul,

> woven right through from the centre to the furthest heaven (*to eschatos ouranos*) and covering it around from outside and turning round on itself had a divine source and beginning (*archē*) of ceaseless rational life for the whole of time.
>
> (*Timaeus* 34e–37a, 41d)

Outside of his written work Plato set his students in the Academy the task of discovering a model for the uniform and ordered

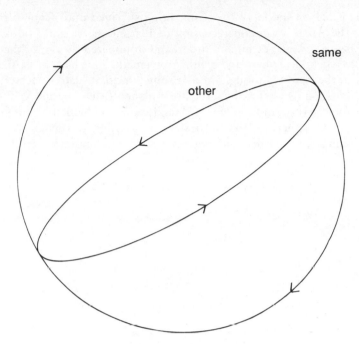

Figure 6 The world soul.
According to the *Timaeus* the outer band (that of the 'same') gives the revolution of the fixed stars, the inner (the 'other') is divided for the planets.

movements of the planets which would 'save the phenomena', i.e., provide a rational explanation for what appeared to be random 'wanderings'. Eudoxus took up the challenge, and approached the problem as a piece of theoretical astrophysics. Using the pattern of the *hippopede* (the figure of eight horse-fetter), he worked out a separate system of spheres for each planet, with a totality of twenty-six; seven more were later added by Callippus. When Aristotle studied the model further he looked on it more as a description of the planets as they actually were, and found a total of fifty-five spheres necessary:

> The result of making the model paramount to the facts and turning it into an actual substance was to complicate the picture to such an extent that no trace of the original intention of simplification remained.
>
> (Sambursky 1956: 62)

The ancient model of the cosmos that survived until Copernicus was the Aristotelian concretisation of Platonic myth and Eudoxan theory, based on reason and order, and dominated by the aesthetic appeal of circle, sphere and orbital movement. This had the earth at rest in the centre (although there is some hint that Plato preferred it revolving on its axis) with moon, lunar planets (Mercury and Venus), sun and the three outer planets (Mars, Jupiter and Saturn) encircling it, and the sphere of the fixed stars in counter-movement at the extremity. The beauty and organisation of this system were thus

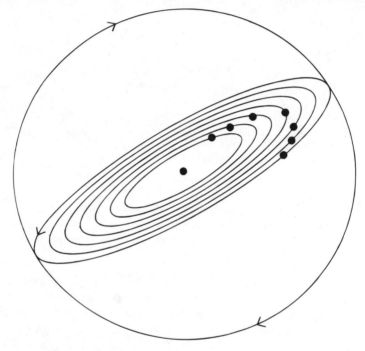

Figure 7 The circles of the planets.
The central earth with the planets encircling it, in order from the centre are Moon, Sun, Mercury, Venus, Mars, Jupiter, Saturn, with the whole enclosed by the sphere of the fixed stars.

taken as proof of divine reason arranging all for the best, and so it prevailed over any attempts to move the earth from the centre. It was not replaced either by the central fire of the Pythagoreans or by the advanced heliocentrism of Aristarchus, which finally put the earth in its proper position as a satellite of the sun.

As observations of the planets became more accurate, the Aristotelian model proved less satisfactory, but, rather than moving the earth, solutions were attempted with a pattern of eccentric circles for the planets, where the centre of the earth did not coincide with the centre of the planetary orbit, or of epicycles, a series of mini-circles traced by the planet as it moved along the broader circuit around the earth. The culmination of this concept of a model that would keep the earth at the centre of a closed cosmos, and still take into account ever-more complex phenomena, came with Ptolemy's construct, and the new device of the equant (a hypothetical centre at which the actual and the ideal were reconciled). This system could then be embodied in the construction of a three-dimensional astrolabe or armilla. The excitement of seeing such a model is reported by Cicero, when he was shown the reconstruction by Posidonius of the armillary sphere of Archimedes:

> When Archimedes showed the movements of the moon, sun, and five planets on a sphere, he did what Plato's god in the *Timaeus* did – he made it possible by a single rotation to control movements at very different speeds. . . . Our friend Posidonius recently constructed one – a single rotation produces the same effect on the sun, moon and five planets as is produced in the sky through one day and night.
> (*Tusculan Disputations* 1.63; *On the Nature of the Gods* 2.88)

The Ptolemaic system was the most sophisticated development of the main trend in ancient cosmology, but there were dissenters within this tradition, not only the Pythagoreans and Hipparchus, who wanted to shift the earth from its central position, but also those following Democritus' lead in abolishing the centre altogether and looking beyond the distant perimeter of this particular world order into an infinity of space. The most famous attempt to establish a boundless universe uses the imagery of a Roman declaration of war, when an official went to the extremity of the home territory and threw a spear over the boundary into the hostile country on the other side. The point may have been made earlier by Archytas of Tarentum, with the instance of an outstretched hand or stick, but Lucretius supplies the main text, using a Roman custom to make a Greek philosophical point:

> If the whole of space had a limit, suppose someone were to run to the furthest boundary, and standing at the very edge throw a spear – do you prefer to say that the spear, hurled with

strength, would continue on its course and fly far, or do you think that something in the way would stop it; you must say one or the other.

(Lucretius 1.968–73)

According to the argument, if an obstacle outside impedes the spear, then the stand was not taken at the very edge and should be further out, which leads to the same question being asked: if there is no obstacle, what happens to the spear? Either way the conclusion abolishes any firm boundary to the cosmos as a whole. Beyond the supposed limit of this world-system, according to the atomists, was 'the empty' (*kenon*), the spatial extension they gave to Parmenides' non-being, which could exist along with 'the full', void as well as atoms.

In the general context of ways of representation comes a wealth of imagery – metaphor, simile, analogy and *paradeigma* – to try to explain the constituents of the cosmos, with the variety and complexity of their phenomena, in simpler terms, and to reconcile the reality of how things are with the perception of them by eyes and ears and the senses generally. A few contrasting examples indicate the working out of some of these early ideas.

The first is Anaximenes' block of ice. The ice is solid, it melts into a liquid, and, when heated this transforms into mist, which, on cooling, is again visible as drops of water that can congeal. The model then became a description of how things are: air, in its neutral state is invisible but essential for life, when thinner and rarer it has the appearance of fire, when thicker and denser that of wind and cloud, then of liquid, and when more compact that of earth and stones, and everything else is from these.

Heraclitus put ordinary objects to cosmic use. He took the bow and lyre as illustrations of the necessary tension between component parts – 'agreeing and disagreeing'. If the string is too tight in relation to the wood or shell it breaks, if too slack the bow does not pull and the lyre is out of tune; a similar tension is essential for the maintenance of the whole (fr. 51). A medicinal barley-drink has to be stirred; if the ingredients rest and separate, there is a failure to function, and so of the world-system (fr. 125). The same road goes up and down, showing, as most things do, an apparent contradiction (fr. 60). A shopping expedition, exchanging goods for gold and gold for goods, illustrates the position of fire as controller of, and a participant in, the transformations of the physical masses of earth, fire and water (fr. 90).

52

And, most enigmatically, 'time (*aiōn*) is a child playing draughts' – which suggests a cosmic player moving on his board such pieces as life and death, waking and sleeping, young and old (frs 52, 88).

Empedocles was the first to posit the four elements of earth, water, air and fire as the ultimate constituents of all things. To show how the different phenomena can be produced from these four, he gave the example of a painter who produces in two dimensions a varied world from the juxtaposition of a few colours:

> As painters decorating temple offerings take in their hands pigments of various colours, and after fitting them in close combination – more of some and less of others – produce from them shapes resembling all things, creating trees and men and women, animals and birds and water-nourished fish, and long-lived gods too, highest in honour, so let not error convince you in your mind that there is any other source for the countless perishables that are seen.
>
> (fr. 23)

In other illustrations he compared primary elemental combinations to saffron-dye in wool, or wet and dry ingredients kneaded together in dough, and unsuitable ones that reject each other to water and oil (frs 93, 34, 91). Love, or Philia, the principle of attraction that produces good combinations, is a forerunner of Plato's divine craftsman; Empedocles describes her work as she 'rivets' elements together for eyes, or, like a busy potter, moistens earth with water, and puts the shaped product into the oven for the fire to harden (frs 87, 73).

The atomists, as one might expect, dispensed with craft analogies. To show the variety of phenomena explicable by an arrangement of atoms and spaces they pointed to letters of the alphabet, where the vivid characters and events in the world of the *Iliad* are conveyed by a limited number of letters – it was a question of the arrangement of the letters with appropriate spaces intervening. Aristotle reports in his history of early philosophy in the first book of the *Metaphysics* that actually the only distinctions recognised in atoms were in contour (*rhysmos*), contact (*diathigē*) and inclination (*tropē*); these rather exotic Greek words for shape, order and position look as if they are quoted directly from Leucippus. The three distinctions were illustrated by letters: A differs from N in shape, AN from NA in order and Z from N in position. Lucretius gives the atomists' answer to the sceptics' doubt that something seen as single and motionless can be really a mass of moving atoms – it is because the atoms are below the range of the senses. A flock of sheep on a distant hillside looks like a still, white blob, but close up there are individual ewes with separate movements, and their lambs frisking and butting; similarly a regiment drilling contains a myriad of soldiers making separate manoeuvres but from afar they look like 'a blaze of light stationary upon the plane'. Comparably, if we had better eyesight (having lynx eyes was the ancient equivalent of looking through a microscope) the structure of myriads of moving atoms would be revealed in what seems to be a continuous and stable mass (Lucretius 2.312–32).

The Pythagoreans tended to account for phenomena by applying arithmetic and harmonic ratios to the structure of their material, but when it was discovered that some numbers were irrational, more complex arithmetic formulae were no longer available as models or explanations. But irrationality did not affect geometric figures in the same way, so that when Plato wanted to show that the cosmos had a mathematical structure he expressed it geometrically.

Plato accepted the four Empedoclean elements of earth, water, air and fire, but realised that they were not basic enough. 'Elements of elements' are needed, and he found these in the two basic types of right-angled triangles, one with equal sides about the right-angle, the other with the hypotenuse double one side. From these atomic triangles, larger equilateral triangles and squares could be constructed, and then, with these used as plane surfaces, the regular solids of the cube (assigned to earth), pyramid (to fire), octahedron (to air) and icosahedron (to water). The cosmos itself was represented as put together by twelve pentagons to give the dodecahedron as the sphere of the whole (like a football made of twelve five-sided pieces of leather). 'Logic and likelihood' made the assignation of the first four solids to the four elements, and Plato commented on the models thus set up:

> We must of course think of the individual units of all four bodies as being far too small to be visible, and only becoming visible when massed together in large numbers; and we must assume that the god duly adjusted the proportions between their numbers, their movements and their other qualities, and brought them in every way to the exactest perfection permitted by the willing consent of necessity.
>
> (*Timaeus* 56b–c, trans. Lee)

Plato's cosmology here is a paradigm blend of mathematics, physics, logic and theology, presented as myth and worked through models.

Finally, there is the range of mythology connected with the phenomena of the day and night sky, which is too vast to be detailed, and is marginal to cosmology as an ancient science. All the main celestial phenomena had their relevant myths, many aetiological, providing explanations for natural events in personalised contexts. Sun, moon, planets, constellations, dawn and the rainbow, thunder and lightning, comets and meteorites, were brought within the compass of a sequence of narratives to provide a structure in which familiar patterns of human experience could be applied to distant and awesome events. Reacting against such ingrained tradition, the early cosmologists struggled to interpret the natural world by theory and argument in the search for a new certainty, whereas Plato maintained that any such confidence in the results of scientific speculation was misplaced, and went back to myth, powerful, imaginative and sophisticated, but still basically storytelling, as the appropriate medium for the explanation of observed phenomena.

4

MACROCOSM AND MICROCOSM

The most important of the models for the cosmos was to see it as a living creature, and this model was so pervasive that it requires separate treatment. It was the atomist Democritus who called the individual a 'microcosm' (*mikros kosmos* fr. 34), and so drew attention to the analogy between an animal as a cosmos in miniature, and a cosmos as a large-scale animal. For the atomists there were innumerable *kosmoi*, since on their theory particular world-systems were continually arising, maturing and disintegrating through the infinite void, but the analogy also held for those who posited the universe as a single cosmos. The theme was progressively developed from both points of view, first tentatively and then quite deliberately. The individual could be regarded as an ordered system comparable to the whole in its composite matter and psychic principle, and the cosmos as a great organism, a massive expansion of a similar elemental arrangement infused with vital powers, and often also with reason and control attributed to it. Between the two stood the body politic – the individual 'writ large' and a small-scale cosmos – so that the political vocabulary of conflict, justice and restitution could be applied in one direction to parts or opposite forces within the individual and in the other to the universe as a whole. The individual was a citizen of the *polis*, but this could broaden, as it did with the Cynics and Stoics, into the concept of citizenship of the world *polis*, the *cosmopolis*. Civic friendship broke through city boundaries to be expressed as love and concern for humanity, and private morality, civic and natural law and cosmic order might be viewed as intrinsically related. Other organisations, such as a household, a theatre or an army, also appeared as medians between the smaller and the greater, analogous in different respects to the cosmos. 'The world's a stage' was an ancient as well as a Shakespearian concept, highlighted by human conflicts acted out in the ancient theatre, which was built on a circular plane on the earth, beneath the bright open sky and in view of the distant sea.

The cosmos as a living organism could be established in various ways and with varying degrees of sophistication, as was its converse, the individual as microcosm. The former is first found in those cosmogonies which viewed the emergence of the main features of the world as comparable to that of plants growing from seeds, birds from eggs, mammals from semen, or as births directly from earth as universal mother. From the earliest texts, the difficulties of deriving the animate from the inanimate was avoided by positing the first principles as themselves vitalistic, and consequent developments as conjunctions, begettings, growths and disjunctions in a continuous genealogy. The Renaissance image of the Great Chain of Being and contemporary mapping of DNA molecules are descendants of an ancient way of regarding all forms of existence from the smallest to the greatest as on the one spectrum of universal life.

In the beginnings, in the ancient Egyptian cosmogony from Heliopolis, this living world was viewed as growing from the seed of the first god Atum. It was thought that he had within himself the primary sexual urge which compelled him to draw out his own body's fluid with his hand, and from the semen thus spilt arose the first pair of divinities: Shu (air) and Tefnut (moisture) who formed a trinity with him. As the watery atmosphere, these then caused the emergence and separation of Geb (earth) and Nut (sky). To complete the Ennead (the sacred nine) these mated and produced the male Osiris and Seth, and the female Isis and Nephthys, the former in each pair as vital principles locked in enduring conflict with the destruction and sterility represented by the latter two. The Babylonian myth of creation, given in Akkadian as *Enuma elish* ('when on high' – from the opening words) has Apsu, the primeval god of fresh waters, mingling with the salt water of the female Tiamat, and so generating the first divinities of earth, sky and sea.

Some of these features came together in Hesiod's *Theogony*, the poem in epic style which combined the succession narrative of the transfer of universal power from Ouranos (the sky) to the youngest son Kronos and then on to his son Zeus with a semi-mythical account through matings and begettings of the emergence of individual features of the universe. In Hesiod's poem Earth, Tartarus and Eros were the first generation to emerge from the primeval Chaos. Here, as in the Egyptian myth, the powerful sexual stimulus of Eros was needed at the very beginning; it activated the generative force within Chaos and Earth, and then drove the male and female cosmic forces together to produce the subsequent phenomena of nature. From Chaos came the spatial darkness of Erebus and the temporal blackness of Night, and then from them their complements in the bright space of Aither, and the bright time of Hēmera, the day. The four are in counterpoints of opposition and balance – space as male, both dark and light, time as female night and day; the first male–female pair were the blackness of space and time, the second the light equivalents set against them and alternating with them in a complex first representation of space and time as vitalistic principles.

Earth (*Gaia*) also emerged from Chaos in the beginning, as the deep-rooted base and firm support for the subsequent structures, but also as the first mother, whose children and grandchildren will comprise the whole of nature. According to the *Theogony* her first child, produced immediately from her own body, was the starry sky, personified as Ouranos, 'equal to herself, to cover her all around' (125–6). She then articulated her own surface into mountains and valleys, and poured out from her solidity the the male Pontus, which was the liquid salt sea, barren and tempestuous, the counterpart to her own fertility and calm.

Once Ouranos had been produced from the earth, he pressed down on her, covering her completely and inseminating her continuously. Offspring were produced – twelve Titans, three one-eyed Cyclops and three monsters with a hundred hands and fifty heads each, but the sky in hatred of them all prevented their birth by keeping them suppressed in earth's womb, and so causing her great pain. The myth goes on to relate how the impasse was broken by the mother plotting with Kronos her youngest son. She made a sharp-edged sickle, gave it to Kronos, and from within her womb he stretched out and castrated his father with its blade. At once the sky moved away from his oppression of earth, the children were born and Kronos usurped his father's power. The severed genitals were cast into the sea, and the goddess Aphrodite came from them, emerging in all her beauty on to the island of Cyprus. The genesis of sky from earth, and the separation of the two as distinct cosmic areas, were thus explained in human terms of male and female, love and hate, oppression and revenge, family feuding and the leitmotif of the success of the youngest son.

The first child of the union of sky and earth was Ocean, physically the freshwater river that was thought to encircle the earth's disc, but also the oldest of the Titans, who mated with his sister Tethys to form another set of primeval cosmic progenitors. Two further pairs of Titans also had an implicit cosmic role. Koios and Phoebe together accounted for the character of the sky as a shining vault, and Hyperion and Thea for the high luminosity in which their children subsequently emerged – sun and moon, and Eos the dawn, begetter of stars and winds. The powerful Titan Themis, personifying the principle of established order and regular procedure in past, present and future, then took up her place. The world was thus completed in its main earthly and celestial configurations, and was ready as a theatre of war for the great cosmic conflict between the generations, when the children of the Titans Kronos and Rhea, headed by the youngest, the new sky-god Zeus, set out to usurp in their turn the power of their parents, and so to establish their own rule.

The Babylonian creation epic started from the freshwater god Apsu, and there was a similar tradition of the primacy of the generative power of fresh water in the Greek description of Ocean. Ocean was known already in Homer as the river surrounding and enclosing the earth's surface at its outer limit, and the source of all existing wells, springs, rivers and seas. The sun was thought to rise from it in the east, and the stars, except for those of the Bears, to bathe in it after their setting in the west (as at *Iliad* 7.422, 18.489, 21.194–8). But there were also hints of it being the primeval begetter in the traditional phrases 'generator of the gods' and 'generator of all' (*Iliad* 14. 200, where Ocean is linked with 'mother Tethys', and 244). Plato was intrigued by the Homeric line 'Ocean, generator of all and mother Tethys', and quoted it three times (*Cratylus* 402b, *Theaetetus* 152e, *Timaeus* 40e), suggesting a link from the etymology of the two names to Heraclitus' view that everything is in a state of continual movement and flux. Plato was not being completely serious, but his suggestion was picked up by Aristotle, who mentioned a tradition of those who made Ocean and Tethys the first parents of the world's generation, thus giving water priority over earth (*Metaphysics* 983b30).

In Aristotle's own systemising of the history of philosophy he introduced the Milesian Thales as the first 'physicist', i.e., the first to tackle topics of natural science in a rational way. Thales, according to Aristotle, supposed that the earth rested on water like a log (as an explanation of its not 'falling down'), but more importantly he took it to be the *archē*, the beginning and first principle of everything. Aristotle provided some possible reasons for this supposition: that nourishment is generally moist, that heat is generated from moisture and fuelled by it (according to the ancient view that the fires of the stars were fed by exhalations from the sea) and that semen is moist. Whether these reasons were Thales' own or the result of Aristotle's prompting, the point was established that water makes up the greater part of the earth's surface and is the major constituent of organisms, and, as a cosmic principle, is living and generative of life. Anaximander took this further in his suggestion that human life first started and survived in water before moving on to earth, a suggestion that is close to some contemporary views on the origin of human life.

As Thales appears to have looked for the source of life in the depersonalised Ocean, so the early Presocratic Xenophanes both removed from Earth the traces of an anthropomorphic mother, and yet recognised in living earth the beginning and end of generation:

> for all things are from earth and into earth all things end.

> (fr. 27)

In one sense this is a truism, for all vegetation grows from the earth and decomposes into it, and animal forms 'come from dust and into dust return'. But Xenophanes also gave to everything a dual parentage of water, now also stripped of mythical connotations, and the soil of earth, so that he could maintain generally that

> all that have generation and growth are earth and water

and in particular that

> we all have our generation from earth and water.

> (frs 29, 33)

Everything was thus envisaged as formed either of earth or (as with clouds and the rainbow) of water, or a combination of both, and this combination significantly includes human life. In this way a physical interpretation was given to myths of humans formed from moistened earth by divine craftsmen, as in Greek tradition by Hephaestos or Prometheus, or, in the Hebrew Book of Genesis, by the creator god.

The concept of stones as the bones of earth is also relevant, and appears in the story of Deucalion and Pyrrha repopulating the earth after the flood. They threw stones ('the bones of their mother', according to the oracle of Themis) over their shoulders – men sprang from the stones thrown by Deucalion, and women from those by Pyrrha. The Athenians thought of themselves as 'autochthonous', i.e., born from the very earth of their land, supposing that their first king arose from the seed of Hephaestos falling on Attic soil, and the first men of Thebans were called 'Spartoi' (those 'seeded in the earth') from the myth of their generation from the dragon's teeth sown by Cadmus. Even the atomist Lucretius opened his poem with a hymn to the fruitfulness of the earth and the joy of life as allegorised in the goddess Venus, and in his fifth book put forward a theory of the first forms of life growing in 'wombs' rooted in the earth and nourished by the earth's juices.

Thales and Xenophanes took the concept of mother earth or primeval waters as living and generators of life out of the realm of myth into the new area of the study of nature. The Milesian Anaximander attempted to go beyond this with his view of 'the indefinite' as a limitless source of generation, while still involved in the basic hylozoism of an animate cosmos. Like all animate creatures Anaximander's cosmos would therefore originate in seed, and his struggle to express new physical ideas in the available biological language is shown in the strained terminology attributed to him. The doxography, probably going back to Theophrastus, reports Anaximander as saying that, at the birth of this cosmos, out of the eternal was separated off a *gonimon* of hot and cold (an unusual neuter word meaning something seed-like that was 'capable of producing' the opposites); out of this a sphere of flame grew, which encased the air about the earth 'like bark round a tree', and then split off into the sun, moon and star rings. The idea of 'seeds' at the beginning which contained within themselves all forms of future life was taken up later by Anaxagoras, but Anaximander's immediate successor Anaximenes had a simpler approach. He made air the vitalistic principle responsible for the beginning and continuation of all that there is – the cosmos itself, its constituents and the forms of animal and human life. The main quotation from his work gives the analogy:

> As our soul, which is air, maintains us, so breath and air surround the whole cosmos.
>
> (Aetius 1.3.4)

The air we breathe, invisible but essential for life, was an obvious candidate for the source of that life; as such Anaximenes envisages it now enclosing the cosmos, and also as the immeasurable vastness from which it first arose. The 'controlling' function of air in the individual animal and in the cosmos as a living organism along with the explicit analogy with human soul (*psychē*) suggest that it had a role more complex than merely that of a vitalistic principle.

This was stated more explicitly in the work of Anaximenes' later follower, Diogenes of Apollonia, for whom more of the original text survives. He explained that 'all that exists are modifications of the same thing, and in fact are the same thing' as variations of air, which would have to be intelligent to 'keep the measure of all things – winter and summer, night and day, rain, winds and fine weather', arranged in the best possible way. So what has and is intelligence was what was called air, guiding and mastering all things, and all things having a share in it. Obviously however there is a range of life and intelligence from the smallest organism to the cosmos itself, and this was explicable by the 'multiform differentiation' that the one principle can take on, as in the innumerable possible variations of it in temperature, humidity, stability and speed of movement. (The account is from Simplicius' *Commentary on Aristotle's Physics* 151–2.)

A cosmos that 'breathes' also featured in Pythagoreanism as quoted by Aristotle in *Physics* 4, ch. 6, and again by Simplicius' commentary on it. According to Aristotle the Pythagoreans said that void exists as a kind of 'unlimited breath', extending in every direction from the surface of the spherical cosmos, and was actually inhaled by it: 'they said that the void enters the cosmos as if in a way it drew in a breath from that which lies outside', and this is taken further in a fragment from Aristotle's *On the Pythagoreans* quoted by Stobaeus (1.18.1):

> The universe [according to the Pythagoreans] is unique, and from the infinite it draws in time, breath and void, which distinguishes the places of separate things.

Void here is 'what separates and divides things which are next to each other', although, in typical Pythagorean fashion, this becomes less clear when Aristotle reports that they say that 'this happens first with numbers – the void separates their natures' (*Physics* 213b27).

Earth, water and air were thus shown by the earliest Greek physicists in their different ways to be accountable for the beginnings of the known world order and its continuation. In being vitalistic principles they signalled the correspondence and even identity of the cosmos with its population in the spectrum of existing things from the smallest to the largest, the universe itself. Heraclitus followed immediately in this tradition, but claimed the priority of a different substance – that this *kosmos* 'was and is and will be – ever-living fire, kindling in measures and being quenched in measures' (fr. 30).

The cosmic *logos*, the 'one wise', was thus incorporated into the physical structure of the world as the constituent of all-controlling fire. It was 'quenched in measures' (but never completely) as in various parts and at various times it was transformed into water and then earth, but there was compensation in the earth being 'poured out' as water and from it corresponding measures of fire rekindled – Heraclitus represented this as through the medium of *prēster*, the energy of lightning flash in rainstorms. These transformations were called *tropai* or 'turnings', and the linking of microcosm and macrocosm was deliberate when these same 'turnings' were also said to characterise the individual *psychē*. *Psychē* as fire dies when it becomes water and earth, which is a physical representation of reason subdued by self-indulgence, but is reborn, recharged almost, when the soul resists desire and fosters reason to become wiser and so physically more fiery.

This way of thinking was taken over eventually by the Stoics, and given a much more sophisticated form. They set up a principle of heat and air combined which they called *pneuma*; the combination was necessary because of the obvious biological facts that the survival of an animate creature depends both on the external air for its breathing and the vital heat within. Soul then was explained not as a fire or breath separate from the individual physical structure, but as one with it. Air and fire as *pneuma* permeated the earth and water of the body, giving it its coherent form, maintaining and controlling it, and in the higher forms of life being responsible for language and reason. The same was thought to hold for the cosmos, where the all-pervading *pneuma* was bound into the elements of earth and water as a cohesive force, self-sufficient and self-nourishing. There could be no void within the enclosed whole because any spaces were immediately filled by the atmospheric *pneuma*. The parts were integral to the whole, and differentiations in their structure and character were accounted for by the constituent proportions of air and fire, and by the gradations of tightness and slackness in their tension. The resulting dynamic continuum in Stoic theory in which matter is informed by energising heat could be seen as an antecedent of some modern physical and cosmobiological concepts.

Fire, air, earth and water were first posited as the four basic elements by Empedocles. He preferred to call them 'roots' (*rhizōmata*), which emphasised their biological character, but he also gave them the names of gods – Zeus, Hera, Aidoneus and Nestis – as the authoritative source of all things, and in their eternal and unchanging nature deserving the respect and wonder traditionally due to gods. They were to be identified with the great visible masses of fire (seen in volcanic fire in Sicily as well as that of the sun), air, earth and sea, but also, in various proportions and arrangements, they constitute the physical bodies that populate those masses:

> for all these – sun and earth and sky and sea – are one with the parts of themselves that have been separated and born in mortal things.
>
> (fr. 22.1–3)

In addition, the cosmos as a whole and the microcosmoi within it were thought to be subject to the same opposing forces of attraction and repulsion ('love' and 'strife' in Empedocles' vitalistic terminology):

> at one time [the whole] grew to be one only from many, and at another again it divided to be many from one . . . and they [the elements] never cease their continual exchange of position, at one time all coming together into one through love, at another being borne away by strife's repulsion.
>
> (frs 17.1–2, 6–8)

This pattern was repeated in the initial conjunction and subsequent disintegration of constituent elemental parts to which the names 'birth' and 'death' are given in the narrative of an individual's life-span. The antecedents of such a force of attraction can be seen in mythical form in Hesiod placing Eros as a dynamic force at the very beginning of his cosmogony, and also in Parmenides 'devising' that same force as the first of all the gods (fr. 13). Empedocles asked us to recognise the elements of which we are composed by looking at sun, sky, sea and earth around us, and, conversely, by noting the character and activity of love on the human scale – 'she is acknowledged to be inborn in mortal bodies, and because of her their thoughts are friendly and they work together' (fr. 17.22–3) – it is possible to come to some understanding of elemental attraction at work in cosmology.

Plato's myth of the *Timaeus* further developed these ideas of the comparability of the cosmos with the kinds of life within it. The myth narrated how all the available supply of elements was used for the body of the world, so that it should be unique, 'as complete a living being as possible' and invulnerable to any external attack. Its shape was to be 'suitable for a living being that was to contain within itself all living beings' (33b) and so spherical, a figure it was thought that contained all possible figures within itself, as well as being complete, self-sufficient and uniform, with every part of its surface being equidistant from the centre; its movement was to be the most rational, that of a continuous rotation on its axis. The world soul, which was to give this body life, movement and reason, was represented as two circular bands, one within the other, circling antithetically to each other. This soul was then fitted to the world's corporeal structure centre to centre, and woven right through it from the centre to the circumference of the outer heaven, which it enveloped from the outside and 'revolving on itself, provided a divine source of continuous rational life for all time' (*Timaeus* 36e).

Human souls were said to be made from the same ingredients as the world soul, from what was left over after its composition (but now in a less pure state), so that they too were capable of harmonious movement and rational thought, but to an inferior degree. The souls were then allotted to stars, to take up bodies and lives on earth at the due time; after this the craftsman-god retired and left lesser gods to continue his work (for otherwise the human race would have been perfect). When the time for a birth came, one of these gods inserted the human soul into a human body, but in the trauma of the birth, which plunged the soul into the violent conflicts of the body's elements, the soul at first was unable to take control (with the visible results that a baby cannot walk or otherwise master its body, or speak a coherent language, the sign of rational thought). With growth, right nurture and appropriate education the soul's orbits would settle down into their correct form and take control, so that the child then learns to walk and talk and eventually to make reasoned judgements. Plato thus portrayed human soul and body as made of the same ingredients as world soul and body, and the whole purpose of human life as the attempt to have the soul's orbits in perfect movement, controlling the body and independently engaged in the activity of reason, in imitation of the orbits of the cosmic soul which keeps the celestial bodies in ordered rotation and has its own rational life. Our failure to match these movements is probably the key to the interpretation of the earlier enigmatic judgement made by the philosopher–physician Alcmaeon:

People die because they cannot join the beginning to the end.

(fr. 2)

Between the time of Alcmaeon and Plato some of the earlier

medical writers in the collection known as the *Hippocratic Corpus* were interested in finding biological connections between the individual human being and the cosmos itself as a living organism. Bruce Lincoln, at the beginning of his *Myth, Cosmos and Society* (1986, in a passage derived from the fourth chapter of G.E.R. Lloyd's *Polarity and Analogy*, 1966) sets out in diagram form the most extreme of these connections, verging on the bizarre, that are to be found in the treatise *On Sevens*. The system was worked out in a series of concentric spheres, where, for the macrocosm, the seven levels of the outer heaven, the stars, the sun, the moon, air, waters and rivers and earth have their counterparts respectively in the heat of the surface skin, that under the skin, internal heat, breath, bodily fluids and blood, and flesh and bone paralleling the clay and rocks of the earth (*On Sevens* 6.1–2; chapter 11 of *On Sevens* even equates geographical sites with bodily parts, and *Regimen* 1.10 has other homologies). One of the Hippocratic works called *Airs, Waters, Places* connected climatic conditions and temperatures with the different physical and personality traits of the local inhabitants. This again linked with elements in the physical structure corresponding to bodily humours and character, in the fourfold medico-Platonic scheme of (i) fire, yellow bile, hot-tempered, (ii) air, phlegm, phlegmatic, (iii) earth, black bile, melancholic and (iv) water, blood, sanguine. There was an alternative threefold atomic scheme outlined in the third book of Lucretius of (i) heat, lion-like and hot-tempered, (ii) air, deer-like and cowardly and (iii) breath, cow-like and placid. The point here was to find common features in the organisation of elements on the larger and the smaller scale, and to locate the health and general well-being of the individual in the harmony and equilibrium of the constituents as an instantation, copy and reflection of cosmic order.

Empedocles was particularly given to such homologies, bringing together the complexities of elements, form and function in plants, animals and humans and the cosmos itself. For example, the famous fragment 82 reads:

> As the same things, hair, leaves, the close-packed feathers of birds, and scales on strong limbs grow.

Leaves on trees that grow on earth relate to scales on fish in water as feathers on birds in the air and hair on humans. In like vein he also related eggs to olives, called the ear a 'sprig', the foetal membrane *amnion* ('lambskin'), and spoke of the hedgehog's sharp-pointed 'hair' and the 'stony-skinned' turtle which has its bone structure on top as the carapace. The older analogue of stones as bones was also recalled in the analysis of bone made within the hollows of the earth with a proportionate combination of earth, fire and water. There is extant a brief mention of a reverse analogy in the phrase of fragment 55: 'sea, sweat of earth', where the observed phenomenon of humans sweating as a result of exertion in the sun is transferred to the salt sea exuding from the earth as it was heated in the initial rotation.

In general, in Empedocles' scheme, the working of the forces of attraction and repulsion on the four elements is, as he says, 'the same' – for plants and trees growing on the earth, fish in the sea, birds in the air, animals and humans, traditional long-lived gods and the cosmos as a whole. Because of this structure the individual was thought to perceive the external world, as in fragment 109:

> with earth we perceive earth, with water water, with air divine air, with fire destructive fire, with love love, and strife with baneful strife.

Such concepts break down the apparent differences in forms of life, with various developments and consequences. Empedocles supposed his elements to be ultimate, and it was the arrangements of their parts that accounted for the variety of appearances. The atomists kept the principle of arrangements of minimum bodies (interspersed with void) for cosmic and individual differentiations, but deprived them of life, allowing only shape, size and weight to be predicated of them. Plato, Aristotle and the Stoics kept the four elements, denied their ultimate primacy and allowed their mutual transformation. In addition, Plato followed the Pythagoreans in positing transmigration of the soul as well the recycling of the bodily structures through the generations of plant, animal, human and divine life.

The works of two Roman authors illustrate later adaptations in a different culture of the breaking down of the old barriers between human, animal and plant life, divine and human, sky and earth. The first is Ovid's *Metamorphoses*, in which not only the population of the earth's landscape but also cosmic features were given mythical origins as former individuals with their own lives and history. As a consequence, wherever the eye turns there is a reminder of human life and tragic emotion. Plants and flowers, trees, insects, reptiles, numerous birds and animals and even fountains, rivers and springs, are represented as victims of frustrated love, jealousy, violence or vindictive spite. Here is Ovid's version of an Empedoclean homology, on the transformation of Daphne into a laurel tree:

> A deep languor took hold of her limbs, her soft breast was enclosed in thin bark, her hair grew into leaves, her arms into branches, and her feet that were lately so swift were held fast by sluggish roots, while her face became the treetop. Nothing was left of her except her shining loveliness.
>
> (*Metamorphoses* 1.548–52)

But stones, rocks, mountains and land masses were also to be seen as formerly living and suffering flesh and blood. Flint, bluestone, adamant, coral and marble have aetiological histories, Pelimela and her five companions became an archipelago, Haemon, Rhodope and Atlas become mountains in changes on a vast scale:

> Atlas was changed into a mountain as huge as the giant he had been. His beard and hair were turned into trees, his hands and shoulders were mountain ridges, and what had been his head was now the mountain top. His bones became rock. Then he increased to a tremendous size, and the whole sky with its many stars rested on him.
>
> (*Metamorphoses* 4.657–62)

Vergil, in the fourth book of the *Aeneid* (246–51), had presented Atlas conversely, as a mountain like a person, rather than a Titan who was changed into a mountain. In another dramatic passage Ovid describes Perimele as she is hurled from a cliff by her father:

> While I was still speaking, land newly formed embraced her floating limbs, and a massive island materialised from her body.
>
> (*Metamorphoses* 8.609–10)

More conventionally Ovid had explanatory myths to tell about the former personal histories of stars, the constellations of the Great and Little Bear, the signs of the zodiac and aurora borealis (as Ariadne's crown, the gift of the god Dionysus and elevated by him to the northern sky).

Ovid's older contemporary, Vergil, in the sixth book of the *Aeneid*, imagined a scene in Elysium in which the spirit of Aeneas' father Anchises identifies individuals waiting by the river Lethe, destined to be born anew as famous Romans. The Platonic/Pythagorean theory of the transmigration of souls was used here to create the opportunity to make a political point about Roman history, and integrated with the Stoic concept of the source of life, the *spermatikos logos*, from which individual organisms were derived. Anchises' explanation began as follows:

> From the beginning a vital principle from within nourishes sky, earth and sea, the moon's shining sphere and the Titan stars, and an intelligence pervading every part blends into the great body and keeps the whole structure in motion. From this combination come humans, animals, birds and the strange creatures under the sea's smooth surface. The force of fire is in their seeds from their origin in the heavens. . . .
>
> *(Aeneid 6.724–31)*

Today one might paraphrase this passage in terms of cosmic energy and mass, whereby the energy-charge in the mass produces differentiation, first, of galactic form, then of this particular galaxy with its sun, moon and earth, and finally the population of living things within it in one continuous and dynamic process.

In the fourth book of Vergil's earlier poem, the *Georgics*, the poet studied the microcosm of the beehive. The community of the hive was pictured as a miniature city ruled by law, with each individual having an allotted task – labouring in the fields, preparing the honeycombs, educating the young, doing sentry duty, town-surveying, busy in their workshops like the Cyclops forging thunderbolts, engaging in wars, sometimes sacrificing their lives in loyalty to their ruler or fellows. Vergil concluded the intricacies of his analogies between beehive, household and city by linking them to the wider scheme, and giving even the bees a cosmic origin and destiny in the energy and consciousness of a divine mind which

> permeates all land and sea and the depths of sky; from this source flocks, herds, men, all wild animals each at their birth derive their frail life, and to that source return.
>
> *(Georgics 4.221–5)*

The beehive cosmos is unique to Vergil in its detailed development, although bees and ants were long recognised as examples of community life with job allocation and mutual cooperation as analogous to, and even a model for human communities. Human communities in turn could provide models for the cosmos. Aristotle, in one passage of *Metaphysics Lambda*, in puzzling over the way in which the universe contains 'the good and the highest good', suggested that it may be as in an army, since the good of an army is to be found both in its ordered formation and in its general, but more so in the general since he is responsible for its order:

> and all things – fish, birds, plants – are in some sort of order, but not all alike, and the cosmos does not have one isolated from another, but they are all connected.
>
> (*Metaphysics* 1075a12–20)

And this order was also compared to that of a well-run household, where the various individuals work together for the good of the whole; the free members have least freedom to act for themselves rather than for the family community, but it is not catastrophic if the inferior ones, the slaves and animals, act at random. This would seem to mean, when the comparison was applied to the cosmos, that the stars and planets are of necessity tied to their orbits, but that activity beneath the moon may be non-rational, but is too inconsequential to affect the whole. Aristotle concluded, with the support of a quotation from Homer, that in any case for the cosmos to be well-governed, as with army, household and state,

> it is not good to have many in command; one ruler let there be.
>
> (*Metaphysics* 1076a4, quoting *Iliad* 2.204)

Aristotle, like Plato before him, tended to impose his own political views on to his cosmology, assuming that the vast order of the universe needed to be seen in terms of the 'monarchy' (literally the 'single rule') of a system ordered according to a master plan. But earlier philosophers were more democratic. They were closer to the time when the city-state, the *polis*, arose as an alternative political system to monarchy. The concept fundamental to the *polis* was of a limited, self-governing and self-defending citizen body bound into a social and political unit, and regulated by its own constitution and laws. It began to be recognised that *eunomia* ('good custom and government') could combine the different classes into a powerful unity when there arose mutual tolerance, respect and recognition of the rights of others. These ideals were put into practice in the institution of the citizen army and the founding of colonies, where in both contexts each individual had equal status and relied on his neighbour for support and even survival.

This political vocabulary of balanced equality, of justice, injustice and reparation maintaining an established order, was then transferred by some of the Presocratics from *polis* to *kosmos*, and a three-term analogy was established, with the city-state as median between the individual and the whole universe. So the individual was like a city, the city the individual 'writ large'; the city in turn could be viewed as a microcosm, and the cosmos as a city. Anaximander provides the first evidence, in the one quotation that survives:

> From the source from which [opposites] arise, to that they return of necessity when they are destroyed, 'for they suffer punishment and make reparation to one another for their injustice according to the assessment of time', as he says in somewhat poetical terms.
>
> (fr. 1 from Simplicius *Commentary on Aristote's Physics* 24.29)

The subjects here, 'opposites' such as hot and cold, wet and dry, were viewed not as qualities but entities, acting and reacting on each other like quarrelsome neighbours. At some time or place one encroaches on its counterpart, and that in turn, at another time or place, makes good the loss and itself becomes the aggressor. Gains and losses balance out overall in a cosmic equilibrium or *isonomia*, exemplified temporally in the succession of hot dry summers and cold wet winters, and spatially in the compensation of floodings by siltings.

This pattern of political metaphor binds city and cosmos, whereas Alcmaeon provided an example of the link between individual and city, to show the same vocabulary continually shifting between the three terms:

> What preserves health is *isonomia* between the powers – wet and dry, cold and hot, bitter and sweet and the rest, and *monarchia* among them is the cause of sickness.
>
> (Alcmaeon at Aetius 5.30.1)

Monarchy in this context was viewed as harmful to individual, state and cosmos, whereas health and survival depended on the 'blending' (*krāsis*) of opposed sides in due measure.

Some fragments of Heraclitus, in their enigmatic way, also used the metaphor of opposition on the cosmic scale, in a parallel to interstate strife:

> War is father of all and king of all; some it shows as gods and others men, some it makes slaves and others free.
>
> (fr. 53)

On the human battlefield war reveals the gods, or more precisely those who will achieve heroic status, and among the survivors some will obviously be slaves and others free. But 'war' was also given the rank of the Homeric Zeus, and, as the principle of universal opposition, was held responsible for all generation and continues to maintain it:

> It is necessary to understand that war is common and strife is justice, and all things come about by strife and necessity.
>
> (fr. 80)

Strife, *eris*, here was put in striking juxtaposition to justice; it represented the permanent tension between the opposed forces that is *dikē*, controlling the structure and functioning of both *polis* and *kosmos*. Yet there had to be a limit to the aggression, and when it was reached a corresponding retreat followed. Even the turning of the sun, which as a concentration of fire had a special place in Heraclitus' system, was subject to this universal law, and that is why it turns regularly at the equinoxes:

> The sun will not overstep its measures; if it does, the Erinyes, the daughters of justice, will search it out.
>
> (fr. 94)

Cosmic justice backed by cosmic law is here sanctioned by the Erinyes, who were traditionally the avengers of any violation of the natural order. The human perspective sees injustice, but Heraclitus pointed to an ultimate reconciliation of the apparent inequalities:

> To god all things are fair and just, but men suppose some are just, others unjust.
>
> (fr. 102)

And in another set of connections Heraclitus linked the one divine law, which maintains the structure and functioning of the universe through its fluctuations, with that human law which binds the *polis* and maintains its integrity even more than the physical encircling defences:

> Those who speak with sense must put their strength in what is common to all, as a city does in its law, and much more strongly, for all human laws are nourished by the one divine; for this has as much power as it wishes, and is enough for all and more than enough.
>
> (fr. 114)

A further example of political vocabulary being applied on the universal scale came in the 'broad oath' in Empedocles' scheme. The incomplete fragment 30 starts:

When great strife had grown in the frame and leapt upward to
its honours as the time was being completed, a time of exchange
for them, which has been defined by a broad oath. . . .

That the predominance of the power of attraction must be recom-
pensed by that of its opposite continued the idea of cosmic justice and
retribution in Anaximander's fragment, and of measures governed by
logos in Heraclitus. The function of the oath was to add solemnity
and certainty to the necessary exchange of times of power for the
cosmic forces, and the connection with the microcosm was reinforced
in fragment 115, when the time for the emergence of human life was
set by 'a decree of necessity, eternal and sealed by broad oaths'.

Finally, in the politicising of the cosmos, comes the notion of the
kosmopolis (in Latin the *mundus communis*), the shared universe
expressed in the vocabulary of a world state governed by natural law.
The concept started perhaps with Socrates, of whom the anecdote is
told that when asked what his native city was he replied that he was
a 'citizen of the cosmos' (*kosmopolitēs*). There had however been a
similar sentiment attributed to Anaxagoras, who was accused of
neglecting politics and not caring about his *patris* (his 'native
country'), and in answer said that he did indeed care about his *patris*,
and pointed to the sky. (The anecdote is given by Diogenes Laertius
2.7.) The general theme of the cosmos as one's true city or country
was taken up by the Socratic school known as the Cynics, and then
developed by the Stoics in the context of world empire, but firmly
based on a particular understanding of human nature.

The argument was that the primary natural instinct is for self-
preservation based on self-love. As the child then becomes more
aware of the external world it draws parents and relatives into affinity
with itself, and evidence from the animal world supports the assumption that family and community ties are based on nature. With
adolescence and the maturing of reason the individual gains a place
in the civic community, and the obligations of justice and social
cooperation begin to be understood. Finally comes the stage at which
civic obligations are seen as widening into the concept of world-
citizenship, cosmopolitanism in its exact sense. So the universe

> is a kind of city (*urbs*) or state (*civitas*) belonging jointly to
> gods (as rational) and humans, each one of us being a part of
> the universe; and the natural result of this is that we put the
> general interest before our own.
>
> (Cicero *On Final Good and Evil* 3.64)

Cities have their particular legal systems, which aim to keep inviolate the associations of their citizens; the cosmos is regulated by natural law, from which the particular city laws are derived and have their authority. Civic friendship, appropriate to a city honouring in justice the status of all the members of the citizen body, gives the pattern for the universal benevolence in the world setting, which is based on due respect for the humanity of others. Cooperation within the state in the interests of the whole community enlarges into universal mutual assistance, for, as Cicero says in the same context,

> On account of our very humanity we should not regard anyone as a stranger.

(3.63)

The interconnection of justice, law, reason and nature was thus in the interests of citizens and world citizens alike. Altruism and utility coincided in both civic justice and philanthropy, for acting justly strengthens the civic ties to the advantage of all citizens, and acting kindly towards a fellow human being enhances the cosmos. The emperor Marcus Aurelius, in this spirit of breaking down city boundaries in the recognition of the wider community under natural law personified by Zeus, offered the following prayer:

> All that is in good harmony with thee, o cosmos, harmonises with me. Nothing that is at thy right time is for me too early or late. All that thy seasons bring, o nature, is my harvest. From thee all comes, with thee all is, into thee all returns. Some say 'dear city of Cecrops', but will you not say 'dear city of Zeus'?
>
> (*Meditations* 4.23)

5

CHAOS AND COSMOGONY

The articulation of the distinct from the indistinct in the cosmogonies of antiquity took on three basic forms: the biological model of the growth of seed, the mechanistic one of a 'separating-out', often as the result of rotation, and the technological construction of an artefact. But these were not mutually exclusive, and one could take over from another, or run parallel to it, in a way comparable to the involvement of a modern cosmologist in a number of sciences, working in fact towards a new unity of the sciences, in accounting for the emergence of order out of disorder and the animate from the inanimate.

The most fundamental distinctions involved oppositions – cold and hot, wet and dry, dense and rare – leading to the victory of light over darkness which brings about the visible earth and sky. These features can be seen first in the oldest, non-Greek cosmogonies. The Babylonians, appropriately for the geography of Mesopotamia, started their account (in the *Epic of Creation*) from the mingling of salt and fresh waters (which have no distinct characteristics), and supposed that sky and earth came from them in the divisions made by the victorious Marduk. In the Egyptian myths the primary god Atum-Re' emerged out of formless water, and from his own seed produced Shu (god of the air) and Tefnut (mist), whose offspring were Nut, the sky goddess, and Geb, the earth. Shu then lifted his star-studded daughter away from her brother to give the basic trilogy of separate world masses of earth, air and sky, as was widely illustrated in Egyptian art. The other main version from Egypt gave the creation as the 'thought and word' of the god Ptah.

Many of these features can also be traced in the opening of the Book of Genesis:

Figure 8 The Egyptian cosmos.
Shu (god of air and light) holds the female sky-god Nut separate from
Geb, the male earth-god.

In the beginning God created sky and earth. And the earth was
a trackless waste and emptiness, and there was darkness over
the deep . . . God said 'Let there be light', and there was light,
and God divided light from darkness. . . . God said 'Let there
be a vault in the waters to divide them in two', and so it was.
. . . God said 'Let the waters under the sky come together into
a single place, and let dry land appear', and so it was God called
the dry land 'earth' and the mass of waters 'sea', and God saw
that it was good.

The cosmogony here emphasises in turn the formlessness of the
initial material, the first opposition of dark and night, the solid dome
of the vault or 'firmament' and the emergence of the standard three
masses of sky, earth and sea. They resulted from the word of God,
to be followed by various forms of life, culminating in the human

race 'male and female'. It is interesting to compare this account with that of the cosmos engendered by the Egyptian god Ptah. It is said of him that through his divine power he thought the universe in his heart and then brought it into being by his words, as in the following extract from the 'Shabaka Stone' (cited in Pritchard 1955: 5):

> The sight of the eyes, the hearing of the ears and smelling the air by the nose are reported to the heart. This causes every completed thought to come forth, and it is the tongue which announces what the heart thinks. Thus all the gods were formed, and all the divine order came into being through what the heart thought and the tongue commanded.

At about the same time as the Book of Genesis, the Greek poet Hesiod was working on his cosmogony, which began:

> First of all came *Chāos*, and then broad-breasted Earth, sure home of all for ever, and misty Tartarus in a recess of the wide-pathed earth, and Eros, fairest among immortal gods.... From *Chāos* came black Erebus and Night, and from Night in turn were generated Aither and Day, whom she conceived and bore after mingling in love with Erebus. And Earth first bore starry sky, equal to herself....
>
> (*Theogony* 116–27)

Hesiod assumes in this passage that from the initial *Chāos* came dark place (Erebus) and dark time (Night) which then produced their counterparts as bright place (Aither) above and the bright time of day. But also from *Chāos* came the mists of Tartarus below, and Earth in the centre. Earth's first child was the sky who was eventually separated from her by the violence of the youngest Titan, and the second was the sea. Again, after the preliminary light–dark distinction, the masses of earth, sky and sea came into their positions and the subsequent details of the natural world emerged, partly through the workings of Eros and partly through the self-generating fertility of the earth.

The especial interest in this account lies in the primacy given to the entity transliterated as *Chāos*. The word connects with 'yawning' and 'gap', and has sometimes been taken to mean the area separating earth and sky, even though it existed before either of these. It seems more like an attempt to name what there was before anything else, and something like 'yawning gap' or 'open chasm' is a fair attempt. Later the concept was adapted for Anaximander's 'indefinite', the atomists' 'void', Plato's 'receptacle' and Aristotelian 'space'. Hesiod had given the genealogy of world-masses a starting-point, but the problem was that *Chāos* itself 'was born' or 'had a genesis' (which are more exact translations than 'came' for the verb *egeneto*), and it would not be long before a bright student like Epicurus would ask what there was before the primary chaos. Hesiod's text provided no answer, and the problem continually recurs. There were three main schools of thought in Greek philosophy on the topic: the monists who gave the cosmos a spatial and temporal start, those who assumed it was ever-existing and those who postulated the continual recurrence of a plurality of cosmoi, either simultaneously through the vastness of space or succeeding each other sempiternally. Most schemes brought with them some version of *chāos*, not in its original Hesiodic sense, but approaching more the contemporary understanding of chaos as a disordered state of affairs that was yet susceptible to certain principles of order arising from it or being imposed on it.

Whereas Thales, the first of the Greek natural philosophers, appears to have been interested in the formlessness but inherent vitality of water as the first prerequisite of a cosmos (whether or not he was influenced by the non-Greek versions from the Near East), a more ambitious solution was attempted by his successor Anaximander. He posited a first principle distinct from water, fire and similar so-called elements, naming it *apeiron*, i.e., that which is 'indefinite'. This is unlimited in time (for it is described as 'eternal' and 'ageless'), without any specific spatial boundaries and has no identifying characteristics apart perhaps from some sort of indefinite shuffling or oscillating movement. The present world order came out of it, starting from a combination of mechanical separation and biological growth, and is still surrounded by it. Anaximander's cosmology is reported as starting from 'that which is capable of generating heat and cold' being separated out of the eternal, and producing a sphere of flame and a dark mist. Part of this was compacted into earth, then surrounded by a layer of air which in turn was enclosed by the fire 'like bark round a tree'. The central earth was cylindrical, one-third as deep as it was broad; it was eventually encircled by sun, moon and stars, which were explained as rings that had broken off from the original fiery 'bark' and were enclosed by part of the dark mist, except for the openings which allowed the inner fire to shine through. Winds and the sea emerged as the result of the heat of the sun then affecting the mist about the earth.

Anaximander's follower Anaximenes continued the thesis that

what was there first, the *archē*, was neutral and indefinite, but his study of atmospheric air suggested that the *archē* would need to be like this. Air is indeterminate, invisible and incessantly in motion, but by a process of compacting caused by changes of temperature it can take on the appearance of liquid or solid masses. Thus it was reasonable to suppose that there would be a complementary 'thinning' as the result of a higher temperature which would produce the appearance of fire. In addition, the fact that breathing is a sign of life and necessary to sustain it would suggest that air had a similar character on a cosmic scale, and so would be a suitable candidate for a principle that vitalised and enclosed the whole. The doxography (especially from [Plutarch] *Stromata* 3) shows how Anaximenes derived his cosmogony from this first principle: the air was initially compacted at the centre where it formed the earth; parts of the earth then 'thinned' into sea, and exhalations rising from this rarefied further to make the celestial bodies. There is also the suggestion that the fire in the celestial bodies was ignited by the speed of their motion.

Some early Pythagoreans were also interested in a 'breathing' cosmos, which started from an undefined 'point' (comparable perhaps to the enigmatic location of the 'big bang'), and then drew in the surrounding 'unlimited' in ever-expanding ripples of inhalation. The testimony, which comes from Aristotle (*Physics* 213b22–6), is by no means clear, but it provides an example of how these first cosmologists wrestled with the problems of accounting for a spatial and temporal beginning to the universe, its natural vitality and the manner of its expansion from one or two simple principles.

The general Milesian and Pythagorean oppositions were brought to a head by Parmenides in his 'Way of Opinion'. There it was shown that if a simple duality is accepted a cosmos can be generated. Parmenides, in the preliminary move towards a theory of elements, opposed fire, which is hot, light and bright, to cold, heavy and dark night, and gave an account of phenomena composed of them in varying proportions. And yet he had already subverted any attempt at a cosmogony in the earlier part of his work, the 'Way of Truth'. There for the first time the very idea of a beginning to what there is was questioned and denied, because the assumption of existence prior to 'is' would involve a contradiction with the rejected 'is not'. And what explanation could there be for starting at any particular time?

What beginning will you find for it? How and from where would it grow? I will not allow you to say or think that it comes

79

from what is not, for 'is not' is unsayable and unthinkable. And what necessity would compel it to emerge from a starting-point of nothing at a later rather than an earlier time?

(fr. 8.6–10)

The 'principle of sufficient reason', used earlier by Anaximander to show that the earth is 'freely suspended' without moving in one direction rather than another, is given a temporal application by Parmenides here ('why one time rather than another?') to strike a devastating blow at any suggestion that the present reality had a specific starting-point.

Parmenides' challenge was taken up most explicitly by Plato, when he contemplated the logical problems involved in a temporal beginning:

As for the whole *ouranos* or *kosmos* or whatever one likes to call it – we must first study the question that has to be asked about anything at the outset: was it always, with no beginning (*archē*) to its generating, or does it have a genesis, having started from some *archē*? It does have a genesis – *for* it is visible and tangible and with a body; all such things are perceptible, and perceptible things were shown to be comprehensible by opinion and perception as they come and came into generation. We also maintain that what was generated must have been so as the result of some cause.

(*Timaeus* 28b–d)

This needs to be interpreted (as Plato indicated with his explanatory 'for') in the light of the metaphysics Timaeus had just summarised. The realm of 'being' is perfect, eternal, unchanging, fully real and accessible to reason, to be contrasted with the imperfect, mortal, changing realm of generation or 'becoming', which belongs with opinion and the senses and has no firm grasp on its own identity. In saying that this cosmos 'has become' (*gegone*) Plato is placing it in the realm of becoming and attributing to it the characteristics of that realm, rather than ascribing a starting-point to it. He goes on to relegate the cosmos to the status of a copy of a model, and assign a craftsman to it – mythically as a 'likely story', rather than as a truthful account of reality. The subsequent narration of the generation of the cosmos *seriatim* as a product of the craftsman's skill is a literary device appropriately chosen to show the ontological dependence of the perceptible realm on the intelligible one and its inferiority to it.

The situation was compared to a geometer constructing a diagram to illustrate a theorem – the diagram is for the sake of instruction and does not affect the truth of the theorem, but it has to be drawn somewhere at some time and in some sequence (the interpretation reported by Aristotle at *De Caelo* 279b). And Plato's statement in this context that time starts simultaneously with the creation of the celestial bodies which mark its passing makes the question of what there is 'before' time and the means of ordering temporal events peculiarly unanswerable.

The craftsman-god of the *Timaeus* is like a common workman – a cobbler with leather, a potter with clay, a sculptor with marble – having to exercise his skill on unformed material which may resist the shape he has in mind and wishes to impose, but what would count as the preliminary material for a cosmos? In one obvious way it can be called 'space' (*chōra*), that 'nurse of all becoming and change', which is so hard to envisage:

> It provides a position for everything that comes to be, apprehended without the senses by a sort of bastard reasoning, hardly reliable as we look at it in a kind of dream and say that everything which exists must be somewhere and in some place, and that what is nowhere on earth or in the sky is nothing.
>
> (*Timaeus* 52b–c)

Plato summarised the character of space as 'invisible and formless, all-embracing, possessed in a most puzzling way of intelligibility, but very hard to grasp'. Yet, since the craftsman's creation is not *ex nihilo*, the *chōra* must somehow have the means within it, what Aristotle would later call the potentiality, to accept the forms of observed phenomena. In this section of the *Timaeus* (49–52) Plato gave a series of analogies to indicate how this might be explained. The main one is that of the mother providing the material for the future child and the father the form it will take (according to the popular biology of the time). But Plato used, as Heraclitus had before him, the similes of a perfume base which has to be as odourless as possible for the scents to be distinctive, and also of wax having its surface completely smoothed out with no marks of its own on it, but receptive of any impression. Another way of regarding the original material would be to say that there is no 'thing' or 'this' in it but only impermanent 'sort of' qualities. It is comparable to a neutral plastic material being continually reshaped, or like gold moulded into shapes, melted down and remoulded – anything made of it could only accurately be described as 'gold'. Explanations like these sound naive, but the attempt to describe what is there initially is still baffling. A recent suggestion, for example, hardly clearer than those of the Greeks, talks of 'quantum foam' which is 'space in fine detail, not actually composed of anything':

> like soapsuds flickering or vibrating with probabilities, but without the soap, or the time in which to flicker.
>
> (Kip Thorne in *The Guardian*, 1 September 1994)

So the description in the *Timaeus* of the state of affairs immediately before order is imposed on the *chōra* is of necessity vague. The receptacle had no homogeneity or balance but swayed uneasily; yet as it did so what were to be the four basic constituents of the cosmos – earth, water, air and fire – began a process of movement and separation of their own accord, a 'winnowing' which sifted the more solid and heavy to one region and the lighter and more insubstantial to another. As a result they began to show some of their character-istics and take up different areas but 'without proportion or measure' (*Timaeus* 53a). According to the myth, the god then reduced them to order by giving them a mathematical structure, and this accounts for their subsequent transformations and eventually for the struc-tures of the observed phenomena.

Plato here was clearly influenced by many strands in the Pre-socratic cosmogonies that preceded him. He was especially indebted to the Pythagoreans (according to one malicious report the whole work was plagiarised from them), and this is clear from the math-ematical, basically geometrical, structure he assigned to the elements. Aristotle later reported that the Pythagoreans were the only philo-sophers before Plato with any competent grasp of 'formal cause', i.e., that the explanation of the essential nature of an individual substance depends on the ordered proportions and ratios imposed on its material. The crucial part played by the four elements of earth, water, air and fire in Plato's cosmogony is heavily indebted to Empedocles, but the types of movement and method of their separation in the emergence of the first masses in the processes of generation had a more complex history.

These topics were tackled in different ways by the pluralists or 'Neo-Ionians', the collective name for the philosophers of natural science – Empedocles, Anaxagoras and the early atomists – who, in the time between Parmenides and Plato, attempted to account for plurality and change in the face of the Eleatic arguments which denied them. And it was with these Neo-Ionians that the crucial antithesis of the roles to be assigned to purpose and chance in cosmogony began to be recognised.

The first Ionian cosmologists attributed the emergence of the world masses to processes of separation that were independent of eastern or Hesiodic-type mythologies, but they did not question when or how these processes started. Once the celestial bodies had been formed they were seen to move in circles, but apparently it was not suggested that they were generated as the *result* of circular movement. This crucial concept of a vortex or *dinē*, a rapid swirl of cosmic matter about a centre, which caused a separation of heavier parts inwards and lighter ones to the periphery, seems to have been used first by Empedocles. In his important but rather enigmatic fragment 35, which belongs with his description of a world order that was something like the present one with its time-scale reversed, he spoke of Strife, the principle of separation, holding its position in the 'lowest depths of the *dinē*'. Here it kept the elements unmixed until the whole was gradually won over into a harmonious blending and slowed down to a state of rest by the contrary power of attraction. But then 'when the time came round' Strife struck at the centre and recommenced the vortex; the consequent separating out from the mixture caused the emergence of the masses in their present recognised order of earth and water surrounded by air and fire. The process however is not yet complete – there are some fires burning in the earth, the sea is not completely in one mass, and air is still swirling around in an apparently random way 'for it chanced to be running in this way then, but often in other ways' (fr. 53). The movement of 'exchanging ways' of immortal elements causes at present the rise of forms of mortal life. When however the movement reached its limit it seemed that Empedocles envisaged a complete *akosmia*, where there was neither absolute rest nor motion, but a kind of mindless and disordered vibration of parts which were no longer able to be combined into any kind of constructive form.

Empedocles supposed that a spatial limit was set at the circumference of the outer heavens to the expansion of the ripples from the vortex, and also a temporal one when necessarily the span of the power of attraction would be countered and balanced by that of repulsion after a set interval. Anaxagoras, writing soon after Empedocles, took a different view on both aspects, and posited an expanding universe with no limit imposed either on the time taken or the area covered. In Anaxagoras' account 'All things were together' at the beginning, and then at some indefinite moment and for no given reason an omnipotent and omniscient Mind (*nous*) caused a vortex to start in the cosmic mixture. Mind here however was not a Platonic-type divine intelligence working purposively to produce the best possible world order, but, as Socrates complained in Plato's *Phaedo*, a device to provide a start (in time and place) for the present world order; once the start was made mechanistic forces took over. The details of the cosmogony are given in the long twelfth fragment in which Anaxagoras attributed the inflationary expansion to the power of *nous*:

> Mind controlled the whole rotation, so that it began to rotate in the beginning. And first it began to rotate from a small area, but now rotates over a wider area, and will continue to rotate ever more widely.

He then described Mind's knowledge and arrangement of past, present and future movements, including the rotation of the celestial bodies. This was started off physically by a revolution (*periphora*) or rotation (*perichōrēsis*) within the original mixture, causing a separating of opposites and then a gathering together at the centre (it is tempting to say a 'gravitation') of the dense, cold, dark parts to form the earth, with the fine, hot and dry moving outwards for the sky (described in fragment 15). To some extent, this account is in agreement with the cosmogony of the atomists Leucippus and Democritus, and may have influenced it. They however go back to Empedocles' word *dinē* ('vortex') and, contrary to Anaxagoras' expansionist cosmos, the ripples from their vortex reach a limit in an outer enclosure of interlocking atomic elements.

Despite the differences in interpretation the basic notion of an initial rotation in a swirl of primary material became a standard explanation for a cosmos being dense and earthy at the centre with water covering it, and for the lighter air, aither and fire beyond that. It was a basic assumption that larger and heavier bodies are carried to the eye of a vortex (whether a whirlpool or a whirlwind) and the lighter ones shift away from it. But Anaxagoras also recognised a counter-tendency for heavy bodies to be swung outwards, as when he said that sun, moon and stars are red-hot stones hurled from the centre and now carried round in the revolutions of the outer aither.

The early atomic cosmogony initiated by a vortex is reported in the *Life of Leucippus* by Diogenes Laertius. This is especially interesting because it seems to preserve some of the imaginative vocabulary of Leucippus himself, who is otherwise generally over-shadowed by his co-atomist Democritus:

> In a 'cutting off (*apotomē*) from the infinite' many bodies with all sorts of shapes move into a great void where they collect together and start a particular vortex; in this they collide with each other and are caught up in various rotations and begin to separate off, like with like. When there are too many to be able to rotate any longer in equilibrium, the slighter ones move to the void outside as if sifted and the rest 'abide together', and becoming 'intertwined' they 'run together' with each other and make an initial spherical structure.
>
> (Diogenes Laertius 9.31)

The origin of the vortex (*dinē*) postulated here is not accounted for. Bodies simply come together and begin to rotate, although some meagre attempts at explanation attribute it to 'chance' or 'spon-taneity' or 'necessity', but these are merely different ways of saying that it is just how things are.

In this atomic theory, once the stage of the spherical structure or 'system' was achieved the consequent growth was envisaged as something like that of a foetus, drawing new material into itself:

> [The sphere] moves apart with something like a 'membrane' enclosing all sorts of bodies within it; while they whirl around because of the counter-pressure from the centre the surround-ing membrane thins as the bodies adjacent to it are continually drawn into the vortex. The earth emerges when those already brought into the centre 'abide together' there, whereas the 'membrane' expands with the intrusion of outside bodies – as it moves around with the vortex, it assimilates whatever comes into contact with it. Some of these bodies become 'intertwined' with it and produce structures that are at first moist and muddy, but they dry out as they are carried round in the vortex of the whole and then ignite, ending up as the substance of the stars.
>
> (Diogenes Laertius 9.31–2, continuing the previous quotation)

The free-standing foetus-like system then developed according to basic physical and biological laws. These were explained more fully by Epicurus (and his Latin exponent Lucretius) who called small molecular atomic compounds 'seeds', and showed how regular growths and ordered structures could take over from an initial haphazard collecting and whirling of atomic particles. A further crucial development here came with the concept of the 'swerve'. Leucippus and Democritus understood the initial chaotic atomic movements to be random like those of 'motes in a sunbeam', but once the implications of atoms having weight were realised, the basic movements were taken to be linear. To start any kind of compound or subsequent cooperative activity it was proposed that any atom, at any time or in any location, could make an inexplicable 'jig', the smallest possible deviation from its path; the 'motes in the sunbeam' type would then be secondary to the disturbance caused by a single atom moving out of line. Obviously only one such atomic swerve would be needed to cause innumerable changes of direction, but, since the swerve also had a part to play in the Epicurean ethics of free will, the potential to swerve was thought to be built into the very nature of the atom, in somewhat the same way as inherent erratic behaviour is now recognised in subnuclear particles. Lucretius' comparison then of the subsequent random movements of atomic matter at microscopic level to the 'motes in a sunbeam' is extraordinarily vivid:

> You will see a multitude of tiny particles mingling in a multitude of ways as though engaged in everlasting conflict, rushing into battle turn and turn about with never a moment's pause in a rapid sequence of unions and separations.

> (2.116–20)

When the sequence involves particles coming together which are capable of mutual reaction they start swirling around in unison; this initial vortex then draws in further particles, and the intake increases until there is a sorting out of appropriate positions from the centre to the extremity of the rotation, certain characteristics emerge from the compounds, and eventually a settled firmament results.

So far this study has been concerned with the genesis of the present world-system, but associated with it is the question of whether the process can or has been repeated at another time or place. Professional and amateur cosmologists alike have always been fascinated by the possibility of another world like ours: are there intelligent creatures 'out there' in space, or rudimentary forms of life or even the conditions for life anywhere else? The possibility was certainly discussed in antiquity, not in terms of alternative or parallel universes, but in a basic dichotomy of one *kosmos* or many *kosmoi*. The monists in favour of one *kosmos* would generally be envisaging 'the whole' as the immediate solar system with earth and sea at the centre, atmospheric air surrounding them and some kind of fiery sky above, containing the observed celestial bodies within a spherical periphery. Those like the atomists who assumed a plurality would have an open universe with many solar systems, galaxies or the like, extending through the infinite space of the whole in various stages of growth and decline. In modified versions of these views (such as that of Anaxagoras) either the immediate system, although one only, would be understood as ever-expanding, or else, beyond the periphery, there might be a limitless stretch of space or void which contained no further structures. The latter concept could be combined with plural *kosmoi* in the sense that the present world-system had others like it in the same location before and after in a series without beginning or end. This, basically, was the position of Empedocles in the fifth century BC and the Stoics in the third.

Plato, in his myth of the craftsman-god of the *Timaeus*, took a firm stand on one cosmos only, for model and copy alike:

> There is one, if it is to be crafted like the original, for that which encloses all intelligible life cannot have a double. . . . so for this to resemble the perfect living creature in its uniqueness, he did not devise two or an infinite number of *kosmoi*; instead this heaven was, is and will continue to be the only one of its kind.
>
> (31a–b)

A plurality of *ouranoi* was sometimes attributed to Anaximander and of *kosmoi* to Anaxagoras, but the evidence is not reliable enough to suppose that these were to be understood as separate world-systems. The indefinite nature of both Anaximander's *apeiron* and Anaxagoras' expanding universe would have allowed for the conditions posited by the atomists, who did conceive of plural worlds, but it is more likely that in these two cases the reference was to the newly recognised antipodes, a world 'down under', where the arrangements of human settlements and the view of the rotating bodies in the day and night skies would be similar to those observed from a Mediterranean standpoint.

If there should be another cosmic system in addition to this one, then obviously there must be some location for it, which raises the preliminary question of what is 'outside' the present space, a question which in some ways complements the temporal enigma of what there could be before the beginning of time. Parmenides had rejected anything outside of what there is in a similar way to his denial of before and after, because it would involve the acceptance of the unacceptable and illogical 'is not'. Empedocles then identified 'is not' with 'empty', and agreed with the rejection of it (although the interesting phrase 'idle matter' occurs in one report of his cosmology). But contrary to Parmenides, Empedocles reinstated movement and argued, as Plato and Aristotle did later, that it could occur without emptiness or void if it was understood as the shifting of parts in any particular location in the *plenum*. Melissus went back to supporting Parmenides on the eternity and immutability of what there is, but claimed that it would be without parts and 'unlimited', and then used this as an argument for uniqueness: 'for if it were two, it could not be unlimited, but they would set limits to each other' (fr. 6). In addition, he argued that it was immobile, homogeneous and 'full', since the empty is nothing, and nothing does not exist. Perhaps, too, there was no 'corporeality', for, in the ninth fragment attributed to Melissus, it is suggested that what there is has no tangible, visible, shaped 'body' or solid 'bulk' or parts, but none the less is spatially and limitlessly extended. This again seems to be an attempt to describe a present state without change or generation which is comparable to that which the pluralists envisaged as prior to any generative process.

The early atomists amalgamated the previous notions of 'is not', 'the empty', the 'limitless' and the 'indefinite' in Presocratic philosophy, and asserted the existence of void ('not-body' or 'not-being') along with atomic matter as the necessary condition for movement. As Epicurus later said:

> If place (*topos*), which we call 'void' (*kenon*) and 'room' (*chōra*) and 'intangible nature' did not exist, bodies would not have anywhere to be or to move through as they are observed to do.
>
> (Diogenes Laertius 10.39–40; Sextus *Against the Mathematicians* 10.2)

'Intangible nature' (*physis*) here is the general term, 'void' when it is empty of body, 'place' when it is occupied by one at rest and *chōra* when bodies move through it.

Void, in the ancient atomic theory, was understood as limitless (for being empty it can contain no extremity to limit it), and the number of atoms would also have to be limitless since otherwise they would be 'lost' in space and could not come into contact with each other to start the interaction necessary for generation. But once these two criteria were established – an infinite amount of material in an endless extent of emptiness – then the 'sum of things' opened out, and the conditions were appropriate not just for this one world-system but for an innumerable or possibly an infinite number of them. Hippolytus preserves a vivid account of the result for Leucippus and Democritus:

> There are innumerable cosmoi differing in size. In some there is no sun or moon, in others they are larger than with us, in others more numerous. The intervals between the cosmoi are unequal: in some places there are more, in others fewer; some are growing, others are fully grown, others again are dying; somewhere worlds are coming to be, elsewhere fading. And they are destroyed when they collide with each other. Some cosmoi have no living creatures or plants, and no water at all.
>
> (*Refutations* 1.13.2–3)

Epicurus, in his 'Letter to Herodotus' (recorded in Diogenes Laertius 10.45), showed later that the number of cosmoi might well be without limit, some like the present one and others different, for there are multitudes of atoms moving ever onwards through the void, and those from which a cosmos could be generated have not all been used. Lucretius developed the point at the end of his second book, reminding the reader of the physical fact of numberless atoms hurtling through a limitless universe in perpetual motion. This cosmos arose from casual collisions and random collections which happened to come into an appropriate rotation to cause a sifting of like to like and the emergence of elemental combinations, but 'it is highly unlikely that this earth and sky is the only one to have been so formed, and that all those particles of matter outside are doing nothing' (2.1052–7). When the space is available and there are no impediments, with an unlimited supply of material and the same natural forces at work, it must surely be admitted that there are other earths, and humans and animals elsewhere. And since there is more than one individual in every known species, it would again be unreasonable to expect this sun, moon and sky to be unique.

The Stoics were also ready to allow an infinite, non-physical void extending outwards from the periphery, but not within it (as the atomists supposed), as a separate entity intermingling with its matter. Void was needed in Stoic cosmology to provide an area in which the world could expand when the fire in it inevitably increased (for fire takes up more room than a comparable amount of air), and also the cosmos, as a living creature, continually breathes in and out in its entirety, and so requires flexible space for respiration at its pulsating edge. Some of the Peripatetic and Epicurean critics of Stoicism claimed that such a theory would mean that the material of which the world was made would disintegrate into the external emptiness, but the reply to this was that it had its own cohesion held in tension by the inherent *pneuma*. Sambursky summarises the Stoic position here:

> This cohesive force, which binds the parts of the cosmos together into a single entity, offsets the dissipating influence of the surrounding infinite void and makes the cosmos a closed universe whose unity is not vitiated by changes in its size.
>
> (1956: 203)

The assumption of only one such cosmic 'island' in the void was dictated mainly by the tenets of Stoic theology, which postulated a unique divine force innate in the dynamics of this system, and anthropocentric in its providential care for this human race.

Some Pythagoreans had earlier made the point that the cosmos as a living creature breathes in and out, inhaling and exhaling the surrounding void. In addition they supposed that, since it was like a living creature, it would have a beginning, a time of maturity and an end, and that therefore a plurality of cosmoi would be generated, not simultaneously but successively, and that there would be an identical recurrence through the series, with everything eventually returning 'in the self-same numerical order'. Empedocles also posited a single cosmos whose generation and dying continues without beginning or end, occurring both when many things come into a unity and again when they separate out, but there was no requirement for an identical repetition. The Stoic cosmogony brought together these and other strands from the Presocratics, for it described a Milesian-type separation out of hot and dry with fire and air arising from it, the air condensing into water and earth solidifying at the centre, but, as with Heraclitus, these 'turnings' were thought to be controlled by divine fire. They then calculated that when this has complete ascendancy, there will be a universal conflagration, an *ekpyrōsis*, from which the process will start afresh, according to a Pythagorean pattern of endlessly repeated cycles.

Although starting from different premises, both Stoics and Epicureans therefore believed that this present cosmos is doomed to extinction, either to give way in the temporal succession of cosmoi to another with identical features, or as one of many simultaneously at different points of the life-span of generation, maturity and decay. From the Stoic point of view there is a slow but steady global warming – the equilibrium between the elements no longer holds and eventually the whole will be engulfed in the cosmic fireball of the conflagration. They found signs of this already in the drying up of swamps and wetlands, and previous habitable regions becoming increasingly arid; the evidence for the ancient theory is cited by Alexander (*Commentary on Aristotle's Meteorology* 90a) but the relevance of these same signs to modern anxieties is clear. The increasing infertility of the earth was also used by the Epicureans as testimony that the world was dying, as graphically described by Lucretius:

> We exhaust the oxen and the strength of the people who work the land, we wear out the plough, and yet the fields scarcely support us – they grudge their harvest and increase our toil. The old ploughman shakes his head and sighs again and again because all his hard work has come to nothing; comparing times present to times past he often praises his father's success.... He does not realise that everything is gradually decaying and on course for shipwreck, worn out by the long years of its old age.
>
> (2.1161–74)

Although the early atomists supposed that worlds might be destroyed by colliding in space, the view later prevailed of a slow decay of a system under the bombardment of external particles at the circumference, and the loss of internal matter without adequate replenishment. Arid landscapes and the deterioration in the earth's fertility are the warning signs that, in its life-span, the present world has reached its maturity and is now past its prime. Eventually the defences of the system, the *moenia mundi*, will be attacked from all sides, and, in the same context as the previous quotation, Lucretius described how they will crack and disintegrate as the whole system collapses in on itself.

It can therefore be seen that in explaining the emergence of an ordered world-system from chaos the ancients were as sensitive in their way as contemporary cosmologists are to many of the basic issues. Some held to a 'steady state' hypothesis of the cosmos, involving continual loss and compensation within a general equilibrium, and others had a version of the 'big bang' theory, with expansion outwards from an initial vortex. And with the latter came the enigma of the very beginnings, and the reason for a starting-point at any particular moment in any particular location. Will the consequent system hold at a certain level or expand indefinitely? Is the growth teleological or mechanistic? Are laws externally imposed or is the material self-regulating? Can the conditions be expected to be duplicated at another place or time? Will there be a corresponding 'big crunch' to balance the beginning, so that the present system can be expected to collapse in on itself at some time? In working on such problems the best minds then as now were characterised by persistent curiosity, creative imagination and unrelenting logic.

6

ELEMENTS AND MATTER

In the *Iliad* Homer tells of how the three sons of Kronos, after defeating their father and his fellow Titans, divided the world into three, and drew lots for the shares: Poseidon had the sea, Hades the misty darkness below and Zeus 'the wide heaven among the aether and the stars', while earth and Olympus, the home of the gods, were open to all (*Iliad* 15.187–93). Sea, sky and nether darkness became areas of control for these divine powers, and, with earth, reflected basic and recognisable world divisions, but there was no suggestion that they formed constituent parts of existing things. Similarly, in Hesiod's *Theogony*, Tartarus, earth, and her first progeny sky and sea, made up the four main general areas of the observed world; they became responsible through further mating and begetting for the increase in population of those areas, but provided explanations for them only in the vague sense of being their progenitors.

The Milesians were the first to be concerned with the basic nature and structure of the world as they attempted to simplify the range of phenomena by finding explanations for the diversity in more fundamental principles, and so rendering the whole intelligible and accessible to rational analysis. According to Aristotle, however, as he looked back on the history of explanations and causes given by his predecessors, the only recognition in the beginning was of 'material cause', that is that the understanding of an object or entity is in terms of an explanation of what it is made of. (He himself thought that it would also be necessary to know its shape, who made it and what it is for – formal, efficient and final causes, as his terminology is traditionally translated.) The passage which discusses this is from the first book of the *Metaphysics*:

> Now the majority of the earliest philosophers thought that the only general principles were those of a material kind. They say

that what all things consist of, and from which they first come and into which they eventually disintegrate – the substance persisting while the attributes change – is the element (*stoicheion*) and principle (*archē*) of things, and because of this they think that there is no generation or destruction at all, since a natural substance (*physis*) of this sort persists throughout ... there always has to be some natural substance, one or more than one, which endures while the rest are generated from it. They do not however all agree on the number and character of such an *archē*. Thales, the founder of this type of philosophy, says that it is water. ...

(983b6–21)

Aristotle's language is anachronistic as he reports the achievements of his predecessors in his own vocabulary of 'matter', 'substance', 'attributes' and 'elements'. There is however some evidence for an early use of the word *archē*. This combines the senses of 'origin', 'basic principle' and 'main constituent', and, although it is too sophisticated for Thales, the concept and the use of the term were attributed on good authority to his successor Anaximander. Thales' significance in the history of philosophy is his search for a simple, naturalistic explanation of the complexity surrounding him in the perceived world, an explanation which did not require the involvement of Homeric or Hesiodic gods. He also seems to have been interested in offering reasoned support for his assumption of the importance of water in the natural world, as occupying a large part of its surface, for example, or as being necessary for life, or a main constituent in living things (as is the case), and Aristotle was ready to suggest others.

The new way of thinking attributed to Thales involved the search for a non-mythical origin for the cosmos and for the supply and maintenance of life within it, but it also required arguments supporting the conclusions reached. Anaximander adopted and furthered this approach, understanding that such arguments needed to show the weaknesses in previous solutions as well as the strengths of those now put forward. In this context belongs a report from Simplicius, which is likely to go back to the first *History of Philosophy* from Aristotle's Lyceum:

Among those who suppose that the *archē* is one thing, moving and infinite, Anaximander ... said that the unlimited (*to apeiron*) is both *archē* and *stoicheion* (element) of what there is, being the first to use this word *archē*. And he says that it is neither water nor any other of the so-called elements, but some other unlimited *physis* (nature), from which come to be all the heavens and the *kosmoi* in them. . . . It is clear that, in observing the change of the four elements into one another, he did not think it appropriate to make any one of these a substratum, but something apart from them.

(*Commentary on Aristotle's Physics* 24.13–20)

The supporting reasoning is given by Aristotle himself, in an indirect reference to Anaximander:

There are those who make something else [alongside earth, air, fire, and water] unlimited, but not air or water, so that the rest of them are not destroyed by the unlimited among them; for these have an opposition one to another – air for example is cold, water moist, fire hot – and if one of them were unlimited, the others would have perished by now; but as it is they maintain that what is unlimited is separate from them, and that they come out of it.

(*Physics* 204b24–9)

No one *archē* or *stoicheion* could be given priority above the others, without the subsequent destruction of that consistent balance and equilibrium which, in the only extant quotation attributed to him, Anaximander claimed as a requisite for the continued maintenance of the universal construct:

for they [the opposites] make atonement to one another for their injustice according to the assessment of time.

The evidence allows us to conclude that Anaximander first used the word *archē* for the indefinite origins of the universe, and named it as *to apeiron* (the 'limitless'). In making a noun from the neuter of the adjective (as Greek linguistic usage allowed) he was able to distance it from any entity with definite characteristics, and in the adjective he chose he was able to cover the senses of being unlimited, inexhaustible and indeterminate. He called it 'divine', but immediately glossed this as meaning 'immortal' and 'indestructible'. It had in itself no internal distinctions, but from it emerged, via some kind of 'seed', opposite qualities still envisaged as entities – hot, cold, dry, wet and possibly others such as light and dark. A world order comes from these, with cold dark earth at the centre and bright fire at the outer edge, which eventually split into the rings of the circuits of sun and moon. Anaximander supposed that the opposites were engaged in acts of aggression against each other, shown physically in excessive seasonal heat or flooding, but always compensated for by their 'atonement' and the counter-aggression of winter cold or silting, so that there is stability overall in the incessant temporal and spatial adjustments. The limitless surrounds the whole, continually and consistently absorbing and regenerating life.

His successor Anaximenes took over much of this theory, keeping to an *archē* that was limitless, indeterminate, indestructible and still surviving at the outer edge, encircling and maintaining the cosmos. The main difference was that he defined the *archē*, giving it the character of air. He accepted the predominance of this and could argue against the need for a neutral origin by claiming the necessity of air as breath for life, and also by using the quantitative changes in air, which produce variations in both temperature and density. In the first reports of observed changes being used as support for a general theory the temperature difference is given in a note from Plutarch on Anaximenes' evidence:

> The breath is chilled by being compressed and condensed with the lips, but when the mouth is loosened the breath escapes and becomes warm because it is thinner.
>
> (*On Cold* 947f.)

Differences in appearance were taken to be the result of the *process* of the quantitative change:

> When air is uniform it is invisible . . . but when its consistency is thinner it becomes fire, but wind again is air condensing, and cloud comes from air that is 'felted'. When it is packed further, water results, then earth, and, at its most condensed, stones.
>
> (Hippolytus 1.7.2–3; also Theophrastus *Physics* fr. 2)

Water congeals as solid ice, melts back into liquid, which in turn can be heated to produce steam, the more solid being colder, the rarer the warmer. It is clear that Anaximenes then inferred that the variety of phenomena could be derived from air in the three densities of solid, liquid and gas (or 'mist' in his terminology), the incessant movement of air being responsible for these variations.

In the exchange and adaptation of ideas concerning basic substance which characterise this early period, Heraclitus, the next important thinker, accepted the process of transformations but in terms which gave priority to fire. Simplicius, again going back to the the *Physical Opinions* of Theophrastus, reports that Heraclitus

> makes the *archē* fire, and produces all things from fire by condensation and rarefaction and resolution back into fire, supposing that this is a single, underlying nature; for Heraclitus says that 'all things are an exchange for fire'.
>
> (*Commentary on Aristotle's Physics* 23.33)

This can be elaborated from two fragments of Heraclitus' own words. The 'exchanges' for fire are as in barter when 'goods are exchanged for gold and gold for goods' (fr. 90) in the sense that fire is a unit in the exchange but also the standard which determines the amount of that exchange. And what is exchanged for fire is water and then earth, and, conversely, in the 'turnings', earth dissolves into sea, and moisture from the sea rises as an exhalation to fuel and is absorbed into the fire above (fr. 31). Air as such is not involved, but water and earth were presented as primary derivatives from the basic 'ever-living' *archē* of fire.

One of the fundamental problems with all these theories of the early Ionians was, as Aristotle saw, that it was not sufficient to define the basis for generation and change (i.e., to give explanations only of what things might be basically made of); a cause or reason for the change itself was also needed. This was a requirement for any physicist after Parmenides, who, in the part of his poem known as the 'Way of Truth', argued that if one used reason and discounted the deceptions of sight, hearing and the other senses, generation, change and plurality would be found to be impossible. Yet in the more fragmentary final section – the 'Way of Opinion' which was labelled deceptive and untrue – he was himself a pioneer of the concept of an element.

Xenophanes, in a simplistic way, had said that everything comes from earth, or is made of earth and water, but Parmenides grasped the point (even if he disparaged it) that a universe could be generated from the minimum plurality of two 'forms'. These were distinguished from each other and characterised as follows:

> on the one hand the aithereal flame of fire, gentle, tenuous, the same as itself in every direction and not the same as the other, but the other is on its own as its opposite – dark night, thick in form and heavy . . .
>
> (fr. 8.56–9)

since all things have been named light and night and the powers assigned to each, the whole is full of light and unclear night, both equal, since nothing is without either.

(fr. 9)

As he struggled with the limitations of the language available, Parmenides in these lines is setting out the ground rules for a theory of elements. A basic pair of permanent and unchanging entities, with inherent and separate characteristics, could in theory account for plurality, change and variety throughout the cosmos according to their proportions as the constituent parts of any particular compound within it.

Empedocles from nearby Sicily reacted to Parmenides on two fronts. He assented to the conclusions from the 'Way of Truth' that there could be no absolute generation or destruction, since these entailed temporal non-existence, nor could the corresponding spatial non-existence in the form of void be admitted to produce gaps in the continuity and homogeneity of being. Furthermore, there could be no addition to or subtraction from the total sum, so that birth and death were merely 'names' mistakenly used in human speech. But Empedocles then developed from the hint of the two forms of light and night in the 'Way of Opinion' the concept of four basic elements, and so reinstated the perceptible world of plurality and variety. He too was a poet wrestling with a new vocabulary, and instead of saying flatly that there are four basic elements of fire, air, earth and water he wrote:

Hear first the four roots of all things: bright Zeus, life-bringing Hera, Aidoneus and Nestis, whose tears are the source of mortal streams.

(fr. 6)

The botanical term 'roots' (*rhizōmata*) indicates the vitality of the substructure, and the divine names their potency and sempiternity. To illustrate the possibility of the wide diversity of phenomena generated from just four elements Empedocles used the simile of a painting, which can show in two dimensions a variety of plant, animal and human life, although it consists basically of pigments of a few basic colours in a particular arrangement. He chose four as the economical minimum number, perhaps from the importance of the opposites of hot and cold, dry and wet for the Milesians, or from a combination of the candidates for the basic *archē* put forward earlier, or possibly from a consideration of the Homeric partition given at the beginning of the chapter. A group of four (the first square number and signifying justice for the Pythagoreans) also allowed for mutual activity within a structure of balance and equilibrium. Most obviously the four comprise the natural masses visible in a coastal town of Sicily – the earth below, the sea at its edge, the air above and fire pouring from the volcanoes and in the bright sun. This accords with one fragment which states that an understanding of the true nature of things can come simply from looking around,

> since all these – sun and earth and sky and sea – are one with the parts of themselves that have been separated off and born in mortal things.

(fr. 22)

The four elements were considered to be basic, unchanging corporeal entities, forming temporary arrangements as their parts were brought into compounds with different forms but not subject to any alteration themselves:

> these are the only real things, but as they run through each other they become different objects at different times, yet they are throughout forever the same.

(fr. 17.34–5)

To explain how the four elements come into compounds and separate into their own masses Empedocles posited opposed principles of attraction and repulsion which, in the vocabulary then available, he called *philia* ('love', 'friendship') and *neikos* ('strife', 'hate'). As the visible masses of earth, sea, sun and sky provided evidence for the four elements and their characteristics in the composition of individual constructs, so a converse inference was drawn from the power which Love and Strife have in human affairs to their behaviour on a cosmic scale; in both areas Love could be seen as constructive and unifying, Strife destructive and separating. The elements then were to be understood to be subject to the opposed forces of Love and Strife working on them with expanding and contracting areas of application as they were brought together or held further apart. In Empedocles' theory the tensions of such attraction and repulsion resulted in the repeated patterns of movements and arrangements of the elements within the cosmos, in the genesis and destruction of successive generations of mortal life and, for individuals, in friendships and enmities.

The assumption that all things, including the variety of forms of life – 'trees, and men and women, animals, birds and fish' – are temporary compounds of elemental parts of earth, air, fire and water in different proportions is not so very different from the contemporary views that the main ingredients are the elements of carbon, hydrogen and oxygen or that the types of life are reducible to arrangements of the four letters of the DNA alphabet. In any case Empedocles' theory of four elements immediately became standard, and was taken into account by philosophers, cosmologists, natural scientists and medical writers throughout antiquity, in the Middle Ages and into modern times.

Plato's adoption and adaptation of Empedocles' theory of four elements is to be found in the one work in which he specifically dealt with physics, cosmology and natural science 'for relaxation' – the *Timaeus*. The account given in this work is in the form of a myth, a 'likely story' and, since the subject-matter is this 'secondary' world, in Plato's metaphysics that of 'becoming' rather than of 'being', the conclusions can be no more than probable, and as such susceptible to modification, revision and improvement. The myth tells of the work of a craftsman-god, the Demiurge, who, by working on a pre-existing material, imposes order on disorder, reason on necessity, to produce the best possible cosmos in the likeness of a perfect model. Plato's use of a mythical narrative, and his general dismissive attitude to the study of natural science, are subversive devices to detract from the intense interest and solid achievements revealed in the work.

The narrative of the construction and composition of the cosmos presented in the *Timaeus* is in three main sections. The first tells of the crafting of world body and world soul, and, from the same ingredients, human body and human soul. The second posits an alternative version of the cosmogony as the imposition of order on a disordered 'receptacle', with the subsequent mixtures and compounds, and the third gives the details (assigned to inferior craftsmen) of the anatomy and biological functioning of the human body in conjunction with its soul. Within these, Plato's views on elements come mainly in the consideration of the world body, and of the pre-cosmic disorder.

For Plato there is only this one world-system, a unique copy of its model. According to the myth, when the craftsman-god engendered it in the realm of 'becoming' it had to be corporeal, visible and tangible. It was however thought impossible for anything to be visible without the light of fire, or solid without earth, so these two elements were requirements, but then it was necessary to have a bond to hold them together. One mean proportion would have been needed for a two-dimensional world, but two for a three-dimensional one, and these were given as water and air. The ratios were such that earth (dry and cold) related to water (cold and wet) as air (wet and hot) to fire (hot and dry) on the pattern of the mutual ratios of the cubes $1 : 3 : 9 : 27$:

> so by these means and from these four constituents the body of the cosmos was engendered, a unity due to the proportions, having concord (*philia*) from these, so that, having come together in unity with itself, it is indissoluble except by what (or who) first bound it together.
>
> (*Timaeus* 32b–c)

Stars with allotted souls were then said to be placed in the outer fire, and the forms of life in the other masses (birds in air, fish in water, animals on earth) inhabited their respective elements, but each was constituted of all four. The result for humans was that their corporeal constitution resisted the attempts by soul to be controlled, so that 'it became a cause of evil to itself', exacerbated by the properties of objects encountered – the impact of fire or the solid mass of earth, the liquid flow of water or the blast of driving winds (*Timaeus* 43b–c).

The second section of the myth takes up the narrative from the perspective of the component material and examines it more closely. Plato's starting-point was a consideration of the transformation of the elements, which is discussed in a passage reminiscent of Anaximenes' theory of fire, liquids and solids explicable as changes of air:

> We see that what we just termed water, in solidifying, becomes stones and earth (so we believe), but in melting and dispersing it becomes wind and air, and that air, when burnt up, becomes fire, and again that fire, when compounded and extinguished, returns to the form of air; air again, in coming together and condensing, becomes cloud and mist, and from these, compressed still further, comes flowing water, and from water come earth and stones in their turn; and in this way it seems they hand over generation to one another in a cycle.
>
> (*Timaeus* 49b–c)

In the pre-cosmic state however earth, air, fire and water were there only as 'traces' of themselves. The enclosing 'receptacle' (which in other aspects was the 'mother' from which the cosmic child would emerge, or space as the realm of becoming) was in a state of continual disordered flux. Nothing was stable enough to be identified as a 'this' but only a 'sort of this', and the elements moved so continuously and randomly that the situation was like objects being formed and re-formed from gold melted down (comparable to the changes of Plasticine models or the casual shapes of play-dough). Earth, water, air and fire, because of these transformations, were obviously not fundamental enough – elements of elements were needed, and these were interpreted as two types of triangle.

Plato was looking for a mathematical basis of matter comparable (although obviously more rudimentary) to the formulae of a modern physicist. Algebra was still in the future, arithmetic was temporarily disgraced after the discovery of irrational numbers and stereometry and calculus were in their infancy; and so geometry was virtually the only mathematical medium available to Plato. He argued there-fore that since earth, water, air and fire were bodies, they would have volume and so surface; rectilinear surfaces break down into two kinds of right-angled triangles – the isosceles, with equal sides about the right-angle, and a scalene, with the hypotenuse double one side.

Developing the work of Theaetetus, who had been a student at the Academy before his death in 369 BC, and 'proceeding according to the reasonable account along with necessity' (*Timaeus* 53d), Plato showed how these triangles could be built up into four regular solids and then assigned to Empedocles' elements. Four of the isosceles triangles could produce a square, and six squares a cube – the solid that represented earth. Six of the scalenes make an equilateral triangle, and four of these form a pyramid (allotted to fire), eight an octahedron (air) and twenty an icosohedron (water). There was a fifth figure, the dodecahedron, made of twelve pentagons, and the god was said to use this for the construction of the sphere of the whole, comparable perhaps to a football which is made of twelve pentagonal pieces of leather sewn together.

Since fire, air and water had been analysed as made of the same type of equilateral triangles (from the scalene), each could dissolve into its component triangles and reform as either of the other two. Since they were all composed of a specific number of the original scalene triangles – fire of 24, air of 48 and water of 120 – Plato was then able to place them in quantitative relation with one another (at *Timaeus* 56d–e) so that

1 water = 1 fire + 2 air
1 air = 2 fire
5 air = 2 water

Furthermore, an explanation could also be given in this way for water (which included all liquids) being 'bigger and heavier', air lighter and the pyramids of fire lightest and sharpest of all, with the most rapid movement. The cube of earth, representative of all solids, moves least, and, according to this scheme, because its triangular structure is different it would not mutate into any of the other elements, but if broken down would reform only as another solid.

The triangle units were described as too small to be visible at the subatomic level. Once their pattern was imposed on the disorder of the original receptacle, and the whole was held within the sphere of the dodecahedron, the recognisable cosmos emerged. The forming and reforming of the elements into and out of their basic units in unceasing movement within the *plenum* was then explained by the revolution of the whole, and within it by the inequality of size of the molecules of the bodies (the smaller penetrating the larger as the fire pyramid entered into air, or the larger water squashing the smaller air) and by the compounds collecting into their separate and respective place: earth at the centre, surrounded by water, then air, then fire. The variety of phenomena consequent on the incessant movement were all to be explained as due to the innumerable possible combinations and transformations of the basic 'elements of elements'. Plato then proceeded to work out some of the combinations as a way of relaxing, of spending one's leisure 'in a way that brings pleasure and no regrets, considering likely accounts of the world of change' (*Timaeus* 59d).

Aristotle's theory of elements has to be pieced together mainly from the *Physics* and *De Caelo*, while his account of their structure and transformations is in *On Generation and Corruption*. He agreed with Empedocles in assuming that everything in the sublunar world is made of earth, water, air and fire, but, like Plato, could not accept them as absolutely elemental and so immutable. However, he parted company with Plato on the mathematical structure of matter, having little sympathy with Plato's objectives, and finding, for example, the idea of the body of fire made of plane triangles to be verging on the absurd. His own theory set out to be qualitative rather than quantitative.

On a cosmic scale, according to Aristotle, the nature of each element tied it in to the structure of the whole, for he assumed, as did his predecessors, that each elemental mass had its own position in relation to the others. According to this notion of 'natural place', each element comes to rest in its proper region when under no constraint. Earth's place lay at the centre of the cosmos; outside of it was the region of water, then that of air, and fire outside of air. (For Aristotle however fire marked the limit of the sublunar region, and between that and the circumference came, as shall be shown in Chapter 7, the realm of a fifth element which he called *aithēr*.)

Along with the idea of natural place goes that of natural motion. An object made up wholly or largely of a particular element will, when it lies outside of its natural place and is unimpeded, move immediately to it. A stone thrown into the air will drop back to the ground or sink in water, water will rise above earth in the form of springs and rivers, air trapped in water will rise to the surface once released, fiery volcanoes erupt from the earth (as Empedocles had pointed out) and flames shoot up through the air. In general, unless an elemental body is kept from its proper place by constraint (and so forced to undergo counter-natural or unnatural movement), it returns there. Aristotle is here taking over the standard formula of 'like to like' from his Presocratic and Platonic inheritance, and giving it a new importance in the history of physics.

The natural movements of the elements were mediated for Aristotle by weight and lightness. Although he spoke of them on different occasions as either quantitative or qualitative, weight and lightness were nevertheless for him primitive or near primitive properties of bodies. He nowhere explicitly showed that he had grasped the notion of 'mass', in the sense of viewing weight as the result of gravitational force applied to bodies; the conclusion from the fourth book of *De Caelo* was that weight and lightness were more like the opposites of hot and cold. In the same way as a body may be hot or cold without qualification, so Aristotle could think in terms of earth being absolutely heavy and fire absolutely light, with the consequence that the natural movement of earth was 'downwards' towards the centre of the cosmos, and that of fire upwards towards the extremity of the sublunar cosmos. Water and air however are *relatively* light and heavy, water being lighter than earth but heavier than air and fire, air lighter than earth and water but heavier than fire, and so their positions would also be relative to the two extremes.

When Aristotle set out to explain the mutual interchanges of the elements in *On Generation and Corruption*, he also drew upon the long tradition of 'opposites' which went back to the first Milesians, and brought them more systematically in line with the tetrad of earth, water, air and fire. Empedocles himself had characterised his roots with qualitative attributes, calling earth heavy and hard, for example, water cold and dark, and fire as the sun white and hot (fr. 21). These seem to be fairly general attributes, and soon after Philistion, in a simplistic way, related hot to fire, cold to air, dry to earth and moist to water. More interestingly, the Hippocratic writers (for example, *On Human Nature* 7) brought the seasons of the year and the bodily humours into the pattern of relationships, which then connected cold and wet winter with phlegm, wet and hot spring with blood, hot and dry summer with yellow bile and dry and cold autumn with black bile.

Aristotle took the final step of allocating to each Empedoclean element one term from each pair of hot and cold, dry and wet. Fire therefore would be dry and hot, air (being something like steam) hot and wet, water wet and cold, and earth cold and dry. This neat fit between the possible combinations of opposites and the simple bodies formed the basis for Aristotle's theory of elemental transformation, since each element could change into any of the others by losing one of the contraries and acquiring its opposite. As air loses its wetness it acquires 'the dry' and becomes fire; water becomes air by exchanging 'the cold' for 'the hot'; earth dissolves into water when dry is destroyed by wet, or rarefies into fire when hot in turn takes the place of cold. An indirect change, as of dry cold earth into hot wet air, would be via the intermediate stages of dry hot fire or cold wet water.

Despite his criticisms of Plato, Aristotle agreed with him in realising that neither the four simple bodies nor their related opposites were fundamental enough, but rather than looking for an ultimate reality in mathematics, he went back to the concept of an *archē* from which would be derived first the opposites and then the foundations of earth, water, air and fire. This basic substratum he called prime matter (*hylē*), indeterminate and impossible to isolate. In Aristotelian terms it was 'potentiality alone', a *capacity* to receive form and then to emerge into the range of perception with the characteristics of the 'so-called' elements.

The systems of Plato and Aristotle accepted the Empedoclean tetrad of earth, water, air and fire, and accommodated them to their cosmology by looking for something more fundamental still: mathematical elements in the one case and prime matter in the other. But there was another line of thought originating, like that of Empedocles, in a reaction to Parmenides, and through its history antagonistic to the basic features of the Platonic Aristotelian cosmology; this was ancient atomism.

The atomist approach to natural philosophy began with the Presocratic Leucippus in the fifth century BC, but only a few rather exotic words are extant from his writing; the first clear articulation of the theory with the supporting arguments belongs to Democritus, his compatriot from Abdera, although the two names were always closely linked. Like Empedocles, they accepted Parmenides' denial of absolute generation and destruction, but posited a basic plurality 'to save the phenomena'. They maintained that what exists are *atoma*, unlimited numbers of uncuttable units (the root meaning of the word), which are solid, eternal, immutable, of different shapes and sizes but all too minute to be visible. To be able to move, and so account for perceptible change, they require room for movement. Here 'what is not', denied by Parmenides, and identified in its spatial application as 'the empty' by Empedocles, was given a paradoxical existence – nothing (*to mēden*) is as real as thing (*to den*).

This breakdown of temporal and spatial boundaries resulted in the assumption of limitless material in the form of an infinite number of atoms moving at random through a limitless expanse of space. On this theory, the present galaxy arose as a consequence of a rotation of a group of atoms, and it was obvious that other world orders would be forming and disintegrating elsewhere. The atomic compounds that emerged within a system on a large and small scale were then explained as due to the arrangements of atom groups interspersed with void. This was compared in some respects to the epic world of Homer's *Iliad*, being basically no more than an arrangement of alphabet letters (for which the same word – *stoicheion* – as for elements was used) in different groupings with different spacings. The only distinctions made between the atoms themselves were in 'contour' or shape, 'contact' or order and 'inclination' or position. Aristotle preserved the original examples from the alphabet letters:

A differs from N in shape, AN from NA in order, and and Z from N in position.

(*Metaphysics* 985b4–19)

Size, shape and relative spatial position were thus the only variations distinguishing one atom from another. Colour, taste and the like were not properties of atoms:

you should not suppose those white objects which you see before your eyes as white to consist of white primary particles, nor those which are black to be the product of black seed, nor that objects dyed any other colour exhibit it because their particles of matter are imbued with the same colour. For particles of matter have absolutely no colour, neither like nor unlike that of objects.

(Lucretius 2.731–8)

Such apparent qualities were to be explained as alterations in the faculties of perception brought about by internal movement and external pressures, for

our understanding shifts in accordance with the disposition of the body and of the things which enter it and of those which push against it.

(Democritus fr. 9)

The atomic theory of Leucippus and Democritus was adopted by Epicurus in the post-Aristotelian era to give the foundation in physics for his ethical theories of freedom from fear and tranquillity of mind. Epicurus' main change was explicitly to assign weight to the atoms, and as a consequence of this to assume that their movement would then be uniform and linear through the void. For any vortex to start it was then necessary to posit a minimum random shift in this movement – the so-called 'atomic swerve'. Such a swerve would cause a collision with a neighbouring atom, a rebound and further collisions, and so the conditions for the first groupings of atoms into molecules would arise. The incessant bombardment of motes in a sunbeam, which Democritus had seen as an exemplum of primary atomic movement, was later recognised to be derivative, and the minute specks of dust, the smallest objects visible to the naked eye, were rightly interpreted as themselves each mini-battlegrounds of even more minute atom molecules. And even when the 'partless' atom was isolated and taken as physically indivisible, Epicurus was ready to counter Aristotelian objections to such bodies being capable of any kind of movement by formulating a theory of 'minimal parts', according to which atoms are themselves at least theoretically divisible into parts, although none could exist in separation from the atom of which they would be the components.

In this as in many other features the atomic theory was perhaps the most remarkable of the theories of elements to come from the ancient world, staying basically true until the 'uncuttable' atom was actually split early in this present century. Its old antagonist, the Stoic concept of matter as a dynamic continuum rather than discrete units, is perhaps now on course to being the more relevant. This topic belongs with the next chapter, on aither as a fifth element and the theory of *pneuma*.

7

AIR, AITHER AND ASTRA

It has always been obvious that earth and water are fundamental to the world's structure from the very division of the world's surface between land and sea. From earth as universal mother come different forms of vegetation and the means of subsistence for living creatures, and everything decomposes into it. Water too sustains life, in the welcome rain, the streams and springs that well up from the earth, and in Egypt in the flooding of the Nile. Fire is a third ingredient, in volcanoes beneath the earth and lightning across the sky, in the light and heat from the sun that is necessary for growth and nourishment and in the controlled fires of hearth and home open for the advancement of human culture. From the beginning these have been used for warmth, comfort and protection, and then with the advance of technology for cooking (which softens tough food and makes it digestible), conversely for turning soft clay utensils, tablets and figurines into hard and enduring objects, and in metallurgy for making the ores drawn from the earth pliable, so that they could be beaten into shape on the anvil in the forge. Air, added as a fourth basic constituent by Empedocles, is more problematic, whether the four are taken as immutable and eternal elements themselves, or as derived from something more fundamental, such as mathematical forms, a substratum of prime matter, atomic molecules or the 'artisan fire' of the Stoics.

Obviously air, like heat, is necessary for life; the corpse is most clearly distinguished from the living body in being cold and without breath. Air could easily be shown to be a substance with bulk and pressure by inflating gourds and wineskins; a famous practical illustration of this occurred when Spartans trapped on the island of Sphacteria had supplies brought to them by swimmers conveyed on inflated skins. Empedocles, in his account of respiration (fr. 100), used the clepsydra, a simple device for drawing water from jars, as evidence for the corporeality of air. With the top covered, air became trapped inside the clepsydra, thus preventing the entry of water when the device was immersed; when the top was uncovered again, water entered the clepsydra, replacing the air. A child playing with a drinking straw and blocking one end will produce a similar effect when the opposite end is in water. Empedocles used the phenomenon as evidence for his conclusion that the pressure of air could match precisely that of a liquid, for example, of water in the clepsydra and of blood in the mechanics of respiration. Later Lucretius, in a splendidly poetic passage, showed that air is not to be despised because it is invisible, but that the damage effected by a hurricane lifting and whirling heavy objects and sweeping all before it could be as devastating as that caused by a flood (1.290–4).

The animate body clearly stays alive as long as it breathes in and out. Breath and wind are air in motion, and for the Presocratics Anaximenes and Diogenes of Apollonia human reasoning powers were also connected with breath as air in motion within the individual. The atomists supposed that the structure of the soul was as material as that of the body, and that thoughts, desires and emotions were explicable as the movements of a *psychē* made of molecules of small swift atom groups. In Epicurus' refinement of this theory, according to Lucretius, the *psychē* was composed of molecules of fire, air, breath and a nameless fourth substance, the finest and thinnest of all, deep within and the very 'soul of soul'. This activated the fire molecules which stirred the air and breath groups, and they in turn, in contact with the atoms of the body, started it moving in a way comparable to the chain reaction from the brain through the nervous system. The Stoics, also assuming a corporeal soul, described it as a fusion of air and fire which they called *pneuma*.

This tendency to conflate air and fire within the microcosm as the source of reason and life was reflected in the macrocosm. Above the air containing mists, fog and clouds there seemed to be a finer or different substance, showing as a clear blue in the day and black at night, in which were suspended the fires of the sun, moon, bright planets and remote twinkling stars. A crucial issue in ancient cosmology, which had a profound effect on subsequent European science and religion, linked and distinguished the usages of *aēr, aithēr* and the composition and nature of the stars (*astra*). As the vastness of the distances involved in cosmological speculation began to be appreciated, two diverse tendencies emerged. One was to cut off the sky above the moon as a completely separate area with a different nature from the sublunar one; the other was to involve the earth and its surroundings in the life of the cosmos as containing the same substances (whether limited or unlimited) and bound into the same natural developments.

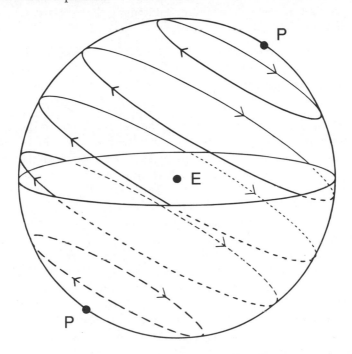

Figure 9 The circles of the stars.
The outer sphere (the *ouranos*) containing the fixed stars revolves with the axis of its poles at an angle to that of the earth's diameter.

A distinction between air and the sky, or between the lower and upper air, had already been made by Homer in the eighth century BC, when, for example, the highest pine tree on Mount Ida was described as reaching through the air to the aither (*Iliad* 14.288). Air at ground level often obscured vision by taking the form of mist or fog, and a hero might be concealed by it when his protecting divinity 'poured out' air about him (as at *Iliad* 3.381, 8.50, *Odyssey* 7.143). Aither, on the other hand, referred to the upper part of the atmosphere, the region from which clouds were formed (*Iliad* 16.365). The distinction between air and aither was not only a

physical and spatial one, but aither was also said to be 'divine' and
the domain of the gods. Zeus 'dwells in the aither', and once received
as his realm 'wide heaven amid the aither and clouds' (*Iliad* 2.412,
15.192). And in the *Odyssey* Athena returned to Olympus, which
here was not the mountain traditionally assigned to it in northern
Greece, but in some upper region containing the ever-secure home
of the gods,

> which no winds shake or rainclouds ever drench or snow
> covers, but cloudless *aithrē* spreads wide, and a white light
> shines, and there the blessed gods are happy all their days.
>
> (*Odyssey* 6.42–6)

Hesiod similiarly described starry heaven (*ouranos*) as the 'ever-
secure home of the gods', born of earth with its roots in Tartarus,
whereas *aithēr* was the bright space generated along with day from
Erebus (dark space) and Night, and *aēr* the mist that came down from
the sky and spread over the earth (*Theogony* 124, 127, 738; *Works
and Days* 548–9). *Aithria*, a dialect version of *aithēr* like the Homeric
aithrē, was later used by Herodotus both for a bright and cloudless
blue sky indicating fine weather and also for clear, cold night air
(2.25, 2.68, 3.86). But the connection with Zeus was still to be found,
for example, in the Zas/aither of Pherecydes, the 'aithrion Zeus' of
Heraclitus (fr. 120) and the identification of Zeus and aither in
Aeschylus (fr. 70) and Euripides (fr. 877), who also used aither in the
traditional sense for the home of the gods (*Bacchae* 393–4).

Among the first philosophers, Anaximenes, as has been shown,
took *aēr* as the limitless and characterless substance from which
everything else is derived by a process of thinning and compacting,
and aither, like fire, was for him simply rarefied air. Heraclitus
ignored both air and aither in his account of the transformations of
fire, which he said was liquefied 'in measures' and then poured out
as earth, which in turn dissolved into sea and then rose as exhalations
to feed the fire (frs 31 and 36), and so started the cycle again.

Empedocles, in his four-element theory, allegorised Zeus as fire
and 'life-bringing Hera' as air. He did not distinguish *aēr* from *aithēr*
as terms for this 'root' as a constituent of organisms, but used the
two indiscriminately, even in the sense of 'breath' in his account of
respiration (fr. 100). As cosmic masses however he listed 'earth and
swelling sea, moist air and Titan sky, whose circle binds all things
fast' (fr. 38). Here the element of air was apparent both in the mist
close to the earth's surface and the bright area above, also called sky

(*ouranos*, fr. 22), which contained and confined the world within itself. The epithet 'Titan' which he attributed to aither would bring to mind the vast size and strength of the giant Atlas, who stood on the earth, while holding fast the sky on his shoulders.

In the system of Anaxagoras, Empedocles' contemporary, the ingredients in the initial universal mixture of all things had no individual recognisable characteristics because in themselves they were diminutive, and were swamped by unlimited air and aither. Once a rotation was engendered by the cosmic intelligence however there was a separation, and

> the dense and moist and cold and dark came together here, where the earth now is, while the rare and hot and dry went outwards to the farther part of the aither.
>
> (fr. 15)

Then water, earth and stones were formed by an Anaximenes-type compacting of the air, while the aither that surrounded the *aēr* 'by virtue of the tension of its whirling motion, snatched stones from the earth and set them ablaze so as to form stars' (Aetius 2.13.3). Anaxagoras thus seems to have been the first to make a clear distinction between the fundamental character and natural place of misty air around the earth and fiery aither above it. In this he was followed by both Plato and Aristotle, although he differed from them, and from other mainstream ancient cosmologists, in supposing that the original rotating was set to continue indefinitely ever outwards, rather than being restrained at the circle of the *ouranos*. Even the atomists supposed that the effect of an initial vortex would reach its limit at the natural periphery of any individual world-system within the infinite void.

Plato in the *Timaeus* took Anaxagoras' differentiation of air and aither further, and within the mythical structure of the work he not only found it necessary to explain the mathematical bases of the four so-called elements of earth, water, air and fire, but hinted at aither as a candidate for an additional fifth fundamental substance for the upper reaches of the sky. When he came to explain the triangular elements which he supposed constituted the Empedoclean roots, he assigned a regular solid to each – to earth the cube, to fire the pyramid, to air the octahedron and to water the icosahedron. And although, following the previous tradition, he had agreed that the celestial bodies were composed 'mostly of fire' (*Timaeus* 40a), for the remaining fifth regular solid, the dodecahedron, Plato added that the god used it for the whole, 'decorating it with constellations' (*diazōgraphōn*, *Timaeus* 55c, a single participle meaning literally 'variously animal-drawing'). The word was puzzling even to the ancients, and was taken by Xenocrates and others to mean that the fifth solid with its living stars indicated a fifth element, comparable to the other four with their related geometric solids and associated forms of life (Xenocrates at Simplicius *Commentary on De Caelo* 12.21–6; Plutarch *On E at Delphi* 390a; aither as an element distinct from air is standard in the *Epinomis*, preserved in the corpus of Plato's works, but unlikely to be by him).

Whether or not aither was already recognised as an element distinct from earth, water, air and fire in the Academy during Aristotle's time there, he was the one who specifically adopted and argued for it, so that it came to be known as the fifth element (the 'quintessence', *quinta essentia* in Latin, although Aristotle's own term was usually 'first body'). In three chapters of the first book of his *De Caelo* Aristotle established the existence and attributes of aither as a fifth element spanning the sky from the moon outwards to the distant enclosing circumference, and constituting the substance of that area and the bodies within it. He used the 'universal consent' argument based on the tradition of gods having their home high in the sky, as well as some questionable etymology (deriving 'aither' from the words *aei thein*, 'always running'). More significantly he used the immutability of the region as evidence:

> The truth of this is clear from the evidence of the senses, enough at least to secure the assent of human belief; for throughout all past time, according to the records handed down from generation to generation, we find no trace of change in the whole of the outermost heaven nor in any one of its proper parts.
> (*De Caelo* 270b12–17)

The aither was distinguished from the Empedoclean elements in its exclusive position above the moon, and also, in contrast to the rectilinear movements of the other four, Aristotle argued that its natural motion was circular: 'We see the heavens turn in a circle' as he said (*De Caelo* 272a5–6), and this perception was supported by the records of past generations. In addition, whereas the downward movements of earth and water were taken as contrary to the upward movements of air and fire, the aither's rotation could have no contrary. And since it could not move upwards or downwards even if it were possible to be constrained, aither could not be either heavy or light, or subject to generation, corruption or change, but rather it was to be understood as engaged sempiternally in circular motion, immutable and impassive. Being above the world of change aither would also have greater honour and purity than earth, water, air or fire, and so be linked with the divine – Homer's 'ever-secure home of the gods' updated. The related cosmological pattern of a central, static spherical earth, with water, air and fire in linear movements in the mortal world of change beneath the moon, and above it the clear, unchanging region where aither rotates for ever and bears in the rotation the divine spheres of planets and stars, was the most influential to survive from the ancient world.

Aristotle's theory of aither, however, had its critics, even among his own school. Theophrastus, Aristotle's successor at the Lyceum, seems to have accepted the idea; Strato of Lampsacus, the next head, perhaps succumbing to Stoic influence, looked upon the aither as a species of fire, much as Anaxagoras had done and as Cicero was to describe it in *On the Nature of the Gods*. The Peripatetic Xenarchus of Seleucia, Cicero's contemporary, attacked Aristotle's concept of aither as a special substance with a natural circular movement in a treatise entitled *Against the Fifth Substance*, partially preserved some centuries later in Simplicius' commentary in the sixth century AD on Aristotle's *De Caelo*. Simplicius also quotes extensively in this commentary from another attack upon the Aristotelian aither – *Against Aristotle on the Eternity of the World* by John Philoponus. Philoponus, as a Christian believing in a beginning to the cosmos in the divine creation, set out to undermine the powerful challenge to that belief of Aristotle's ever-existing world.

Simplicius however defended Aristotle against the attack by Philoponus, and the theory of aither continued to be influential. It was basic to the serious as well as the more dubious aspects of alchemy; Cartesian physics had a role for aether as the field of interstellar space, and Boyle introduced it in the context of various non-mechanical phenomena. In a paper sent to the Royal Society towards the end of 1675, Isaac Newton postulated 'an aetherial medium, much of the same constitution with air but far rarer, subtler, and more strongly elastic'. This medium, conceived as vibrating in a manner 'like air', was said to be at a 'greater degree of rarity in those pores of natural bodies than in the free aetherial spaces'. Newton then introduced into his own theories a version of the Aristotelian aither, which, taken as an intermediary, was used in explanations of gravity, optical phenomena and in general the relationship between light and body. By the nineteenth century, aither (as *ether*) came to be regarded as the medium responsible for the transmission of light and electromagnetic waves. It was not until Einstein's paper on relativity in 1905 that Aristotle's theory was finally laid to rest, although the term for the medium of communication lives on in the contemporary 'ethernet'.

Aristotle had connected the nature and function of the celestial aither to that of *pneuma* in animal life, and when this was adapted by the Stoics to their theory of a dynamic continuum, another potentially interesting link between the ancient world and the modern emerges. Before this can be pursued further however some explanation of the origin and meaning of *pneuma* is required.

In early Greek epic poetry atmospheric air (*aēr*) was usually thought of as having a certain density, enough to shroud a hero and make him invisible, or hide a mountain top from view; Tartarus, the region beneath the earth, could also be 'airy' in the sense of being dim and misty. Air in motion however is perceptible as 'the winds that blow', and it was the etymology here that linked the winds with the breath of animals, for the verb *pnein* can be translated both by 'to blow' with reference to winds and breezes, and 'to breathe' of animals; 'to breathe', like 'to see the light', would then be simply an alternative expression for 'to be alive' (as with Homer, for example, at *Iliad* 17.447, or Sophocles *Trachiniae* 1160). The cognate noun *pnoē* similarly was used for the wind's breath and for air in respiration. A second noun *pneuma* was a later derivation from *pnein*, and like it was initially applied to the blowing of the winds (as by Herodotus at 7.16.1) as well as to air that is breathed. The reference then broadened to the 'breath of life' and to the human *psychē* generally – Sophocles could even say that a human being is '*pneuma* and shadow only' (fr. 13). Eventually in Christian literature it became the standard term for the third person of the Trinity – the Holy Spirit (*hagion pneuma*).

A connection of the cosmos with this constituent of atmospheric air and human breath is first found in the frequently quoted fragment of the early Presocratic Anaximenes in the sixth century BC:

> As our *psychē* which is *aēr* maintains us, so do *pneuma* and *aēr* surround the whole *kosmos*.

The breath of life, which holds together, strengthens and controls the individual, was here directly linked in constitution and function to the pneumatic air that envelopes the whole and ensures its survival.

116

It was also related to temperature, for the air that condenses, in Anaximenes' theory, into liquids and solids is colder, and becomes warmer as it rarefies in proportion to its distance from the earth. He produced evidence for this from a common observation:

> Breath (*pnoē*) is chilled when compressed and compacted by the lips, but when the mouth opens and the breath is exhaled it becomes warm because it is thinner.
>
> (quoted by Plutarch *On Cold* 947f.)

As has been explained in Chapter 4 (p. 62), Aristotle attributed to the Pythagoreans the concept of a cosmos that 'breathes', reporting their claim that it inhales (*anapnein*) the boundless *pneuma* that surrounds it (*Physics* 213b). Another version is given in the *Metaphysics*, at 1091a, specifically said to be in the language of natural science:

> when the unit (*monad*) had been constructed, whether from planes or surfaces or seed or elements or whatever, immediately the nearest part of the unlimited began to be drawn in and to be limited by the limit.

The mathematics of basic principles were here linked with cosmobiology, when the 'drawing in' of the unlimited (which would then be defined in arithmetic and geometric terms) was also the 'inhaling' by the animate cosmos of the external *pneuma* to maintain its own life.

Since in these systems the seed from which the world first grew was thought to be of a fiery nature, there emerged a further analogy, suggested by the fifth-century BC Pythagorean, Philolaus. The first breath which the new-born animal takes in from the outside air cools its innate heat and the subsequent exhaling restores the body temperature to the appropriate level, and so with the subsequent breaths in and out ('like taking in credit and repaying a debt' (Menon 44A27)). According to a similar pattern the heat of the whole is cooled and regulated by the external *pneuma* which moves in and out in the vast process of cosmic respiration. The connection between breathing on the small and the large scale was confirmed when cosmic and animal *pneuma* were identified and used as the basis for the kinship of all forms of life. The reason for this kinship, reported by Plato in the *Meno* as an 'old story', was explained by Sextus in terms of *pneuma*. He quoted the Pythagoreans as saying that

117

we have a certain community not only among ourselves and with the gods, but also with unreasoning animals. For a single *pneuma* pervades the whole world as *psychē*, and this also unites us with them.

(*Against the Mathematicians* 9.127)

The last Presocratic, Diogenes of Apollonia, rejected the post-Parmenidean pluralism of Empedocles, Anaxagoras and the atomists, and returned to Anaximenes' monistic *archē* of air, but with various elaborations that took account of some of the intervening theories. Diogenes supposed air to be the individual psychic principle, responsible for life and reasoning:

Humans and other animals stay alive because of *aēr*, by breathing it in. And this is for them both *psychē* and thought . . . and, if they are deprived of this, thought fails and they die.

(fr. 4)

In another fragment Diogenes proposed air as the basic element both of the individual and of the cosmos as a whole since it was able to take on the basic opposites and other characteristics. It was also subject to variations in temperature – warmer within us, cooler outside, but then hotter again in the higher reaches:

There is no single thing that does not have some share of air; yet no one thing has a share of it in the same way that another does, but there are many forms both of air itself and of thought. For it is multi-form, being hotter and colder and drier and moister and more stable and more swiftly moving, and in it are many other differentiations both of taste and colour, unlimited in number. And the soul of all living creatures is the same thing, air that is warmer than that outside in which we live, but much cooler than that near the sun.

(fr. 5)

The further linking of the individual to the cosmos came in the report that Diogenes described animal semen as 'of the nature of *pneuma*', so that in body and soul a continuity between the individual life-form and the cosmic whole could be traced.

Aristotle later picked up the particular biological point made by Diogenes, and also argued that *pneuma* was contained in semen, and it was therefore *pneuma*'s vitalistic properties that caused the material provided by the female in reproduction to develop into a living animal. (The main argument is in *On Generation of Animals*, 2.2.) Furthermore, Aristotle suggested that the *pneuma* transmitted to the individual at birth had a part to play throughout its time, not only as the principle of life, but also as an intermediary in the stimulus to action. Movement obviously was perceived to arise in an organism as the result of desire (*orexis*), and this was explained as a stimulus to the body which triggered it into physical locomotion by means of the *pneuma* contained in the heart and blood-vessels of animals and humans.

Pneuma for Aristotle was a combination of breath (understood as air in motion) and heat, and it was *pneuma* as the bearer of 'what is called hot' that made it the generative factor in semen. Aristotle however was careful to make it clear that the natural substance which was in the *pneuma* was not fire, but was analogous to the element that makes up the stars. The reasoning was that

> fire does not generate any animal, and no animal is seen to be
> formed either in fluid or solid substances while they are under
> the influence of fire, whereas the heat of the sun and the heat
> of animals do bring about generation . . .
> (*On Generation of Animals* 737a1–3)

The fire that we see about us was understood as destructive, burning up whatever is available as fuel, whereas the sun's heat is clearly generative, and fosters birth and growth on earth. As has been shown, the sun, like the other celestial bodies, was thought by Aristotle to be made of aither, the additional element which he called 'first body', and it is to this that *pneuma* in animals was analogous by virtue of its generative heat.

Aristotle pursued the analogy between *pneuma* and celestial aither further into the life of the animal. In its role as initiator of animal movement, *pneuma* was responsive to the faculty of desire, and so was the cause of movement without itself being altered qualitatively (*On Movement of Animals* 703a25), in much the same way as aither was the cause of cosmic movements while remaining independently ever the same. In addition the mediation of *pneuma* between the immaterial (the faculty of desire) and the material (the animal body) could be compared to the role of aither as the link between the immaterial 'unmoved mover' and the sublunar region of change, the material and the mortal.

The Stoics brought some of the features of Aristotle's *pneuma* into the creative technology of the universal fire which they called *pur technikon.* This worked within the enclosed spherical cosmos assumed by Plato and Aristotle, but the Stoics argued that, rather than staying for ever in the same condition, the cosmos was subject to a periodic conflagration when this fire engulfed everything in its flames, and then with that same regularity regenerated the cosmos. As the conflagration died down it was thought that its fiery substance was transformed into hot air and then condensed into moisture, and from this were derived the familiar earth, water, air and fire which, from Empedocles onwards, had been viewed as standard constituents of the present world-system.

In a simpler scheme than the Aristotelian complexity of transformation through alternate opposites, the Stoics allocated a single quality to each body – earth was dry, water moist, air cold and fire hot. *Pneuma,* which could also be called aither, was then explained as a combination of cold and heat, air and fire, acting on the passive bodies of earth and water. It was thought to pervade the cosmos, and intermingle with all its constituents, as thoroughly as the fire and air mingled with one another in the *pneuma* itself. The complete interpenetration of fire and air as *pneuma* with their opposites earth and water resulted then in a dynamic and unbroken continuum, of the kind in which a butterfly movement in one part would affect the whole, or, in the Stoic version: 'Nothing stops a single drop of wine from mixing with the sea.'

In a concept of cosmic conflict going back to Heraclitus, the Stoics supposed that the combination of air and fire, which permeated and activated the cosmos in the form of *pneuma,* was in a state of continual tension or *tonos.* This had two aspects – an outward movement of the *pneuma,* for which fire was responsible by virtue of its warm 'elastic' nature, and an inward movement back into itself, which was due to the contractive and chilling properties of air. These movements were thought of as continuous mutual reactions, such that the resulting tension in the *pneuma* might explain both the cohesion, unity and internal stability of bodies, and their external dimensions and qualities. In plants *pneuma* was in this way held responsible for their life, nourishment and growth, in animals for perception and locomotion in addition to these, and in humans for intelligence. In each case the variety of functions was related to the proportions of fire and air in the constituent *pneuma,* and their survival to the preservation of the tension between them. *Pneuma* was thus the vital ingredient of the Stoic cosmos, maintaining the whole as well as the bodies within it. It maintained the earth in equilibrium at the centre, kept the whole stationary and prevented it from disintegrating into the surrounding void by using the same 'holding' function that was observable in the maintenance of the structure of its parts. The Stoic Chrysippus even went so far as to suggest that the theory involved a precursor to the theory of gravitation in the implications of a universal attraction of all the parts towards the centre, which, in a sphere, coincides with 'below' from every aspect of the periphery. (The evidence is discussed by Sambursky 1959: 110–15.)

The consequence of this way of thinking was a literal *sympatheia* or 'being affected together' in the interaction of the parts, and between the parts and the whole. The Stoics provided a new context for the earlier identification of 'those who breathe' with 'those who live' in the cosmos itself. This now came to be regarded directly, without metaphor or analogy, as a living entity in its own right, which had in *pneuma* its own vital breathing and perceptive faculty, and the power of reason. The parts within its closed system might be imperfect, with relative temporal and spatial gains and losses, but as a whole, in the sum total of its parts, the Stoics regarded the cosmos as self-sufficient, independent and complete.

There was a special way in which the sympathy of the parts of the cosmos with the whole could be shown, and the apparent gulf between life on earth and events in the distant aither might be bridged, and that was in a link between the individual and the stars above, found in mythology, popular thought and the more philosophical concept of 'astral eschatology' – the theory that the origin of the human soul was in the stars, and that it would return there after its separation from the body at death.

These beliefs are first found in ancient Egypt, some implying that the dead are reborn with the new sun when it is renewed either beneath the earth or beyond the sky, and others indicating a connection, at least for the Pharaohs, with the stars of Orion and Sirius. The pyramids were called 'the mansions of eternity', and some of their texts proclaim the relationship:

> I fly upwards; I am not of the earth, I am of the sky. I am the essence of a god. My soul is a star of gold.

The lines are quoted by Bauval and Gilbert in *The Orion Mystery* (1994) in the course of their general argument that the three Khufu pyramids were deliberately aligned with the belt of Orion, and that their 'star shafts' allowed for instant access to these stars for the

Phaoronic souls. Even if the authors' conclusions are unacceptable in detail, it seems undeniable that the Milky Way was considered to be the celestial counterpart to the river Nile, overseen by the stars of Orion and Sirius as on earth the Pharoah and his queen protected the kingdom of Egypt. The numerous tomb paintings of the night sky clearly imply a journey to a permanent abode in the stars for the soul, while the body was preserved indefinitely in its mummified state.

The general belief that the souls of the dead connect with the stars appears to have been well established in Greece by the late fifth century, although it is difficult to assess the influence here of eastern or Egyptian mythology. Whatever the antecedents, the language of the texts is in that tradition. In 432 BC, for example, after the battle of Potideia, a monument to the Athenian dead was raised with the inscription:

Aither received their souls, earth their bodies.

Two representative quotations from the fifth-century tragedian Euripides offer further supporting evidence for a continuing tradition of astral eschatology. In his *Suppliant Women* he distinguished *pneuma* from aither in this context:

Let the dead be covered by the earth, and, whence each part came to light, there let it return – *pneuma* to aither, the body to earth.

(531–4)

Towards the close of the play the chorus says of the dead children of Iphis that 'the aither holds them now' (1140). The relationship between the containing aither and the human soul is further clarified in the *Helen* (1014–16):

The mind (*nous*) of the dead has lived its life, but an immortal power is preserved, once it has entered immortal aither.

There is also support for this way of thinking in the eschatology of the famous Gold Leaves that were found in the Greek colonies of south Italy. They belong roughly to the same era, but have features which link them with Babylonian and biblical texts. These leaves or *lamellae* were enclosed in amulets and placed in coffins. They gave guidance on what was expected to happen after death: there would be a tree of shining dark cypress (comparable to a Tree of Life or Tree of Knowledge) growing by refreshing waters, and protected by guardians who need to be propitiated. The formula of propitiation for the soul to recite would be:

I am child of Earth and starry Sky.

In this way earth would take back the body, and an astral destiny could be claimed by the soul, compatible with its origins. (The Gold Leaves are discussed by Zuntz 1971: 355–93.)

Animals and humans were allotted a specific place in the sky in the mythology known as *catasterism* ('star-transformation') in which a particular group of stars, suggesting a certain shape, was linked to a story of an event on earth which resulted in the appearance of that constellation. Some of these stories go back to Babylonian and Egyptian sources, and link with ancient astrologies across the world, but the Greek versions were collected by Eratosthenes in Alexandria in the work known as *Catasterismi* and preserved at some length in secondary sources. (The fragments are collected by Charles Robert (1963).) The signs of the zodiac were all to be explained by catasterisms but with many alternative versions. The Twins, for example, were identified as Amphion and Zethus of Thebes or Castor and Pollux, Virgo might be Justice, Fortuna, Ceres or Erigone, and the Water-carrier Asclepius or Ganymede. Heroes were connected to some of the animal signs, for example, Hercules to Cancer and Leo, and Aries to Jason, whereas Orion, his belt, his dog and the scorpion that killed him were all catasterised. Sometimes the myths told of women who were turned into stars as the Pleiads, Andromeda and Ursa major and minor, and Ariadne was honoured by the god Dionysus when her crown, made by Hephaestus, was set into the northern sky as aurora borealis. Such myths proliferated in countless forms, but one of the strangest is the aetiology which links mother's milk with 'galaxy' (the etymology of the word), and explained the Milky Way (in Greek *kuklos galaxias* and in Latin *circulus lacteus*) with the milk spilled from the goddess Hera when she refused to suckle the baby Hercules, or in another version in which he vomitted in his greed.

The serious, *philosophical* link between terrestial life and the celestial heights first appeared in Anaximenes in his comparison of air, controlling and maintaining life as *psyche* in humans, with that of air as *pneuma* in relation to the whole cosmos. The identification was made more explicit by Diogenes of Apollonia in the claim that the pervasive and all-powerful air also constitutes the soul and thought of men. It is traceable in Empedocles, who found a home for the elemental souls (which he calls *daimons*) between the cycles of regeneration in the outer limits of the cosmic sphere. And the link continues through to Aristotle who in different contexts – in biology (*On Generation of Animals* 736b–737a) and ethics (*Eudemian Ethics* 1248a) as well as in *De Caelo* – relates the *psychē* to the encircling fifth element, eternal and invariant.

Plato, more than any other ancient philosopher, argued for an immortal soul in his constant campaign against those he saw as immoral atheists in their reduction of the soul to a temporary existence that would cease when its matter disintegrated along with the body at death. In his myths he supplemented his counter-arguments with a narrative of a journey for the soul after death which in the most meritorious cases (i.e., for those who had devoted themselves to philosophy) could result in a time of limited or eternal duration in a god-like existence way beyond the confines of this earth. At the end of the *Phaedo*, for example, in the myth that follows the arguments for immortality, Plato suggested, through Socrates as narrator, that the soul which had divorced itself as far as possible from the demands of the body would go 'to a pure home that is above'. Philosophers were to ascend 'to mansions even more beautiful than these' which, Socrates added diplomatically, there was not the time to describe (*Phaedo* 114b–c; the passage is perhaps to be taken with 81a, with the mention of 'the company of the gods' enjoyed by some souls). The destiny of the souls in the Myth of Er at the end of the *Republic* was also given a cosmic setting, linked with the Pythagorean theory of the 'harmony of the spheres' (a theory that belongs more with the discussion of time). In the *Timaeus*, too, the souls were linked to the sky, each one in that myth allotted a 'consort star' when it was said that they were 'sown into the instruments of time'. Plato envisaged as many stars as souls, with the numbers perhaps kept constant by 'recycling'. The souls came to earth and continually transmigrated up and down a hierarchy of lives, but when, as a rare occurrence, a soul lived a human life in righteousness, that soul was then promised 'a return to the habitation of its consort star' and subsequent bliss (*Timaeus* 41–2).

In the well-known myth in another Platonic dialogue, the *Phaedrus*, Socrates as narrator compared the tripartite soul to a winged chariot, with reason as charioteer, and the horses representing spirit and desire. Before birth the team was described as encircling the outer perimeter of the sky in the company of the gods and gazing at 'what is beyond there' (a way of describing the Platonic world of true being), and so gaining an understanding of the ultimate nature of virtue and knowledge. The chariots of the gods were said to encircle the perimeter indefinitely, but the human teams crash to earth and take on mortal lives. From what remembrance each one has (and can develop) of the earlier time, and in the company of a beloved friend, the human soul attempts to regain its wings, and return after death to its celestial origin. Plato here gave a little more detail than in the *Phaedo*:

> The region beyond the sky no poet in the past has hymned as it deserves nor will any in the future, but it is like this . . . the region belongs to being as it really is – without colour or shape, untouchable, perceptible only to the soul's charioteer, the intellect, which is concerned with the genus of true knowledge.
>
> (*Phaedrus* 247c)

These myths therefore, which identify a celestial origin and destiny for humanity, linked themes from Plato's own philosophy – his metaphysics, epistemology and theories of transmigration and recollection – with the more widespread belief that souls, made of air, breath or *pneuma*, make their last journey on the death of the body to the upper aither. When Cicero adapted these concepts to Roman values in his Latin version of a Platonic myth known as *The Dream of Scipio*, he too suggested that 'humans have been endowed with souls made out of the everlasting fires called stars and constellations', but the way that leads back to these fires, more specifically the constellations in the Milky Way (the *circuleus lacteus*) where 'a habitation for all eternity' is envisaged, is by means of the political life, a life devoted to the care and service of one's country.

8

TIME AND ETERNITY

Past, present and future events were once embraced by the wisdom of the prophet who, in the standard phrase, knew 'the things that are and will be and were before' (*Iliad* 1.70). The first philosophical confrontation of the problems the concept of time poses is found in the Presocratic Parmenides, who said of what there is:

> It never was nor will be, since it is now all at once one and continuous; what beginning will you seek for it?
>
> (fr. 8.5–6)

He answered the ever-puzzling question of what was there before anything else by denying past and future, and holding existence in a tenseless and immutable 'now'. Those who, subsequently, were anxious to 'save the phenomena' by restoring plurality and change returned to an acceptance of past and future, but supposed that the basic ingredients (whether elements, atoms or 'prime matter') from which the world was constituted were themselves without beginning or end. Parmenides' denial of non-being meant that from then onwards immortality and eternity implied the denial of both starting and finishing, for a beginning of being required non-being before it and an end non-being after. The 'mixed' notion of a cosmos or god or an individual soul that could have a beginning and then continue without end was unacceptable because of the contradictions involved.

The regular progress of time through past, present and future was first and most obviously marked by the apparent changes in sun and moon. The rising and setting of the sun and the stretch of darkness marked the day, the waxing and waning of the moon the lunar month, and the turnings of the sun with the corresponding seasonal changes limited the year. Within human life there were similar markers: the female menstrual cycle, the ten lunar months of

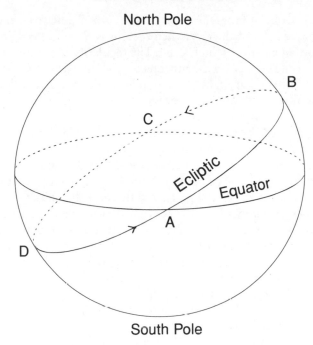

Figure 10 The path of the sun along the ecliptic.
BD is the sun's path March–September (dotted curve) and September–
March; B marks the longest day, D the shortest, A and C the equinoxes
with equal days and nights.

pregnancy and the passing of generations through approximately thirty-year periods within which the son replaced the father, the father aged, and his life was renewed in the grandson. In popular belief the measure of life for any individual was taken to be fixed by the length of the thread which was spun, measured and cut by the three sisters, the Moirai or Fates.

Scientific advance in the ancient world was hampered generally by the lack of a reliable means of calculating time. The six so-called 'hours' of the day and the four 'watches' of the night varied in length according to the time of year, the hours of the day being longer in summer and shorter in winter, and the night watches correspondingly shorter and longer. The months of the year were haphazard, and the Greek city-states were so fiercely independent that they often had different names and different starting days for their months. Methods of naming the year according to the chief officials, or by the series of four-year Olympiads, or in Rome from the year of the foundation of the city when there was no consensus for that date, were all hopelessly inefficient. The regularity of the movements of the celestial bodies, on the other hand, contrasted with this human muddle. The stars at night were a guide to the mariner in locating him spatially, and they came to be widely used to place the individual and his country in a temporal sequence.

Awareness of the order and periodicity of the heavens and their phenomena received its initial impetus from simple observation of the daily movement of the sun across the sky by day and of the moon and stars by night. The connections of the seasons with variations in the sun's latitude and in the pattern of the stars then hinted at larger regularities. A sharpening of this original awareness came with the advances in accuracy of observational astronomy, and the careful recording in Babylonia of the results. Over the course of centuries, astronomers uncovered more and more signs of the consistent orderliness of the movements of stars and planets.

An inevitable consequence of this was to find an unbridgeable divide between the changeless realm of the sky and the human realm of birth, change, decay and mortality. The tradition from the earliest time was to see the sky as the home of the divine, and this tradition was confirmed in Homer and Hesiod with the standard description of the *ouranos* as 'the ever-secure abode of the gods'. Here 'the deathless ones' were represented as being endlessly free from care, pain, illness and old age, sometimes watching with interest the sufferings of humans in their brief life-spans on earth. Despite the opposition from the atomists, who maintained that the present world-system was past its prime and on course for inevitable collapse and disintegration into its atomic constituents, the contrast between the celestial and the sublunar regions persisted in Aristotle and beyond. According to his own testimony, Aristotle was the first to affirm the everlasting existence of the heavens and the unceasing nature of their movement, but he also saw his sophisticated cosmology as being firmly in the older Homeric tradition:

> Therefore it is well to assure oneself that the ancient accounts, especially those of our own people, are true – that there is something immortal and divine among those things that possess a motion such that it has no limit, but is, rather, the limit of others ... the ancients apportioned *ouranos* – the upper region – to the gods on the grounds that it alone is immortal; and the present argument testifies that it is imperishable and

ungenerated, and, further, that it is not susceptible to any mortal trouble; in addition it is free from toil, since it has no need of any forceful constraint to contain it and prevent it from moving in a fashion according to its own tendency.

(*De Caelo* 284a)

The movement of the heavens, everlasting and continual, then secured the base for Aristotle's conception of aither, that 'first body' which in his theory (as explained in Chapter 7) constituted the region above the moon. He considered aither prior to earth, air, fire and water, and more divine than them, and, in the further account given in the *Meteorology* (1.2–3), he described it as separated from them, with its purity increasing in proportion to its distance from the sublunar world. The celestial bodies within the *aithēr* – sun, moon, planets and stars – were themselves also 'the most divine of visible bodies'. The consequence of this way of thinking was to suppose that the cosmos itself, enclosed by aither from the circumference to the moon, would also be ever-existing – neither generated nor created, and with no end to its future life. His subsequent antagonism to the impending disintegration threatened by the atomists is preserved in a report on an early work of his:

Aristotle was surely speaking piously when he maintained that the world is ungenerated and imperishable, and he convicted of grave ungodliness those who maintained the opposite and thought that the great visible god, which contains in truth sun and moon and the remaining pantheon of planets and fixed stars, is no different from an artefact; he used to say in mockery (we are told) that in the past he had been afraid for his home lest it be destroyed by violent winds or by fierce storms or by time or by lack of proper maintenance, but that now a greater fear hung over him, from those who by their argument were destroying the whole world.

(fr. 18 trans. Ross)

The large-scale structure of the world was immutable according to Aristotelian physics: the stars would always turn in their courses, heavy bodies when unconstrained would invariably tend towards the centre of the cosmos, and lighter ones away from it. However, although Aristotle supposed that aither would thus rotate for ever, with this locomotion as its only variation, events beneath the moon were obviously subject to change. Plants, animals and humans in their life on earth were seen to be continually involved in birth and death, growth, decline and decay, and the four simple bodies in constant processes of transformations. Living creatures would experience a quasi-permanence in the propagation of their species, yet individually each inevitably reached an end of life, caught up in the transience that is an essential characteristic of the sublunar world in virtue of the indeterminate nature of the material of which it is composed.

Aristotle's understanding of time in relation to the regions both above and below the moon, and to the sempiternity of the cosmos as a whole, connected with his views on the time word *aiōn* (transliterated as 'eon'). This had a separate but related history to that of the more abstract *chronos*, and needs some amplification, since it is a key term in much of Greek speculation on time in cosmology, and in Aristotle's own theory.

In Homer *aiōn* signified the vitality or vital substance which keeps a human alive, and leaves the body together with the breath at death (for example, at *Iliad* 5.696). This connection with life then led to the term meaning length of life, for humans and also for gods (as in Aeschylus *Suppliants* 574). From there it was associated with immortal life, and so with time itself. '*Aiōn*', said Heraclitus enigmatically, 'is a child at play, playing chequers; the kingdom is a child's' (fr. 52), a line which suggested that human lifetimes are playthings of cosmic time. Empedocles moved between the different senses, applying the word to an individual's lifetime, to human generations and to cosmic time, as when he stated that 'boundless *aiōn*' would never be emptied of the principles of attraction and repulsion working on the elements (frs 16, 110 and 129).

Later, in the *Timaeus*, Plato described the work of the craftsman-god generating the cosmos as an image of an ever-living and divine original. In the complexities of the time distinctions involved here Plato used *aiōn* as an intermediate term for the life of both the original model and its present copy (coining a new adjective *aiōnios* for the purpose):

> The nature of the living creature was eternal (*aiōnios*), and it was not possible to confer this attribute completely upon the created copy; but he resolved to make a moving likeness of eternity (*aiōn*), and when he set the *ouranos* in order he made a likeness, which was *aiōnios* progressing numerically, of the *aiōn* that remains in unity – this is what we call time (*chronos*).

For days and nights and months and years did not exist before the *ouranos* came into being, but at the moment when he framed it he devised their generation; all these are parts of time, and 'was' and 'will be' are created species of time.

(Timaeus 37d–e)

Plato here was looking for a solution in a new context for the problems raised by Parmenides, struggling like his predecessor with the constraints of the language in which it had to be expressed. The solution he suggested here of an *aiōn* that has neither past nor future was later taken to be a foreshadowing of the concept of the atemporal eternity of the Christian God.

Contrasted with the tenseless eternity of the craftsman's model, Plato set the everlasting generations and destructions of the world of becoming. But the continuation of the copy was unlike the eternity of the model, for this world 'progresses numerically' through past, present and future. According to this theory, therefore, time as *chronos* is to be defined as the eternal image (*aiōnios eikōn*) of eternal life; past, present and future are its 'species' (*eidē*), and days, months and years its parts.

In the narration of the myth of the *Timaeus* Plato spoke of the simultaneous appearance of time and the *ouranos*, but this does not imply that he supposed either to have had a starting-point. A serial description of a complex artefact has to begin somewhere, even if as in this case the parts might not have been constructed in a temporal series, but considered to be always there. Plato's successor Xenocrates suggested a comparison with geometrical diagrams, which are drawn at a specific moment for the sake of instruction about truths that do not have a beginning. In any case, when Plato used the verb *gegonen* at 28b it was in the peculiar Greek perfect tense which refers to the present ('is now as the result of generation') and need mean little more than that it belongs with *genesis* (the world of 'becoming') rather than with *ousia* (the world of 'being'). Plato in fact apologised for describing the world body before the world soul, explaining that an account has to have some kind of sequence, and 'our narrative is bound to reflect much of our own contingent and accidental state' (*Timaeus* 34c).

Elsewhere in the same work Plato wrote of how 'the sight of days and nights and months and the cycles and turnings of the years produced number and gave us the concept of time and the power of inquiry into the nature of the cosmos' (*Timaeus* 47a). The revolution of the heavens, by which the number of days, months and years – the parts of time – are marked off, resulted therefore in a numerical conception of time. Time 'progressing numerically' then would be closely associated with number, and time-reckoning was clearly a form of calculation or enumeration. Time, as numerable, could in this way be distinguished from the eternal model from which it derives its own eternity, for the model 'remains in unity', and unity or 'the one' was for Plato (as for Greek mathematics generally) the beginning or principle of number, but not itself a number. Time can thus 'imitate eternity' or be 'a moving image of eternity' in that it rotates 'in accordance with number', so that Aristotle in the *Physics* was ready to interpret such language as an identification of time with the rotation of the heavens, and so bring Plato into line with his own way of thinking (218a–b).

Aristotle himself defined time in this context as 'the number of motion in respect of before-and-after' (*Physics* 219b2). In explaining this definition, Aristotle was careful to point out that 'number' could be understood in two senses: time is not a number by which we enumerate (like the natural numbers 3, 4, 5 . . .), but that which is numerated. The rotation of the heavens could then be accepted as the measure of all other movements because of its continuity, regularity, and sempiternity. This again produced the conclusion that time just is the rotation of the heavens (as at *De Caelo* 287a and *Physics* 223b).

Plato's attribution of eternal being to the model in his *Timaeus* was based upon the metaphysics of contrasting worlds of being and becoming which was afterwards rejected by Aristotle. But there is one interesting passage in which Aristotle adumbrated the idea of immunity to time or timelessness where, at the conclusion to his argument against the possibility of a plurality of worlds, he drew the corollary that there would be no place, void or time outside of the cosmos:

> Time is the number of motion – but there is no motion without physical body. And it has been shown that neither is there nor can there be body outside of the cosmos. Therefore it is clear that no place, void, or time is outside of it; and that is why the things there (*ta ekei*) are not such as to be in place, nor does time make them age, nor is there change at all of anything set beyond the outermost locomotion of the heavens, but, free from alteration and suffering, in possessing the best and most independent life they continue for the whole of eternity (*aiōn*).
>
> (*De Caelo* 279a)

Where Plato in the *Timaeus* had ascribed eternity (*aiōn*) to the model used by the Demiurge in fashioning the cosmos, Aristotle related it to 'the things there' outside the cosmos. 'The things there' (*ta ekei*) was a standard phrase for what was most especially beyond human experience, namely Hades and the world of the dead, and so Aristotle found it convenient to transfer its application to another unknowable region, that beyond the periphery of the outer heavens. There was a similar development later, when the Epicureans banished their gods from their traditional home on Mount Olympus to calm areas between galaxies – the *intermundia* – untouched by the formation, growth and disintegration of atomic compounds in world-systems, and by the turbulence through the void. The description of these regions at the beginning of the third book of Lucretius deliberately recalls the early Homeric account of the calm, bright home of the gods 'ever-secure'.

Both Plato and Aristotle thought of time as a direct serial ordering mapped by numbers. But for Plato the time of the existence of the perceived cosmos could not be given a numerical series, nor could the preposition 'before' be applicable to the pre-cosmic disorder. Since in the narration of the *Timaeus* (34c, 53d) time and order were initiated with the creation of the heavens, the disordered state could only be said to exist before time itself in some metaphorical or analogical sense. Similarly, Aristotle's theory implied that, whereas all things within the cosmos were measured in time, the cosmos as a whole could no more exist in time and answer a question 'when?' than it could be in a place and answer a question 'where?'.

Within the whole and beneath the moon Aristotle assigned to each living creature a natural life-span according to its species, a development of the traditional theme of the thread of life spun, measured and cut by the three Fates, 'for all things have order, and every time and life is measured' (*On Generation and Corruption* 336b). And this time of life was tied to the cosmic regularities of celestial phenomena:

In all cases the times of the processes of gestation and birth and of lives are measured by periods according to nature – day and night and month and year and the times measured by them, as well as those of the moon (which contributes to all the processes of birth and maturation) . . . the movements of these heavenly bodies control the limit of these processes, both their beginnings and their ends.

(*On Generation of Animals* 777b17–31)

133

Aristotle thus claimed that the annual movement of the sun and the monthly waxing and waning of the moon control not only biological processes in the sublunar world, but also the length of animate lives (each of which is from one point of view the sum of a series of such processes), as well as various inanimate physical processes such as the increase and decrease of the forces of the winds. Similar influences were found at work in the human body by the medical writers, who as a rule recommended letting diseases run their course (as suggested by Plato himself at *Timaeus* 89b4–c7) rather than interfering with their natural ebb and flow by prescribing drugs. In other examples the moon obviously seemed to affect menstruation, and to give the time for pregnancy (regularly measured by ten lunar rather than nine solar months), and it was also recognised as controlling in its phases the periodicity of the ocean tides (as reported by Strabo *Geographia* 3.5.8).

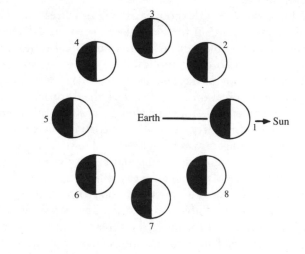

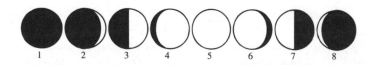

Figure 11 The phases of the moon.
As the (spherical) moon circles the (spherical) earth it reflects the sun's light, and appears in succession as dark, crescent, half-full, gibbous, full, gibbous, half-full and crescent.

Such correspondences between the solar and lunar cycles and terrestrial events were explained within the context of naturalistic theories and beliefs, and expressed in terms of the make-up of bodies (animate and inanimate) and their processes. A related correspondence between celestial phenomena and human affairs formed the basis for astrology, and in time, as Stoic ideas gained currency, belief in astrology came to be viewed in terms of the Stoic idea of a cosmic, universal 'sympathy' (the basis, for example, of the theory of the tides). This Stoic 'sympathy' related all parts of the cosmos to each other and to the whole through the pervasive presence and activity of *pneuma*. There were in addition three further famous and influential doctrines which brought together the concepts of time, eternity and the regularity of the celestial bodies, and which had obvious repercussions for human life. These theories were generally known as the harmony of the spheres, the Great Year and eternal recurrence.

The first of these, the harmony of the spheres, is probably to be attributed to the early Pythagoreans of the sixth century BC (who called astronomy and harmony 'sister sciences' according to Plato *Republic* 530d7–8), and was almost certainly known to Plato's Pythagorean friend, Archytas of Tarentum. Basic astronomical knowledge of the number, order and relative movement of the planets was obviously required to postulate such a theory, as well as some expertise in harmonics. When it was discovered that notes produced by plucking a musical string varied according to its length, and that the octave, and the ratios of fourth and fifth, depended on corresponding precise measurement of the strings, tones were then measurable, and pitch was linked to the frequency of vibration. Similar ratios might then be applicable to the concentric movements of the planets in proportional distance from the centre, and our deafness to the resulting celestial music could be explained by habituation, as with the noise of a blacksmith's anvil or the cataracts of the Nile, unnoticed by those who live near them. There was also likely to have been a link with the purificatory aspect of Pythagoreanism involving the idea of psychic therapy, and which in this context had the aim of attuning the individual soul to the music of the spheres.

Aristotle reported an early version of the Pythagorean theory which explained how the planets as they rotate produce individual sounds which are in harmony:

Some think that a sound has to arise from moving bodies of such a size, since even among us here moving bodies that are neither equal in bulk nor speed do so; and since the sun and the moon, as well as the stars (which are so great in number and size) move with such speed, it is impossible, they say, for an unimaginably great sound not to arise. Assuming these things and that the speeds have the ratios of a concord on the basis of their distances, they say that the sound that arises from the stars as they rotate is harmonious.

(*De Caelo* 290b)

Aristotle himself rejected the theory somewhat abruptly by observing that the force of thunderclaps can shatter stones, so that the sound of the stars in their movement, being much greater, would cause correspondingly more havoc on the objects about us, which is clearly not the case.

Alexander's commentary on Aristotle's *Metaphysics* (from the third century AD) reports the Pythagorean argument that led to their belief in the music of the spheres:

Since the bodies that move about the centre have their distances in proportion, and some move faster, others slower, the slower producing a low sound in their movement, the faster a high sound, then these sounds that arise in proportion to their distance would produce a harmony.

(39.24–40.1)

The distances suggested in this passage are based on that of the moon from the earth, with the sun twice that far, Venus three times, Mercury four times and the others in similar arithmetic proportion. The moon with a shorter perimeter for each revolution would have fewer vibrations in its movement and so produce a lower note, the outer planets with more distance to travel at a faster speed would give off higher notes. Once the lengths and speeds were assumed to be proportionate, the sum of the sounds emitted would then be concordant.

There was some disagreement on the number of notes involved, whether earth should be included for the lowest or whether it was silent and stationary, whether Venus and Mercury gave the same note or not, and how a counter-revolution of the outer circle of the fixed stars might affect the whole. The theory of harmony clearly started from the construction of the lyre, which had seven and then in the fifth century BC eight strings; they were all of equal length, and the differences in pitch were regulated by their tension as well perhaps as their thickness. The two most detailed accounts of the harmony of the spheres are in Plato and Cicero. In the Myth of Er which ends the *Republic*, Plato gave his adaptation of the Pythagorean theory with a system of eight concentric whorls (each of which differs in colour and breadth) representing the sphere of the fixed stars and the seven planets – sun, moon and, in their better known Latin names, Mercury, Venus, Mars, Jupiter, Saturn. The whole system of whorls

> turned on the lap of Necessity. And above each of its circles stood a Siren, carried about with it and uttering a single sound, one note; and from all eight arose the concord of a single harmony. And three others sat about at an equal distance, each on a chair, the daughters of Necessity, the Fates, dressed in white with garlands on their heads, Lachesis, Clotho, and Atropos, singing in accompaniment to the harmony of the Sirens, Lachesis of things past, Clotho of things that are, Atropos of things that shall be.
>
> (*Republic* 617b–c)

Plato implies that each whorl emits a sound to give eight notes in all. Later, however, in the first century BC, Cicero concluded his own *Republic* with a cosmological account along the lines of Plato's Myth of Er, and this account, known as the 'Dream of Scipio', has a slightly different version of the harmony of the spheres:

> The sound that you hear is produced by the onward rush and motion of the spheres themselves. The intervals between them, though unequal, are arranged in a fixed proportion, and by an agreeable blending of high and low tones various harmonies are produced; for such mighty motions cannot be carried on so swiftly in silence, and nature has provided that one extreme shall produce low tones while the other gives forth high. Therefore this uppermost sphere of heaven which bears the stars produces a high, shrill tone as it revolves more rapidly, whereas the lowest revolving sphere, that of the moon, gives forth the lowest tone; for the earthly sphere, the ninth, remains ever motionless and stationary in its position in the centre of the universe. But the other eight spheres, two of which move with the same velocity, produce seven different sounds, a number which is the key to almost everything.
>
> (*On the Republic* 6.18–19)

Cicero's account thus put the number of notes at seven, with the spheres of Venus and Mercury on the same circuit, and so having the same speed and note. Another late report, by Theon of Smyrna in the second century AD, mentioned a harmony of *nine* notes (*Exposition* 140.5–141.4), allowing for eight separate notes, and the lowest from earth rotating on its axis.

Such variations for the ratios between the sounds, speeds and distances of the moving bodies and the sum of notes involved do not however show any significant departure from the premises on which the theory was originally based. The imaginative combination of principles of mathematics, astronomy and harmonics with poetic expression and religious fervour in this concept of the surpassingly beautiful music of the spheres has had an enduring fascination. Cicero suggested in his myth that a gifted minstrel might be able to reproduce or imitate the sounds, and as late as the seventeenth century Kepler was trying to transcribe this music. Despite the obvious errors involved in the theory and the improbability of finding supporting evidence, it shows that scientific laws that are true for us must hold in the cosmos, and that cosmic events may be hypothesised and used as valuable subjects for theorising and problem-solving.

The second influential theory concerning planetary motion was that of the Great Year. On its astronomical definition, the Great Year is the period of time that it takes the sun, moon and the five 'wanderers' (the planets Mercury, Venus, Mars, Jupiter and Saturn) to complete their rotations and return simultaneously to a similar earlier position with respect to the background of the fixed stars. The awareness of such a cycle for the totality of the planets on the pattern of those for the moon and sun is very old, going back to the observations recorded in ancient Egypt and Mesopotamia, but the principles were first spelled out in the extant texts by Plato in the *Timaeus*. After describing the rotations of the sun and moon that give the measurements of the day, the month and the year, he detailed the difficulties of calculating the complete revolution of the planets:

> Only a few have made out the periods of the others, nor do people have a name for them or compare them and measure them off against one another in numerical terms, so that they do not realise that time in a way *is* their wanderings, although incredibly numerous and amazingly intricate. Still it is none the less possible to understand that the perfect number of time

fulfils the perfect year when the relative speeds of all eight periods accomplish their course together and reach their starting-point, being measured by the circle of the same and uniformly moving.

(*Timaeus* 39b–d)

Plato himself did not give a length for this 'perfect year', but Censorinus later recorded various calculations (in *De Die Natali* 18.8–11) by Democritus and Philolaus on a small scale of 82 and 59 solar years respectively, and more broadly by Aristarchus with 2,484 years. The Egyptian precession of the planets was calculated at 26,000 years, Persian and Hindu writings report 12,000 and other figures are variously 1,000, 10,000, 18,000 and 30,000 years. One calculation of 10,800 attributed to Heraclitus was reached by multiplying one human generation of 30 years by the 360 days of the solar year.

Plato, also in the *Timaeus*, referred to the ancient records of the Egyptians as reported to Solon in the context of the introduction of the myth of Atlantis. These mentioned recurring large-scale periodic devastations that resulted in the destruction of many lands and peoples, which could be interpreted as floods in the Great Year's winter and the consequences of the intense heat of its summer. In the Greek mythological tradition memories of these extremes emerge in the narration of the flood survived by Deucalion (the Greek Noah) and the catastrophe of Phaethon's fall when driving the chariot of the sun. Both myths show the destruction as a consequence of mortal presumption, but Plato in this context was prepared to suggest that explanations for the alternate flooding and conflagration to which the earth is subject have celestial origins not as retribution but in their coincidence with certain configurations of the planets in their rotations through the course of the Great Year.

Plato appealed to the notion of long-term cycles in two other dialogues. In the *Republic*, when considering the possible duration of his ideal state before the onset of its degeneration, he discussed the times of divine and mortal existence; for the divine he assigned a period defined by an unspecified 'perfect number', for mortal creatures one involving a complex calculation, which seems to take 3,600 years as its base unit (cf. *Republic* 546b). There have been numerous attempts at determining the significance of these numbers, but the 'perfect number' here is obviously a forerunner of the 'perfect number of time' of the *Timaeus*, which does refer to the period of the Great Year.

The *Statesman*, the other Platonic dialogue relevant in this context, suggests a different model for cyclic time:

> God himself at times assists the cosmos on its way and aids it in its rotation, at others he lets it go, when its periods have reached the measure of time appropriate to it, and it goes back in the opposite direction by itself, being a living creature that derives its reason from the one who constructed it in the beginning.
>
> (269c4–d2)

The cosmos here, again in the narration of a myth, is said to alternate between two states of rotation, one propelled by the hand of god, the other, when the divine assistance is withdrawn, is an 'unravelling', as the cosmos goes back on itself, expending the energy built up in the first rotation. Plato continued with a description of the consequences that would result from the god again taking over the rotation of the cosmos. Given the complete reversal of direction that marks this phase, it would be reasonable to expect that life within the cosmos would similarly be reversed: each living creature would cease to age and in fact rejuvenate, with old men losing their white hair and the young reverting to infancy; the generations of the dead would emerge from the earth in which they had long been buried, reborn in the earth and returning to life once more, resurrected in accordance with the reversal of the cosmic rotation (*Statesman* 270–1). This notion of a cosmos oscillating between periods of forward and reverse counter-revolutions is within Plato's general scheme of planetary movements and the periodicity and seasonal cataclysms of the Great Year, but its particular vision of backward-running time has strange and striking modern parallels, in particular in the concept of 'Time's arrow'.

Plato's main scheme was taken over by his pupil Aristotle, but with some modifications. In general agreement with Plato, Aristotle supposed that the celestial bodies kept to the same revolutions in the aither in perpetuity, and that there were also certain cyclic patterns on earth, despite the constant changes and transformations beneath the moon. He claimed that the same opinions repeatedly occurred throughout the human race as knowledge and skills were discovered and subsequently lost, only to be rediscovered later. (The subject is treated at *De Caelo* 270b, *Meteorology* 339b, *Metaphysics* 1074b and *Politics* 1329b.) The cyclical nature of scientific and technical invention would in this way reconcile the time of particular inventions with the sempiternity of the cosmos. But it involved an explanation of how knowledge was lost as well as gained, and Aristotle's approach here can be inferred from his discussion of the sporadic evaporation of the sea:

> It is clear that since time will not give out and the cosmos is everlasting, neither the Tanais nor the Nile always flowed, but the place whence they flow was once dry; for their action has a limit, but time has not. It will be equally true to say this in the case of other rivers. Yet if even rivers come to be and perish and not always the same regions of the earth are watery, the sea must equally change. And if in some parts the sea fails, while in others it encroaches, it is clear that the same parts of the earth are not always sea or land, but all change in time.
>
> (*Meteorology* 353a15–24)

Aristotle here followed the earlier tradition of a Great Year which is completed when the spheres of the sun, moon and planets return to the same position that they held at an earlier time. The winters of such a year would be marked by catastrophic floods, the summers by excessive heat, but the disorders would be local and there would be compensatory gains and losses elsewhere and at other times. In this Aristotle goes further back to Anaximander, finding as his predecessor did a universal equilibrium in the meteorological 'aggressions' and 'atonements', but also including in it the patterns of human progress and regress.

The form in which the Stoics adapted the assumption of the Great Year links with the third topic relevant to time and the cosmos, that of eternal recurrence. The Stoics took over much of the physical theory of the Presocratic Heraclitus, and furthered the supremacy of fire in his system by supposing that the Great Year ends with a cosmic conflagration (for which the technical term was *ekpyrōsis*, a 'burn-up'). In accordance with the fated procession of events, it was thought that the physical aspect of the divine as 'technical' fire periodically absorbed the whole cosmos and controlled it completely. But it contained within itself the seminal principles from which the new cosmos would be reborn, first by the fire being reformed into the traditional four elements in a complete transfusion, and then by the other kinds of life emerging from them.

During the conflagration, the world was taken to be in a state of homogeneity, a notion that again has Presocratic roots, both in Empedocles' concept of a sphere from which the world was generated, and the original condition when 'all things were together' in Anaxagoras' scheme. In such a state there could be no distinction between the celestial and terrestrial domains, since the world in its material aspect was the same all over. This then raises the question of the compatibility of this assumption with the definition of time put forward by Zeno of Citium, the founder of the school, as an extension or dimension (*diastēma*) of movement and a measure of speed and slowness. Zeno appears to have left unspecified the body or bodies to which this movement applied, but Chrysippus later suggested that it was 'an extension of the movement of the cosmos' (Stobaeus 1.104 and 106), here agreeing with Aristotle that the rotation of the heavens marked out the order of time by its serial nature.

If this is the case, what could be said of time during periods of conflagration, in which there would be no distinction between the celestial and terrestrial realms, and consequently no rotation of celestial bodies to mark time? And if time, on Chrysippus' definition, could not occur during periods of conflagration, and all con-flagrations have the same character, how could a cosmic period (*diakosmēsis*) that follows any conflagration be identified as specific-ally after that one or before the next? It would seem to follow that there would be no distinction, and events in each cycle would follow the same pattern.

Empedocles had supposed that there would be recurring cycles in which the elements separated, grouped into compounds as in the perceived world and separated again:

> A twofold tale I shall tell: at one time it grew to be one only from many, and at another again it divided to be many from one. There is a double birth of what is mortal, and a double passing away; for the uniting of all things brings one genera-tion into being and destroys it, and the other is reared and scattered as they are again being divided. . . . So, in so far as one is accustomed to rise from many and many are produced from one as it is again being divided, to this extent they are born and have no abiding life; but in so far as they never cease their continual exchange, so far they are forever unaltered in the cycle.
>
> (fr. 17.1–13)

Simplicius, commenting on Aristotle's discussion of this passage at *Physics* 250b23, explained that although Empedocles has change and motion as eternal, there is a sense in which everything is always the same: there is a periodic move from many to one and from one to many, but after each move a re-establishment of the *eidos*, the general character, of the one and many respectively.

Empedocles' scheme did not explicitly rule out variations in human life within the overall pattern of cosmic unity and separation, but the Pythagoreans did press the point to its logical conclusion. Eudemus even made a joke about it to his students:

> If you believe what the Pythagoreans say, everything comes back in the same numerical order, and I shall deliver this lecture again to you with my staff in my hand as you sit there in the same way as now, and everything else shall be the same. It is also then reasonable to claim that time is the same, for if a movement is one and the same, and the before and after in identical sequences are the same, then this will also be true of number and of time as well.
>
> (*Physics* fr. 51)

Porphyry reported (in his *Life of Pythagoras* 19) that one of the few beliefs that was attributed with some certainty to Pythagoras was that events recur in certain cycles. And since the Pythagoreans measured time by the movements of the planets, and their positions are indistinguishable at the beginning and end of each Great Year, they held that the same time recurs by virtue of the same celestial movements recurring. When time is further tied in with the *numerical* sequence of events staying the same, then the history of what happens in each cycle will be endlessly repeated.

Although the evidence on this, as on many topics, cannot be conclusive as far as the Pythagoreans are concerned, the Stoics certainly did not flinch from the logical consequences of their own beliefs in the Great Year, periodic universal conflagration and eternal recurrence. The evidence from Nemesius (*On Human Nature* 38, *SVF* 2.625) goes back directly to Chrysippus, who makes the Stoic position explicit:

> The Stoics say that when the planets return to the same point in longitude and latitude, where each was at the beginning when the cosmos was first formed, at specific periods of time they bring about a conflagration and destruction of the world, and then return the cosmos to the same state. When the stars are brought back to the same position everything that happened in the previous period is repeated in exactly the same way. There

will again be a Socrates and a Plato and everyone else along with the same friends and fellow-citizens; the same things will happen to them and they will do the same things again, and every city and village and field will return. The restoration of the whole occurs not once, but many times – indeed without end into infinity.... There will be nothing strange compared with what happened before, but all will be exactly the same right down to the smallest detail.

Even if there are very slight differences (not having freckles the next time round was one example given), the formal distinction is so slight as to be meaningless. If Socrates does not recur, someone indistinguishable from him will, who will marry someone indistinguishable from Xanthippe and be accused by people indistinguishable from Anytus and Meletus (cf. Origen *Against Celsus*, *SVF* 2.626).

The Stoics by this line of reasoning linked periodic thermal destruction and regeneration with cycles of eternal recurrence for the cosmos and individual, with far-reaching results. As Sambursky observes (1959: 200–1), the move in the nineteenth century to apply the second law of thermodynamics to statistical mechanics and the idea of 'the return of the individual' is a cogent reminder of the ancient theory.

9

THE MATHEMATICAL BASES OF GREEK COSMOLOGY

> We shall treat astronomy as setting us problems for solution and ignore the things in the sky if we intend to study the subject properly, and do something useful with our natural intelligence.
>
> *(Republic* 530c)

This statement, as extraordinary to those who first heard it as it is to today's readers, comes in Plato's discussion of the higher education programme for those who are in training to be philosopher-governors. In his scheme Plato recommended that the mathematical sciences should be investigated to clarify their underlying principles, and not for any practical purposes or even with reference to the observed phenomena. Proper arithmetic, for example, 'draws the mind upwards and compels it into a dialogue about pure numbers, and will not be distracted by anyone bringing countable objects into the discusssion'. Geometry is not a science of practical measurement but it deals with knowledge of the eternal in two dimensions. Stereometry takes up the subject of solid bodies, and astronomy is the calculation of the speeds, distances and movements of bodies in three dimensions; it no more deals with bodies that are seen than harmonics with sounds that are heard (*Republic* 525–31). Before this the problems of cosmology had tended to be tackled with speculative reasoning along with conclusions drawn from observation, from the use of models or from analogies with natural phenomena, animal and human behaviour and technologies. The result might be a 'theory of everything', but one which lacked the sure foundation of a set of established principles. Plato's syllabus in pure mathematics as proposed in the *Republic* shows that he is likely to have been the first to recognise the need for such a base before any individual difficulties could be tackled.

145

This assumption is reinforced by the report from Aristotle's pupil, Eudemus (quoted by Simplicius *Commentary on Aristotle's De Caelo* 488.22–4), that Plato set the students of the Academy the problem of discovering by a method of hypothesis 'what regular and ordered motions would account for the phenomena of planetary movements'. There are no grounds for doubting the authenticity of the report, and it shows Plato giving a clear indication of what he understood to be the correct theoretical approach to cosmology.

An answer to Plato's problem needed to explain the following: the heavens rotated in a westerly direction approximately once every twenty-four hours; the planets, of which seven were recognised (moon, sun, Mercury, Venus, Mars, Jupiter, Saturn), while participating in this overall westerly motion, also rotated gradually in the opposite direction. In mapping the paths of the planetary motions, however, it had soon been realised that the courses of certain planets were neither regular nor unbroken: at certain points in their rotation, some of the planets were liable to halt in their easterly motion and thereafter move westwards for a time at a greater rate than the heavens as a whole. This phenomenon (known as retrogradation), when set against the opposite velocity of the fixed stars on an axis of a different inclination, resulted in the course of a planet turning back on itself. Further irregularities emerged when it was noticed that the planets, in addition to these variations in longitude, also differed latitudinally with respect to the celestial ecliptic (the path of the sun through the heavens). The problem for any theory was to present a model that would explain all such variations by hypothesising regular and ordered motions.

The first attempt at a solution was soon made by one of the most learned in the Academy, Eudoxus of Cnidus. In response to Plato's problem, Eudoxus used a mathematical model in a theory of homocentric spheres, which he explained in a treatise 'On Speeds'. (Although this is no longer extant, the core of it can be reconstructed from the twelfth book of Aristotle's *Metaphysics* and the Aristotelian commentaries of Simplicius.) Two main theoretical assumptions were made: first, the earth lies at the centre of the celestial system; second, the motions of the planets may be explained if each of them is viewed as consequent on the motions of a series of spheres concentric with the earth. By postulating four spheres each for Mercury, Venus, Mars, Jupiter and Saturn, and three spheres each for the sun and moon, Eudoxus endeavoured, by an appropriate configuration of spheres for each planet, to explain retrograde

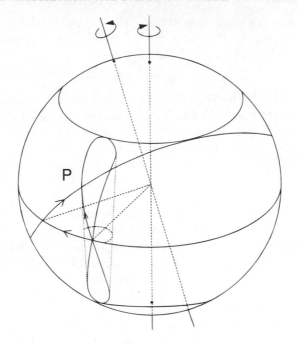

Figure 12 The *hippopede* ('horse-fetter') of Eudoxus.
In its path through the zodiac the planet P describes a figure of eight,
the curve of intersection of a sphere with a cylinder; the angle of
intersection is fixed by the axes of contrary rotation of the planet's
other two spheres.

phenomena and variations in latitude. The orbits on the axes of
different inclinations were also shown to follow a regular pattern,
that of the figure 8, which Eudoxus called a *hippopede* or 'horse-
fetter'. The theory as a whole was a highly sophisticated geometrical
calculation, producing 'tolerably accurate' results (as Heath shows
in the comparison with modern values (1959: 208)). Eudoxus intended his work as a solution to the given problem, a solution that
would account for present observed facts and allow for future
predictions, but without drawing any conclusions as to the nature of
the heavens themselves.

The *Timaeus* in its mythical narrative contains the main features
of Plato's own cosmology, indebted in part to Eudoxus. Like
Eudoxus, Plato has the earth firmly at the centre of an enclosed,
spherical cosmos, but not necessarily at rest:

the earth our nurse, wound about the axis positioned through the cosmos, the Demiurge devised as guardian and maker of night and day, first and oldest of all the gods.

(40b–c)

There is considerable disagreement about the word 'wound' in this passage. Some have interpreted it as meaning that the earth is close-packed or 'globed' (Heath 1959: 174) about the central axis, but Aristotle's interpretation suggests a movement of the earth (*De Caelo* 293b30–2). The concept of the earth actually rotating on its axis is not ruled out by the Greek (the verb is *illesthai*), and is in fact favoured by the immediate mention of the diurnal alternations in connection with it, for 'if the earth had no axial rotation of its own, it would simply be carried round in the same motion as the fixed stars, and there would be no day and night' (Guthrie 1953: 222; the commentary on text and translation of *De Caelo* 293b3). At increasing distances from the earth, the seven planets rotate about the cosmic axis, in the order of moon, sun, Mercury, Venus, Mars, Jupiter, Saturn, as in the theory of Eudoxus.

The phenomena of the heavens then had to be explained on the assumption that the movements which the planets perform are circular and concentric to a central earth. In the myth, the Demiurge, after forming the ingredients necessary for the world-soul into a strip, divided the strip in half, crossed the two halves one over the other, and finally bent them round so as to form circles. He then caused these two circular strips to rotate in opposite directions in such a fashion that the one carried the other about beneath it; the underlying one was then further subdivided into seven unequal circles, in which were set the planets (*Timaeus* 36b–d). This scheme allowed Plato to attribute at least two circular movements to each of the planets – one corresponding to the diurnal westward movement of the outer sky and the other to the eastward movement of the planets – so that the apparent movement of each planet was like that of the sun.

Plato's concern with the circularity of planetary movement may also be seen in the Myth of Er in the final book of the *Republic*, composed earlier than the *Timaeus* but still probably under the influence of Eudoxus (cf. the earlier discussions, pp. 46/7, 137). In the myth, the warrior Er came back to life after having died in battle, and reported what he saw 'there', where the souls go after death. He described how his soul journeyed along with others to a place of judgement, whence, after several days, they moved on until they came to a 'straight light, like a column'. To this light was attached the 'spindle of Necessity, through which all the heavenly rotations turned'; the shaft and hook of the spindle were made of adamant, the whorl from a mixture of adamant and other kinds of material. The whorl was similar to those on earth, but, according to Er's description,

> we must imagine that it was as if within one great hollow carved-out whorl another smaller one of the same kind were slotted in (like basins which fit inside one another), and then a third and fourth fitted in the same way, and so on with four more. For there were eight whorls in all, fixed inside one another, their rims visible as circles above, producing the surface of a single, continuous whorl around the shaft, and the shaft was driven right through the centre of the eighth whorl. The round lip of the outer whorl, the first, was the broadest, the second broadest was that of the sixth, the third that of the fourth (and so on . . .). The circle of the largest whorl was spangled; that of the seventh was brightest; that of the eighth reflected the colour of the light of the seventh; those of the second and fifth were similar to one another, and were yellower than the others; the third had the whitest sheen, the fourth was reddish, while the sixth was second whitest.

(Republic 616d–617a)

On the movement of these whorls:

> the spindle as a whole revolved in the same orbit, but within it as it turned the seven inner circles gently rotated in the opposite direction to the whole. The eighth of these moved the fastest; next, at the same speed as one another, were the seventh, sixth and fifth; the third fastest was the fourth, whose movement, as they thought, involved an additional revolution; fourth fastest was the third, and fifth fastest the second.

(Republic 617a–b)

The description offered here, despite the sometimes convoluted language, represents a fairly simple model of the celestial system, with the outermost whorl standing for the swift orbit of the fixed stars, and the inner whorls for the slower planetary orbits, rotating in concentric circles at different speeds contrary to it, and in proportion to their relative distances. The celestial bodies and their

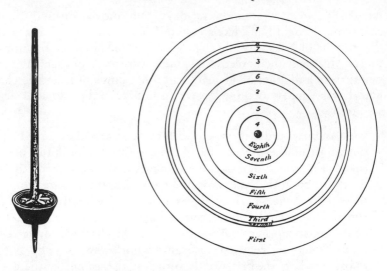

Figure 13 The spindle of Necessity.
The spindle with shaft and cup; the nest of 'whorls' in the cup
explains the paths of the planets about the earth, the relative distances
and speeds, and the notes for the 'harmony of the spheres'.

movements in this way formed an ordered system, appropriately expressed by the term *kosmos*.

In the eighth chapter of *Metaphysics Lambda*, Aristotle presented the earliest surviving account of Eudoxus' theory, and also the modifications of it by Callippus, who thought it necessary to add two spheres each in the case of the sun and moon and one each for Venus, Mars and Mercury 'to account for the phenomena' (*Metaphysics* 1073b36–7). Aristotle, in turn, made his own basic shift: whereas Eudoxus and Callippus worked in purely geometrical terms, Aristotle mechanised the theory, introducing corporeal spheres where the astronomers previously had posited theoretical entities. It was therefore easy to move to the suggestion that the stars and planets rotated because they were attached in some way to a series of rotating spherical bodies.

This mechanisation of the theory of homocentric spheres (i.e., of spheres with a common centre) led Aristotle to realise that a further revision was required. Once the homocentric spheres were regarded as corporeal, and the theory was no longer a model of pure mathematics, the mechanized version had to present some account of the dynamics involved. Eudoxus, and presumably Callippus as well, had regarded the configuration of each planet's spheres as independent – the spheres of Saturn, for example, while lying outside of those of Jupiter, in no way interacted with them. In the light of Aristotle's revision, the following problem had arisen: since each outer sphere was assumed to be in contact with the next innermost sphere, even in the case of spheres that formed parts of different planetary systems, the movements of each sphere would be transmitted to its innerlying sphere. Unless some counter-measures were taken, the motion of the moon, according to this mechanised version of the theory, would then be consequent on the movements of all the other spheres.

In order to maintain the same independence for the system of spheres a planet had possessed on the mathematical model, Aristotle concluded that

> if all the spheres combined are to give an account of the phenomena, then for each planet there must be other spheres, less by one [than those assigned by Eudoxus and Callippus], which counteract and restore to the same position the first sphere of the innerlying planet, for only in this way will the whole system produce the required motion of the planets.
>
> (*Metaphysics Lambda* 1073b38–74a5)

According to Eudoxus' theory, a total of twenty-six concentric spheres was sufficient to explain the workings of the heavens, but with Callippus' revision that total was raised to thirty-three. For Aristotle's mechanised version a sum of fifty-five spheres was necessary – thirty-three spheres to produce the observed phenomena of the heavens, the remaining twenty-two to act as 'reagent' spheres, nullifying the effects of one planet's spheres on the next.

Along with Plato, Aristotle accepted the two fundamental assumptions of the theory of homocentric spheres: geocentricity and the explanation of planetary motion by means of resolution into component circular motions concentric with the earth. Aristotle however went further. In attempting to place the theory within the general context of his natural philosophy, he tried to provide arguments for the two hypotheses that underpinned the theory of homocentric spheres, and to make them workable by means of physical principles. His four books of *De Caelo* attempted to set cosmology on a firm basis by positing certain principles concerning the natural motions (and places) of the so-called elements (earth, water, air and fire). By

151

appealing to such principles and working from them, Aristotle set out to establish a finite, unique and everlasting cosmos, with earth in position at its centre.

Aristotle also had arguments to demonstrate the existence of his fifth element, the 'first body' or *aithēr*, in addition to earth, water, air and fire. He supposed that the only simple motions were in a straight line and round in a circle, and so divided all motion into rectilinear, circular or a mixture of the two (*De Caelo* 268b, *Physics* 261b). Rectilinear motion was further subdivided into two types – motion away from the centre of the cosmos (so-called 'upward motion') and motion towards the centre of the cosmos ('downward motion') – to give three forms of simple motion: motion about the centre of the cosmos (circular), and motion to or from the centre (rectilinear). Aristotle also assumed that each element (or simple body) had a characteristic motion intrinsic to its nature, so that fire and air naturally moved upward, earth and water downward. In addition, following from this argument, a simple body would be required which had circular motion as its natural characteristic, and this was named as *aithēr*. From this element then were composed the homocentric spheres that rotate around the earth as their centre.

Aristotle thus attempted to place cosmology on a quasi-mathematical footing using the basic hypotheses of his predecessors in astronomy – an enclosed spherical cosmos, with an outer moving shell of fixed stars, a series of planets in counter-rotation to it, and a central earth. But his subject was now the actual heavens, and contrary to Plato's warnings, he looked upwards and set out to explain what was to be seen there. Too close a dependence upon the Eudoxian model for an explanation of how the world actually is left Aristotle susceptible to some severe criticisms. The following passage from Sosigenes (quoted in Simplicius' commentary on Aristotle's *De Caelo*) gives some of the failings of the theory:

> The theories of Eudoxus' school do not save the phenomena, not only those discovered later, but even those recognised before and accepted by the school. . . . I mean the fact that at times the planets appear to be near, at times distant from us. In the case of some planets, this is quite obvious to the eye; for the so-called star of Venus, as also that of Mars, in the middle of their retrogradations, appear many times larger, so that the star of Venus actually makes bodies cast shadows on moonless nights. The moon too, even to the naked eye, clearly does not

always lie at an equal distance from us, due to the fact that it is not seen to possess the same size when the same circumstances under which it is observed hold. The same fact is established by observing the moon using instruments, since at times it has a disc of eleven finger-breadths, at others of twelve finger-breadths. In addition in total solar eclipses when the centres of the sun and moon are in our line of sight, similar effects are not always observed; but at one time the sun itself is comprehended by the cone that takes in the moon and has our eye as its apex, when the sun even remains invisible to us for a certain time, while at another time the sun is so much greater that its outer edge to a certain extent is still left visible at the mid-point of the eclipse. And so we would need to accept that the apparent differences in their sizes is due to the inequalities in their distances even though similar atmospheric conditions hold.

(Simplicius *Commentary on Aristotle's De Caelo* 504.17–505.11)

According to the theory of homocentric spheres, both in its geometric and mechanised form, the planets would be at a constant distance from the earth. The theory could not therefore explain the variations in brightness that certain of the planets displayed, nor the occurrence of total and annular eclipses. These phenomena were later correctly explained by the varying distances of individual planets from the earth in their courses.

The possibility of the earth itself moving, adumbrated by Plato in the *Timaeus* and then rejected by Aristotle, was confirmed in the mid-fourth century BC by Heraclides of Pontus, possibly while engaged like Eudoxus in trying to solve the problem put by Plato to the Academy. Heraclides assumed in his explanation of the celestial phenomena that the earth (rather than the stars) revolved approximately once every twenty-four hours, while keeping to its place at the centre of the cosmos. His second startling assumption was that the spheres of the planets did not need to be concentric with the earth. To account for their movements more accurately, he set the circles of Venus and Mercury around the sun as centre. This theory of planets as satellites of the sun in turn contributed to two subsequent developments: the heliocentric theory of Aristarchus of Samos (which anticipated that of Copernicus), and the epicylic and eccentric theories, which culminated in the *Amalgest* of Ptolemy.

The heliocentric theory of Aristarchus in the third century BC

153

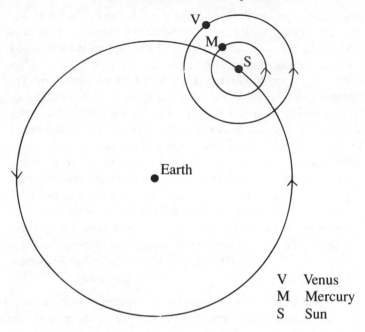

V   Venus
M   Mercury
S   Sun

Figure 14 Epicycles.
Mercury and Venus rotate about the sun as it encircles the earth; the
theory probably begins with Eudoxus.

seems, like the theory of homocentric spheres, to have started from
mathematical principles. The original text is no longer extant, but the
fundamental hypotheses can be found near the beginning of Archimedes' work *Sand-Reckoner* (*Arenarius*) in his address to Gelon,
ruler of Syracuse:

> You know that *kosmos* is the name given by most astronomers
> to the sphere of which the centre is the earth's centre, and the
> radius of which equals the straight line between the centre of
> the sun and the centre of the earth. Aristarchus of Samos,
> however, published writings consisting of certain hypotheses
> in which the assumptions laid down lead to the result that the
> cosmos is many times larger than that one just mentioned. For
> he hypothesises that the fixed stars and the sun remain un-
> moved, that the earth turns about the sun along the circum-
> ference of a circle, the sun lying in the centre of its course, and
> that the sphere of the fixed stars, lying about the same centre

154

as the sun, is so great in size that the circle about which he hypothesises the earth to turn has the same ratio to the distance of the fixed stars as the centre of a sphere has to its surface.

(Sand-Reckoner 1.4–5)

Aristarchus' theory as described here is close to the later Copernican theory, and in a passage which he subsequently suppressed Copernicus mentioned his ancient predecessor (as reported by Heath 1959: 301). The main difference between the two heliocentric theories is in Aristarchus' estimate of the size of the sphere of the fixed stars, which is given the same ratio to the orbit of the earth that the surface of a sphere has to its centre. On such a ratio, the sphere of the fixed stars would seem to be at an incomparable distance from the earth's orbit. Aristarchus' motive is not hard to find, for a perennial objection to a heliocentric hypothesis had been the absence of stellar parallax; by supposing the stars to be at an immense distance, Aristarchus intended to preclude any objection to his theory on this basis. It is worth noting that the first sure measurements of stellar parallax were made eventually by Bessel in 1838, some 2,000 years later.

Apart from Heraclides' transference of the planets Venus and Mercury to be satellites of the sun, the only other move to diminish the central importance of earth was the claim attributed to the Pythagorean Philolaus that the earth was a star, and that the sun, moon and other planets moved around a central fire, an idea criticised by Aristotle in *De Caelo* 2.13–14. After Aristarchus the heliocentric theory had very little influence on subsequent cosmology, and was adopted only by a minor figure in the second century BC, Seleucus from Babylon. Immediately on its appearance the theory was attacked on religious grounds, especially by the Stoics. A character in Plutarch, for example, says:

Don't prosecute us for impiety as Cleanthes thought that the Greeks should charge Aristarchus the Samian on the grounds that he was disturbing the hearth of the universe, when he tried to save the phenomena by assuming that the heaven is at rest while the earth revolves along the ecliptic, and simultaneously rotates about its own axis.

(On the Face of the Moon 923a)

There is also evidence for a similar opposition in a quotation preserved by Theon of Smyrna of one who rejects with abhorrence those who have brought to rest things that move, and have set in motion things that are by nature and position immobile, believing it to be contrary to the hypotheses of mathematics.

(200.10–12 on Dercillides)

As with the later history of the heliocentric hypothesis, the notion of a moving earth seems to have been too incredible to have been seriously entertained. The problem was compounded by the inability of contemporary mechanics to deal with the issue, for there appeared to be no explanation in Aristarchus' theory for the behaviour of heavy objects moving through the air and tending to fall to earth as towards the centre; as late a writer as Ptolemy was offering arguments for a stationary earth that were much the same as those used by Aristotle five centuries earlier. Failings in the heliocentric theory itself also led to its neglect in antiquity. Not until Kepler in the sixteenth century was it realised that the planets do not describe circles in their movements about the sun; Aristarchus had still not shaken off the same concern with concentricity that had characterised his predecessors.

During the second half of the third century BC, the foundations for a new theoretical approach were laid by relinquishing the hypothesis that the movements of the planets should be explained by resolution into rotations concentric with the centre of the cosmos. Apollonius of Perga, working near the end of the century, is generally assumed to be responsible for the next development, which was to explain the planetary movements by means of the epicycle and eccentric.

Heraclides in the fourth century had already suggested something like an epicyclic theory when he made Venus and Mercury satellites of the sun, while the sun itself was still thought to circle the earth. It is difficult to know what influences might have been at work between the time of Heraclides and Apollonius, especially from Babylonia; perhaps there was the mediation of the Babylonian teacher Berossos, who migrated to Cos towards the end of the third century BC. The Babylonians were using the principles of arithmetic rather than geometry in plotting planetary movements, not to establish underlying mathematical principles, but to supply the data for observations of the night sky, and especially for purposes of astrology. Although the procedures were highly sophisticated, no theoretical advances could be made since a geometrical model was first needed, and then the arithmetical deductions would follow (cf. Neugebauer 1962:

157–8, who points out in this context the importance of the methods of locating latitudes used in mathematical geography). Whatever the contemporary influences, and despite the lack of original texts, Apollonius deserves the credit for the pioneering work on epicycles and eccentrics.

On the theory of epicycles the motion of a planet was analysed in the following way: a circle, known as the deferent, is constructed around the earth as its centre, which carries in its rotation a second, smaller circle fixed to a point on its circumference; the planet moves about the circumference of this second circle, the epicycle. The alternative technique for representing the movements of the planets was known as the eccentric. On this construction, a small 'eccentric' circle is hypothesised as rotating about the earth, and a point on the circumference of this circle is taken to be the centre of a second, larger circle such that the larger circle is carried round in the rotation of the smaller; the planet is then envisaged as moving about the

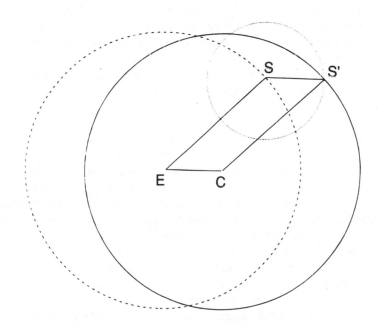

Figure 15 Eccentric, epicycle and deferent.
The dotted circle about the earth E is the deferent which carries the epicycle with centre S; the eccentric circle of the path of the sun (S') is around the hypothetical centre C.

circumference of the larger circle. This is particularly useful as an explanation of the inequality of the seasons, and observed variations in the distance of the sun from the earth.

The epicyclic and the eccentric models in the end produce almost equivalent results, and it is likely that Apollonius knew and demonstrated this (cf. Lloyd 1973: 61–5, Heath 1959: 264–6). He was then able to make use of either as appropriate, allocating the eccentric technique to Mars, Jupiter and Saturn – 'the three planets that can reach any elongation from the sun' (Ptolemy *Amalgest* 12.1) – and epicycles to the others. Hipparchus seems later to have moved Venus and Mercury into the eccentric model, but an epicycle for the sun was kept as better able to explain solar phenomena. The flexibility possible between the two techniques made it possible for them to survive and be integrated into the complexities of Ptolemy's own model, and later into the remarkably similar system of Tycho Brahe in the sixteenth century.

Apollonius' work was carried further in the second century BC by Hipparchus, who provided a firmer observational basis for the theories developed by his predecessors, and it was this which led to his discovery of the precession of the equinoxes. His move of Venus and Mercury from the epicyclic to the eccentric model was in line with the general principle of Apollonius that either should be used according to the better explanation of the points at which a planet appears to be stationary and then retrogrades.

Ptolemy's great *Amalgest*, written in the second century AD, is a complete exposition of the mathematical astronomy then current, and comes as the fitting climax to these developments in Greek cosmology. From the immense riches and sophisticated techniques in this text, it is relevant to point out here Ptolemy's dependence on the work of his predecessors in his use of eccentric and epicyclic models, and to note his introduction of the equant. Given his geocentrism, and the theory of deferent and epicycle, Ptolemy found it necessary to add this further variation (in his tenth book) in order to explain the planetary motions more explicitly. The equant is a point imagined outside of the earth's periphery which provides the hypothetical centre for the rotation of the deferent, i.e., the outer circle along which the planets travel in epicycles. The point at which the epicycle is set on the deferent moves at a uniform *angular* velocity with respect to a point that lies twice as far from the earth and along the same line as the deferent's centre. As Lloyd explains (1973: 128), although Ptolemy's aim was to provide an account that was both mathematically exact and physically true, he concentrated on the mathematics as he set out to provide a geometric model from which the motions of the sun, moon and planets could be computed.

These developments began the split between astronomy and physics as separate disciplines. Astronomy, in its concern to account for the motions of the celestial bodies, looked for geometrical constructions that allowed a description of observed events; yet, in attempting to 'save the phenomena', it eschewed the search for causes demanded by the physicists. They, on the other hand, could no longer appeal to the spherical bodies that Aristotle had introduced to explain the make-up of the heavens without sacrificing the simplicity of the original model. On what understanding of reality could the epicycles and eccentrics of the astronomers now be based?

The division between the two sciences is illustrated in the following passage from Simplicius' commentary on Aristotle's *Physics*, which goes back to a summary from the first century BC:

It is the business of physical investigation to examine the substance of the heavens and of the stars, their force and quality, their generation and destruction, and indeed it can also demonstrate their size, shape, and order. Astronomy, however, endeavours to speak of no such thing, but proves the order of the heavenly bodies by giving an account of the heavens as a true cosmos, and speaks about the shapes, sizes, and distances of the earth, sun, and moon, and about eclipses and conjunctions of the stars, and about their type and amount of motion. For this reason, since it is connected with the investigation of quantity, size, and quality of shape, it obviously needed arithmetic and geometry . . . but although the astronomer and physicist will often propose to prove the same point, e.g. that the sun is large, or that the earth is spherical, they will not go by the same paths. For the one proves each point by proceeding from substance, force, or from its being better that things are so, or from generation and change, the other by proceeding from the effects consequent on their shapes or sizes, or from the extent of movement or from the time appropriate to it. The physicist will often grasp the cause by looking towards the productive force, whereas the astronomer, when he argues from external effects, does not gain a sufficient view of the cause. . . . For in general it is not the astronomer's task to know what is at rest by nature and what sort of things are able to move, but, by introducing hypotheses concerning such things as are at rest and in motion, he considers which hypotheses will result in the phenomena of the sky. He must adopt the physicist's principles, namely that the motions of the stars are simple, regular, and ordered, and according to these principles he will show that all the celestial motions are circular, some of them turning in parallel, others in oblique circles.

(Simplicius *Commentary on Aristotle's Physics* 291.23–292.29)

The astronomer here is content if he finds a mathematical theory that can account for the apparent motions of the celestial bodies, but the physicist would rather push the explanation further on the basis of *his* principles so that the true (circular) motion of each celestial body can be shown. But these physical principles to which the astronomer is expected to defer differ little, if at all, from those Plato established in the fourth century BC. While astronomical theory was capable of advancing hypotheses that were innovative and daring, as with Heraclides and Aristarchus, physical theory clung steadfastly to ideas that fitted less and less with contemporary astronomical models. The two disciplines that had started out as one and in harmony were moving further apart.

One interesting attempt at bridge-building is known. Theon of Smyrna wrote his *Exposition of Mathematics as a Guide to Reading Plato* around AD 120, some time before Ptolemy's *Amalgest*, and it contains a great deal of information on the development of astronomy from the earliest times. In one passage Theon criticised Hipparchus for his general preference for epicyclic models:

Hipparchus approves the epicyclic hypothesis as especially his own, saying that it is more plausible for all the celestial bodies to lie evenly balanced and equally joined together towards the centre of the universe; yet even he, not being versed in natural philosophy, did not know for sure what was the natural and thus true motion and what the incidental and apparent.

(188.15–24)

Theon charged Hipparchus with failing to give a sufficient account of the superiority of the epicyclic over the eccentric hypothesis. In the preceding pages however Theon presented a theory that offered a physical explanation for this superiority, taken from a work on Plato's *Timaeus* by Adrastus of Aphrodisiensis, a Peripatetic of the second century AD, but already familiar to Dercyllides, a Platonist who is said to have lived before the reign of Tiberius in Rome (AD 12–28). The theory itself was derived from Aristotle's assumption of homocentric spheres, to which two modifications were made: the extra reagent spheres introduced by Aristotle were rejected, and the epicycle of a planet was then assumed to be a circle on a sphere rolled between two hollow spheres which were themselves either concentric or eccentric with the earth.

One benefit of such a theory was that it allowed some conception of a reality behind the astronomers' theories. Adrastus had asked how bodies as great as the planets could be fixed on incorporeal circles such as the astronomers assumed (Theon 178.17–19). On the new theory of spheres, an epicycle was no longer an idealised circle, but the equator of a sphere rolled between the two concentric, hollow spheres that contained it. This explanation also showed why the epicyclic model of the astronomers was to be preferred to the eccentric one for all the planets, since the physical reality was now thought to correspond more closely to it. Yet, though the theory could to that extent satisfy the physicist, a concession had to be made. Unlike its Aristotelian predecessor, the new theory dispensed with the idea that all movement should be concentric with the centre of the universe, for the sphere upon which the planet was fixed was now said to rotate about its own centre.

This explanation of the planetary system reported by Theon offered a compromise between the physicists and the astronomers, but it did not survive the publication of Ptolemy's *Amalgest*, with its theory of the equant. Ptolemy himself came near to despairing of any mechanical model which might explain the celestial system he had brought to light when he wrote:

> One should try as far as possible to fit the simpler hypotheses to the celestial motions, and if this does not succeed, to apply hypotheses which do fit. For provided that each of the phenomena is duly saved by the hypotheses, why should anyone think it strange that such complications can characterise the motions of the heavens when their nature is such as to afford no hindrance, but of a kind to yield and give way to the natural motions of each part, even if the motions are opposed to one another? Thus, quite simply, all the bodies can easily pass through their own element and be seen through the others, and this ease of movement applies not only to the individual circles, but to the spheres themselves and the axes of revolution. We

see that in the models constructed on earth the fitting together of these bodies to represent the different motions is laborious, and difficult to achieve in such a way that the motions do not hinder each other, while in the heavens no obstruction whatever is caused by such combinations.

(13.2, trans. Toomer)

When astronomy was placed on a new footing by Copernicus in the fifteenth century, the principles that formed its groundwork were intended to simplify the heavily-laden Ptolemaic astronomy. An integral element in this simplification was the elimination of the equant, as Copernicus wrote:

for here too [the ancient astronomers] admit a circular motion can be uniform with respect to an extraneous centre not its own, a concept of which Scipio in Cicero would hardly have dreamed. . . . These and similar situations [the cases of Mercury and the moon] gave me the occasion to consider the motion of the earth and other ways of preserving uniform motion and the principles of the science, as well as of making the computation of the apparent non-uniform motion more enduring.

(*On the Revolution of the Celestial Spheres* 5,2; trans. Rosen)

In certain respects, Copernicus' astronomy represents a return to a principle that Ptolemy had discarded in pursuit of a faithful computation of the planetary movements: uniform motion with respect to a centre. As for the equant, Copernicus considered that 'It is improper to conceive any such defect in objects constituted in the best order' (1.4).

10

THE COSMOS AND GOD

> Hail to thee, Amon-Re'
> Eldest of heaven, first-born of earth
> Lord of what is, enduring all things,
> Lord of truth and father of the gods
> The chief one, who made the whole earth,
> Lord of eternity.
>
> *(Egyptian Hymns, ANET* 365)

From the earliest texts, as in this one from the middle of the second millennium BC, god was closely connected with cosmology. The first cosmic masses of water, earth and sky were viewed as numinous powers which generated the natural features that arose from them – rivers and springs, mountains and valleys, sun, moon, stars and storms, with varying emphases according to the geography of the different regions in the ancient Near East. The masses and their articulated features, which at first tended to be regarded as animate, became identified with various divinities, and then were represented as the locations in which those divinities resided. Mesopotamia occupied the marshlands of the river basin between the Tigris and Euphrates, and so, as might be expected, their primary cosmic masses related to them. They were named the waters of Apsu and Tiamat, as given in the Akkadian creation epic roughly contemporary with the opening Egyptian text:

> When on high the heaven had not been named
> Firm ground below had not been called by name,
> Naught but primordial Apsu, their begetter,
> And Mummu-Tiamat, she who bore them all,
> Their waters commingling as a single body. . . .
> Then it was that the gods were formed within them.
>
> *(ANET* 60–1)

For Egypt the centrality of the Nile secured the importance of cosmic water so that as well as Amon-Re' there was also the recognition of 'the great god who came into being by himself':

> Who is he? He is water, he is Nun, the father of the gods.
>
> (*ANET* 4)

As old, or in some regions perhaps even older, was the earth-mother-goddess, the principle and source of life, spoken of as Ishtar in Akkadian, Inanna in Sumerian, Isis in Egypt, recognisable also as the goddess of Minoan Crete and Hesiod's Gaia. The sky in all these cultures was also considered divine at first, and later became the area in which the sky-god lived, as Hades was the dark part beneath the earth and then the god of that realm. On the same pattern came the next generation – the sun as sun-god Utu in Sumeria and Horus-Re' in Egypt, honoured especially at Heliopolis, his own 'Sun-City'. More unusually the sun-god among the Hittites was female, her consort was the weather-god, and there were various divinities connected with storms and mountains, reflecting the wilder Hurrian landscape; a common prayer in this context was of the type:

> Hattian Storm-god, my lord, save my life!
>
> (quoted in the Hittite prayer, *ANET* 394–6)

Similarly the moon was consistently considered divine (male in Mesopotamia, female generally elsewhere), as the most prominent of the celestial phenomena at night, as the personification of that phenomenon, and subsequently as the dwelling of the god.

In this way cosmic theology moved into the realm of myth. Natural explanations of the emergence of land from primordial waters, of the earth's surface articulating into mountains and valleys, the enclosure of the vault of the sky above and a corresponding dark area beneath, were told as narratives involving conception, child-bearing and birth, and battles between the generations of gods before the present world order was established. Such myths tended to be characterised by sex and violence, but there was also the idea of a more kindly god as creator or father. In Mesopotamia, for example, Marduk took over the powers of the earlier forces and was responsible for the consequent forms of life. A similar role was given in Egypt to Atum, who was said to have created the next generation of gods and then to have claimed, 'I am yesterday, while I know tomorrow', as in Memphis creation was attributed to Ptah in the words:

the whole divine order came into being through what his heart
thought and tongue commanded.

(ANET 4–5)

Most notably, at about the same time as Hesiod was giving the divine
genealogy of the cosmic masses in his *Theogony*, the author of the
Book of Genesis opened with: 'In the beginning God created sky and
earth', and explained how, through the word of God, the primordial
waters were separated and these first two contrasting areas emerged.

The basic tradition and character of the pantheon of the Greeks,
as Herodotus observed, was fixed by the Homeric *Iliad* and *Odyssey*
and by Hesiod's *Theogony*. In Hesiod the genealogy of gods from
earth to sky, from their Titan progeny to the senior Olympians and
into the subsequent generation of the younger gods, shows an
increasing detachment from the emergence of the phenomena of the
known world to the establishment of personalised gods of cult and
myth. In Homer the Olympians were fully independent individuals,
and only rarely, as in such long-established epithets as 'cloud-
gatherer' of Zeus or 'earth-shaker' of Poseidon, was there a glimpse
of an earlier 'cosmic' role. Together they were portrayed as an
anthropomorphic family, differing from mortals in power and
sometimes knowledge, in being free from toil and suffering and
especially from death, but only too human in character and emotion.
As such they earned Xenophanes' criticism:

> Homer and Hesiod have attributed to the gods all that brings
> disgrace and reproach among men – stealing, adultery, and
> cheating each another.

(fr. 11)

And it was this poetic inheritance that he and the other early Greek
cosmologists aimed to counter.

In his education curriculum in the second book of the *Republic*,
Plato was in general agreement with such criticism; he had no wish
for children to be brought up on immoral tales of the gods, or for
young citizens to claim from them precedents for their own dis-
respect for parents and other offences. But at least the old poets
accepted that gods existed, whereas atheistic scientists presented a
much more powerful opposition to Plato's own moral theology. In
a famous passage from the tenth book of his last work, the *Laws*, he
castigated an anonymous group of 'those who impress the young as
wise' for the mischief they cause in denying the divinity of sun, moon

and stars, and alleging that they were produced by 'agents without soul' (896d). Plato set out an irreconcilable hostility between those who maintained that the cosmos arose from elemental masses as a result of the workings of chance and their own nature, with soul and mind as later developments, and those on the side of his legislator, supporting the old beliefs that gods exist and care for the human race, and claiming the pre-existence of divine soul (*psychē*), with the elementary bodies derived from it. The tension between the two points of view was given dramatic form in the tenth book of the *Laws* in a 'gentle persuasion' for the cosmic primacy of the divine that the founder of Magnesium would bring to bear on a student physicist (a training in science then as now being considered generally hostile to religious orthodoxy).

Plato's 'young atheist' here encapsulates the whole tradition of early Greek science on the genesis, structure and maintenance of the present world order, and serves to introduce an assessment of the place of the divine in the scheme of the first cosmologists. Basically there was a search for new non-mythical explanations, but the discarding of the old was not wholly negative. Xenophanes, as has been shown, rejected the gods of Homer and Hesiod, and also recognised that their form related to their particular cultural contexts (black people, for example, portray gods as black, horses would have gods like horses), but there was a more positive side, as shown in the following fragments (23–6):

One god, greatest among gods and men, not like to immortals at all either in body or in thought.
As a whole he sees, as a whole thinks, and as a whole hears.
Always he remains in the same place, moving not at all, and it is not fitting for him to change places from one time to another.
But without toil, by the power of his mind, he causes everything to vibrate.

Despite Xenophanes' vague terms the features of a cosmic divinity can be recognised here as non-anthropomorphic, one and unchanging, immobile itself but characterised by an intellectual dynamism that keeps the whole cosmic structure moving. The unity and all-pervasiveness is reinforced by Aristotle's comment that 'looking up at the whole sky, [Xenophanes] said that the one was god' (*Metaphysics* 986b20). This is natural theology, a way of putting old terminology to a new use in an explanation of power and movement inherent in the world order, a source of wonder, perhaps, but not of fear. In this Xenophanes is in the tradition of Thales, at the beginning of European thought, if Aristotle's report of him that he said 'all things are full of gods' is to be believed (*De Anima* 411a8). The phrase came to be a tag, used by Plato for his own religious beliefs (*Laws* 899b), and by Aristotle himself in a different context (*On Generation of Animals* 762a21), in which he substituted 'soul' (*psychē*) for gods to make a point about the universal connection of psychic heat with forms of life. Any appropriate interpretation for Thales and his time of 'all things full of gods' would involve a connection with life, and perhaps also with movement, since the discovery that a magnetic stone could move iron was attributed to him in the Aristotelian tradition (*De Anima* 405a21), and this might well suggest that other seemingly inanimate objects have similar unseen powers. At the least the word *theos* had been stripped of connotations of cult, ritual and myth and given a new context in the natural world.

Greater sophistication (and with more documentation) comes with the notion of *archē* as applied to the *apeiron* of Thales' successor Anaximander, and to air by the third Milesian, Anaximenes. Such an *archē* represents a scientific principle characterised by theological attributes in a non-theological context – reason enough for Plato to regard natural philosophers as atheists. The noun *archē*, like the related verb *archō*, has the ambiguities of the English 'first' (as in both 'archaic' and 'archangel') in referring to priority in time and in power. The *archē* of the early philosophers names what there was before there was anything else; it has a role as providing a causal explanation for the world and its phenomena, but does not itself have to be explained. Similarly, it is a 'beginning' for other things, but without having a beginning itself, nor indeed any end to its continuing existence, so that it is 'deathless', *athanatos*, the Homeric synonym for a god. Also (in what is probably Anaximander's own terminology) it 'surrounds' and 'steers' everything, containing the whole and in some way responsible for and explaining its direction. When Anaximenes gives such an *archē* the character of air it again 'surrounds' but also 'maintains' the whole as *psychē* provides breath and life for the body. In addition, it is the basic 'stuff' of the world, taking on different appearances as the result of qualitative changes – fiery when 'thinner', liquid and solid when more compacted.

To this cluster of concepts, of continuity and deathlessness, pervasiveness, control and psychic vitality, Xenophanes, as shown above, added mind in the activity of unified thought, and also some power of initiating and sustaining movement. These were carried further by Heraclitus in his account of wisdom and *logos*, that 'one wise' which can be called Zeus in virtue of primacy, intelligence and power, but not in any anthropomorphic sense. Heraclitus, like Xenophanes, subverted the authority of Homer and Hesiod, and also deliberately flouted traditional prayer and ritual and respect for the dead (as in fragments 5, 14–15, 40, 42, 56–7 and 96). He substituted 'war' for the Homeric 'Zeus' as having the standard title 'father of all and king of all' (fr. 53), and paradoxically juxtaposed immortals and mortals as opposed aspects of a single process (fr. 62). *Theos* was then reintroduced into the new philosophy of nature as a means of explaining the crucial identity of opposites:

> God: day–night, winter–summer, war–peace, satiety–hunger, changing in the way that oil, when it is mixed with perfumes, is separately named according to the smell of each.

> (fr. 67)

And this explanation, called *logos*, brought together the senses of speech and thought, wisdom and unity:

> Listening not to me but to the *logos*, it is wise to agree that all things are one.

> (fr. 50)

In other fragments Heraclitus stated that the divine, not the human, had knowledge (*gnōmē*), and that the relation of human to divine in such knowledge was as that of child to adult (frs 78–9).

As with the Milesians there is a 'steering' of the world (Heraclitus repeated the same verb in fr. 41 and a synonym of it in fr. 64) linked to the basic 'stuff' from which it arose and which accounts for its composition. For Heraclitus, this is fire, which in its 'turnings' is measured out and exchanged for water and earth, and in its cosmic role it is assigned the standard divine attribute of eternal life (fr. 30). The vitality of fiery *psychē* and the wisdom of *logos* (as with Anaximenes' air) pervades both the cosmos and the individual, controlling and connecting the two. The whole was thought to be regulated according to justice (*dikē*) and law (*nomos*), but this no more carries a *moral* implication than it did for Anaximander; the terms are a means of expressing the principles of order, measure and limit regulating the workings of the cosmos and the patterns of movement of the celestial bodies within it. Praise and blame belong only with the effort of the individual to foster the psychic *logos* within.

Parmenides did not use the word *theos* in the extant fragments, although his account was given authority and due solemnity by being represented in the prologue as the speech of a goddess, who was approached via a gateway controlled by justice (*dikē*, who appears later as the guarantee of the validity of the logic being used). In the cosmology section it is said that a female divinity, a *daimōn*, 'steers all things' (fr. 12.3; the same metaphor as used for the Milesian *archē* and Heraclitean fire). The two parts of Parmenides' poem however distinguished metaphysics (the way of truth) from the natural world of plurality and change (named as the way of opinion and deception), and the way of truth set out a relentless deduction of 'signs' characterising what there is in defiance of the apparently obvious. First, its very existence was proved, then a rigorous sempiternity, without beginning or end, past or future, since 'is' applies 'now, all at once' (fr. 8.5). Further it has to be one, homogeneous, motionless and stable, and in the uniformity within its limits comparable to 'a well-rounded sphere'. The effect of Parmenides' arguments was to set up an unbridgeable divide between reality and appearance, reason and perception, one and many, rest and movement, what is and what is not. In this context there was no god, no divine mind, no plan or purpose or explanation; Parmenides' sense of the fundamental *irrelevance* of the physical world to logic and truth had to be faced.

Empedocles' riposte was to attempt to reconcile the Milesian *archē* with Parmenides' metaphysics by applying the criteria of being to a fourfold materialism. Whereas earlier thinkers had disregarded traditional gods in their natural theology (except for Heraclitus' reassessment of Zeus), Empedocles named his four elements and their related cosmic masses after Homeric gods. Fire was called Zeus or Hephaestus, air Hera, earth Aidoneus or Gaia and water after the less familiar local deity Nestis. In denying birth, death and qualitative change to his elements, while using them as explanations in their arrangements and rearrangements for the variety of phenomena, Empedocles suggested that they were worthy of the respect and wonder accorded traditional divinities. Two further gods from Homer and Hesiod, Aphrodite and Eris, were also provided with new and awesome cosmic roles: Aphrodite was to be viewed as a principle of attraction continually at work on the elements to bring them into harmonious compounds, and Eris in permanent conflict with her, pulling them apart. Aristotle was ready to interpret the former as the cause of good and the other as evil, and, although

Empedocles did not say so explicitly, in the adjectives he gave them and in such synonyms as Joy and Love as against Strife and Hate there emerged, for the first time in the philosophers, implicit and explicit moral judgements on the processes and changes in the natural world, and on the part the individual plays in it.

Empedocles prayed for assistance from his Muse as he unfolded a true account of the gods to counteract a 'dark opinion' that was prevalent (frs 131–2). His new *logos* involved the claim that the four elements, and the principles working on them, were truly divine, whereas traditional gods, 'gods highest in honour', were combinations of these elements brought together in the same way as those that result in plants, animals and humans, but longer-lasting. Another fragment, specifically said to describe the divine by Ammonius and Tzetzes who quote it, brings in the connection with thinking which was important also for Xenophanes and Heraclitus:

> He is not equipped with a human head on a body, he has no feet, no swift knees, no shaggy genitals, but he is mind alone, holy and inexpressible, darting through the whole cosmos with swift thought.
>
> (fr. 134)

Now the god of the sphere, when the cosmos was completely under Love, was characterised by the complete commingling of the elemental parts, so that the divine was given a stable physical basis; this was true also of its mode of thinking, which related (like human thought) to the harmony of commingling elements. 'Holy mind' in the fragment quoted relates to the present condition and activity of the sphere-god during the processes of generation now taking place. In sum therefore Empedocles' new theology covered the cosmos as a whole, the material of which it is made, the agencies that bring about the forms of life within it and the thoughts of a 'holy mind' darting through it.

Empedocles' contemporary, Anaxagoras, approached the problem of god in the cosmos in a different way. For him the material of the cosmos, while always there, was not in itself imbued with life. He denied any divinity to celestial phenomena, maintaining that the sun, the moon and all the stars were fiery stones carried round by the rotation of the aither, and used as evidence a meteorite that fell to earth at Aegospotami in 467 BC. In more detail he is reported as having called the sun a hot stone, larger than the Peloponnese, and the rainbow the reflection of the sun in the clouds, and having said that there were hills and ravines on the moon, and that it was inhabited (Diogenes Laertius 2.8–10 and fr. 19); for such claims he was brought to trial on a charge of impiety. Yet Anaxagoras required an explanation for movement and change to meet Parmenides' arguments, and, while not accepting a role for god or gods in the cosmos, he developed more forcefully the concept (already recognised by Xenophanes, Heraclitus and Empedocles) of a mind at work throughout it, 'present and responsible for the whole and its ordering', which won him Aristotle's approval (*Metaphysics* 984b15–18).

The long twelfth fragment of Anaxagoras is concerned with the nature and activity of this cosmic intelligence or *nous*; the language is theological but the word *theos* and its derivatives are carefully avoided:

> Other things have a share in everything, but mind is unlimited and self-controlling, and with no mixture of anything else, but alone by itself ... it is the finest of all things and the purest, and it has recognition (*gnōmē*) of everything and the greatest strength, and all that has life (*psychē*), the greater and the smaller, mind controls. And it controlled the whole rotation, so that it started to rotate in the beginning ... and it recognised everything as it was mingling and separating – what was going to be and what was, and what now is and will be; mind put them all into a *kosmos*, including this rotation, in which now rotate the stars and sun and moon and air and aither as they are separating.

This cosmic mind then has neither spatial nor temporal limit; it is independent, holding to its own identity in the midst of change, knowing or more exactly 'recognising' the ingredients of the cosmos, and having the power to start and maintain their rotation in due order. It is still material, but the superlatives 'finest' and 'purest' bring it close to the boundary of the abstract. Anaxagoras' successor, Diogenes of Apollonia, with his usual eclecticism went on to connect this invisible, intangible mind with the *archē* of air which Anaximenes had first suggested, arguing that the order, divisions and measures in nature, shown in the regular alternation of summer and winter, day and night, rain and sunshine and many other similar examples, supplied evidence for an all-pervasive cosmic intelligence. After the many previous hints and implications Diogenes finally named the intelligent and eternal *archē* as god, described as the one that 'has reached everything and arranged everything and is in everything' (frs 3 and 5).

If the Milesian *archē* was an aspect of the natural world then any identification of it with the divine along these lines would still produce what was little more than a naturalistic theology. This was Socrates' particular worry. In the autobiography which Plato wrote for him in the *Phaedo* (97b–98c) Socrates says that he was delighted to read in a book bought in the market that Anaxagoras posited a mind (*nous*) that arranged the cosmos and was responsible for it, but was then disappointed to find that *nous* in effect was only introduced to start the initial rotation, and that Anaxagoras' cosmology was thereafter explained not according to purpose or an intellect planning for the best possible world but by the mechanistic working of elemental masses.

At about the same time the atomists Leucippus and Democritus took the further step of removing the mind of god altogether from their cosmology, even from the initial rotation. The movement which drew some atoms in the void into a vortex or *dinē* was a mechanistic affair, a coincidental result of the atoms being as they are ('according to necessity' was the terminology for this), and the consequent emergence of the system of this present world or of any of the innumerable others in the extent of unlimited space was not therefore part of any divine plan. The atomists found no role for gods in the structure or workings of nature or indeed in human life, and explained the general conception of them as due to 'idols', thin atomic compounds with a certain form, that impinge on the mind like images in dreams.

The controversy on the connection of the divine with nature and human life, and even on the very existence of gods, was a significant feature of the intellectual life of Athens in the fifth century BC. The horrors of the plague, as Thucydides recorded, resulted in the breakdown of traditional morality in the struggle for survival, and the defeat in the Peloponnesian War, followed by the imposition of the rule of the Thirty Tyrants, undermined any expectations of divine protection. The sophists who came to the city as professional educators found ready listeners for their sometimes subversive teaching. A famous example was the beginning of Protagoras' work *On the Gods*:

> I am unable to discover whether the gods exist or not, or what they are like; there are so many obstacles – the obscurity of the topic and the shortness of human life.

Such scepticism about truth and the means of verification were sharpened by the sophists' anthropological interests and the continuing debate about the claims of convention versus nature. When language, city, law and justice came to be viewed as human constructs emerging at stages in human history, the origins of religion were also to be explained sociologically, and the most potent explanations were based on fear of meteorological phenomena. It was suggested that humans at first were unable to account for the frightening and seemingly random occurrence of thunderstorms, eclipses, earthquakes and the like, and so they invented gods who were responsible for them, and attributed these events to divine anger with mortals which had to be placated with prayers, ritual and sacrifice.

The fifth-century attacks on traditional attitudes to the gods were found not only in conversations in the *agora* and lectures by the sophists but also on the stage in the three main genres of drama. Euripides used the medium of tragedy to question the morality and even the existence of the gods in the face of human suffering. Critias, in a fragment from a satyr-play called *Sisyphus*, presented the character of a cunning statesman who 'quenched lawlessness with laws' by inventing omniscient gods who lived among the stars (described as 'the fair embroidery of Time's skilled craft'); this statesman frightened the people into behaving by telling them that such gods know about unseen crimes that elude civic justice, and retaliate by sending down meteorites and rainstorms on the miscreant. Comedy showed another side of the new rationalism, when Aristophanes portrayed Socrates in *The Clouds* as running a college, and giving the following lesson in theology:

Socrates: These clouds are the only truly divine beings – all the rest belong in fairy tales.
Strepsiades: What! You mean you don't believe in Zeus?
So: Zeus? Who's Zeus?
St: Zeus who lives on Olympus of course.
So: Now really, you should know better. There is no Zeus.
St: What? Well, who sends the rain, then? Answer me that.
So: Why our friends the clouds do that, and I'll prove it. Have you ever seen it raining when the sky was blue? Surely Zeus, if it was him, would be able to send rain even when the clouds were out of town.
St: That certainly backs your argument. I wonder why I was so naive to think that rain was just Zeus pissing into a sieve. Well, that's one thing; but who is it that thunders and sends shivers up my spine?

173

So: The clouds do that too – when they get in a whirl.

St: I can see I'm never going to trip you. But what do you mean, a whirl?

So: Well you see, being suspended in the air, when they get swollen with rain they are necessarily set in motion, and of course they collide with one another, and because of their weight they get broken and let out this great noise . . .

St: I get it – Zeus is dead, and now Whirl (*dinē*) is the new king.

(*Clouds* 365–81, trans. Summerstein)

Socrates later strongly denied that he ran a school, taught for a fee or had any interest in natural science, but Aristophanes' caricature was not forgotten. Socrates was eventually brought to trial and executed on charges of disregarding the city's gods and corrupting the young; in his defence speech he laid much of the blame on the confusion of him with the sophists and a misunderstanding of his fundamental attitude to god and the world (Plato *Apology* 18–19).

Some insight into Socrates' approach has been shown in his criticism of Anaxagoras' theory of mind, which he found inadequate on the grounds that any proper explanation must find a purpose in the cosmic structure – that all is for the best in the best of all possible worlds (*Phaedo* 98c). That this might well be a genuine Socratic approach (rather than Plato putting words in his mouth) is supported by the evidence of Xenophon in his *Memorabilia*, in which he reports many of Socrates' street conversations. These show three main lines of reasoning that were to have a long life in the history of theology. The first is the providential care of gods for men which is shown especially in the light of the sun and its finely judged equinoxes, the phases of the moon, the fertility of the earth and the gifts of water and fire; the well-being of the human race is represented as the purpose of the cosmos. Second, such gods who are working unseen for our benefit should be recognised, honoured and scrupulously propitiated, and in the third place the continued preservation of the cosmos is a continuing witness of the nature of the divine:

He that orders and holds together the whole universe in which are all things beautiful and good, and who preserves it for us to enjoy always unimpaired, undisordered and undecaying, obeying his will more swiftly than thought and with all regularity, is manifest himself only in the performance of his mighty works, being invisible to us while he controls them.

(*Memorabilia* 4.3.13, and cf. 3.3–15 *passim*)

174

On the assumption that a defining property of the human intelligence is an ability to form plans and to decide upon goals, intellectual activity will be expected to be purposive and goal-directed, and the same would be the case with the divine. From the fifth century BC onwards therefore the division became unbridgeable between those like Socrates who viewed the world as largely purposive in the sense that phenomena occur not just for a reason but for some end as well, and so require divine planning, and the sophists and atomists who were ready with naturalistic explanations for phenomena, from random or obscure beginnings, and driven only by the mechanical operation of necessity or 'the way things are'. God and teleology came to be seen as concomitants: without god there could be no purpose in things, and an order to the universe required a divine intelligence to maintain it. On the other hand, the grandeur, complexity and intricacy of the cosmos could be accepted as they are, without the assumption of an initial divine move or all-pervasive purpose and planning. In the former scheme the universe was bounded with the human race at its centre; in the latter there were no boundaries, and humans had to make their own way, without the assistance or care of gods in a non-anthropocentric, wholly natural environment.

Plato recognised the attractions of this mechanistic world-view, and the dangers implicit in it for a law-abiding state. That gods exist, care for humans and are not to be won over by prayer or bribed by sacrifice were axioms central to his programme for the community that he described at the end of his life in the *Laws*. Proving these axioms, or as he put it, 'getting the gods to argue for their own existence', was one of his hardest tasks, especially to the young with an interest in natural science. The atheist whom the legislator specifically addressed in the tenth book of the *Laws* (see p. 165) represented those sophists and physicists who identified nature as the source of all things, attributing generation to the elements of which bodies are made – earth, air, fire and water and the like – and claiming that gods and minds were derived from them (*Laws* 891c). Consequently they supposed that soul and its activities were also secondary, due merely to art (*technē*) and convention (*nomos*). The refutation of this position involved a complex argument (that Aristotle would subsequently adapt) to the effect that a principle of movement is prior to the movement it causes, and the principle of the very first movements in the cosmos must be self-moving, since there would be nothing else available to start or preserve the present world order. Soul or god or mind (the terms become practically interchangeable) therefore has cosmic priority over body and elements, initiating and maintaining everything in heaven, on earth and in the sea by its own movements:

> Concerning all the planets and the moon, the years, months, and all the seasons, what other account shall we give than just this, that since soul or souls, good in all virtue, have turned out to be responsible for them, then these souls are gods, whether as living beings inside bodies arranging the whole universe, or in some other way?
>
> (*Laws* 898b)

Plato himself had suggested two other ways in which this might be the case. Earlier, in the great digressions of books five to seven of the *Republic*, he had set the 'form of the good' at the summit of his metaphysics. This was explained as the source of the being of all things and of our knowledge of them as the sun is of life and of our vision of whatever has life. It was also represented as the culmination of the educational journey that started with watching shadows in a cave, and ended with the sight of the sun in the upper world. The form of the good was the goal of human endeavour as well as the standard by which human virtue was to be measured, and the explanation for the ultimate values pertaining in the cosmos. But, as Plato himself realised in his later dialogue, *Parmenides*, there were many difficulties with such a concept, in particular the question of how phenomena in a world of change could partake of, share in or be accounted for by such an eternal, unchanging entity. It was not referred to again, except for the mention of a lecture Plato was said to have given on 'The Nature of the Good'; the vast audience attracted to it by its title gradually drifted away when the resulting explanation of the secret of the cosmos turned out to be a discourse on pure mathematics.

Plato's second approach was a mythological one. Since the present world was in his view one of plurality and change set against the unique unchanging realm of being, then an account of it could only be probable at best, a likely 'myth' rather than a 'logos' which had the certainty of truth. In the *Timaeus* therefore, through the dialogue's main character, Plato gave a mythical narrative of a divine craftsman or 'demiurge', who constructed the world as an artefact, imposing order on pre-existing disorderly material to produce in time and space a copy (an *eikōn*) as close as possible to the perfect atemporal model, the *paradeigma*. And because the divine craftsman fashions his divine artefact in a rational and deliberative way analogous to skilled and intelligent human craftsmanship his method of structuring the cosmos was presumed to be open to human understanding.

This craftsman was initially called the 'maker and father of the cosmos' but was soon referred to as god. According to the myth, he constructed the world body from the four elements of earth, water, air and fire, and the soul which imbues it with life and intelligence from the 'intermediate' mixture (i.e., between being and becoming) of the Same, which provided for the regular motion of the sphere of the fixed stars, and the Other, governing the paths of the planets. Human bodies and souls were composed of the same ingredients as the world body and soul, but the task of their 'interweaving' was handed over to lesser gods with inferior skills (for otherwise humans would have been 'equal to gods', *Timaeus* 41b). These secondary gods, which included those from Homer and Hesiod, were clearly a device within the mythical framework to explain the 'mechanical' working of forces of kinetic change on elemental compounds, but (unlike Anaxagoras' use of 'Mind') the whole was set within the teleological framework of the providential care and purposive action of the divine craftsman, who is without the *phthonos* ('grudging envy') usually attributed to the Olympians. Therefore, according to these principles, the myth of the *Timaeus* provided for the uniqueness of the cosmos, its deathlessness and self-sufficiency, as well as its spherical shape and unfailing perfect rotation, so that it too could be described as 'a blessed god'.

In addition, the endowment of the cosmos and of the creatures within it with soul (*psyche*) established the principle of 'psycho-kinesis', according to which all movement ultimately derives from psychic function. The superior movements and configurations of the celestial bodies were therefore testimony, in Plato's view, to their superior soul and intelligence, so that they were more deserving of the name of gods than those of traditional religion, who were relegated to the status of inferior and not very efficient assistants. Humans however, who by upbringing, education and their own efforts, succeed in adapting the movements of their individual souls to those of the cosmos, are promised a share in the greater divinity of the world-soul when they return 'home' after their allotted time on earth to their native stars (*Timaeus* 42b).

The myth of the *Timaeus* basically opposed god to nature in terms of form being imposed on random material, of reason mastering necessity or of male controlling female in the act of conception. Such an opposition was soon attacked by Aristotle for a number of reasons. Reading the myth literally he objected that Plato offered no adequate explanation for the present structure of the cosmos, and was incorrect in attributing a beginning to it in the divine craftsman's initial construction of his artefact; Aristotle followed Heraclitus in being a 'steady state' theorist, maintaining that the cosmos stays ever as it is, without beginning or end. Then, although agreeing that the circular movements of the celestial bodies are the best possible, Aristotle reasoned that they were due to the natural tendencies of these superior bodies to move in the best way, rather than being the result of constraint imposed by a world-soul. Aristotle preferred the concept of divinity cooperating with nature instead of coercing it, and in general followed a Presocratic type of rationalism, with structure, change and movement explained by being 'according to nature', or, more precisely, according to the nature of the bodies involved.

There are however some Aristotelian passages that are more sympathetic to a Platonic theology, and relate the existence and dependence of the cosmos to divine power, whether as initiator of movement or as final cause. In the eighth book of the *Physics* Aristotle argued that movement is imperishable, and that everything moving is moved by something; to avoid a continual regress some initial mover that is itself unmoved must therefore be assumed:

> Since there must always be motion, and without intermission, it is necessary for there to be a first instigator of motion (whether one or many) and for this first mover to be unmoved.
> (*Physics* 258b10–12)

Such an unmoved mover would ultimately be the source or principle of the motions of the celestial bodies, but separate from them, one and eternal. The topic however was not developed, the mover was not named as divine in the *Physics* and no explanation was provided for a means of transmitting the movement. The only hint of this comes from the brief essay *On Movement of Animals*, in which it was suggested by analogy that just as animals require a point of rest outside of themselves if they are to move, so too the celestial movements require an unmoved *archē*, here also called the 'first mover' (698b–700a). A complementary text, the second book of Aristotle's *De Caelo*, looks to the finalisation of movement rather than its beginning. It affirms that the stars and planets are alive and active, that their activity is not random but directed towards some end-purpose or *telos*, described as 'that which is in the best state' (292b). The sphere of the stars, which comes closest to this *telos*, is involved in the least movement, with the planets in increasingly varied movement in proportion to their distances from it.

The main text in this context, and the best known, is the twelfth book (usually known as book *Lambda*) of the *Metaphysics*. Here Aristotle argued that what is responsible for the ever constant movement of the sphere of the stars in the 'first heaven' must be pure form – an entity eternal, unmoved, non-material and fully actual. If this is the case, such a being (henceforward called 'the god') could not cause the outer movement by physical contact, and so its (or his) pulling power can only be explained in relation to the object of desire. He attracts 'as a beloved' (1072b), and the stars in their sphere, in

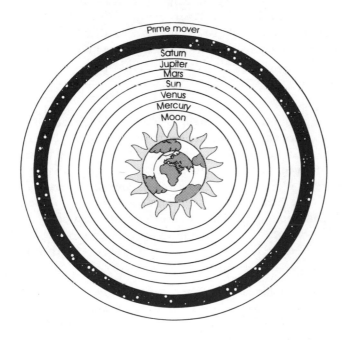

Figure 16 The cosmic system of Aristotle.
The central earth with water round it, air and fire above in the sub-lunar region; the spheres of the planets and the circle of the fixed stars rotate perpetually under the ultimate control of the first mover.

their desire for god and to be perfect as he is, engage in the best activity of which they are capable – incessant regular circular movement. They then transmit this movement to the planets, which in turn are responsible for the sublunar changes (with a significant role allotted to the sun), so that the whole cosmos is viewed as ultimately dependent on the god as both first and final cause. Aristotle may soon have become aware of difficulties inherent in this theory of a divine unmoved mover who maintains the course of the cosmos non-physically, for he did not pursue the topic further himself in the extant writings. There were indeed some criticisms immediately raised by his pupil Theophrastus, the gist of which survives in his own book of *Metaphysics*:

> If the mover is one, it is absurd that it does not move all things with the same movement; and if each thing is moved by a different mover and the principles are more than one, then the harmony of those things moving towards the best [object of] desire is in no way clear. As to the number of the spheres, a greater discussion of its reason is needed; for that of the astronomers is not sufficient. It is also unclear how, though the heavenly bodies have a natural desire, they pursue not rest but movement.

> (*Metaphysics* 5a14–25)

The Presocratics (apart from the atomists) had tended to integrate the divine with the physical structure of the cosmos, but, once the two were separated, further problems arose concerning in particular the 'location' of Aristotle's prime mover as well as that of Plato's creator god. None the less the *Timaeus* and *Metaphysics Lambda* survive as the most enduring and influential texts from the ancient world to harmonise the claims of theology and cosmology.

The Stoics in the following century were the first to adapt the basic principles of these texts for their own purposes, as in the following summary:

> The Stoics think that there are two principles (*archai*) of the universe, the active and the passive. The passive is unqualified substance – matter; the active is the *logos* in it – god. And this, being eternal, fashions (*dēmiorgei*) each thing through the whole of matter.

> (Diogenes Laertius 7.134)

The god represented here, who inherits many of the characteristics of Heraclitus' divine *logos*, moulds shapeless material in the manner of Plato's creator-craftsman, the *Dēmiourgos*, but also contrasts with it as Aristotelian form does with matter. Various Stoic arguments, many of them preserved in the second book of Cicero's *On the Nature of the Gods*, polished the logic of Plato's underlying assumption in the *Timaeus* that, as any recognisable artefact necessarily points to a craftsman, so the cosmos, as artefact *par excellence*, presupposes a supreme craftsman. On the other hand, the teleology derives more from Aristotle, since, as well as initiating the formation of the cosmos, the Stoic god maintains its pattern within the framework of past, present and future happenings:

> The nexus and consequence of these is fate, knowledge, truth, and an inescapable and inevitable law of things that are. In this way all things in the cosmos are managed as in a well-ordered city.
>
> (Aristocles *SVF* 1.98)

This simile of the management of the cosmic city also recalls Aristotle's comparison of god at work in the universe to a general aligning his troops or to a master organising his household with 'all things ordered together to one end' (*Metaphysics* 1075a11–25).

The Stoics however differed from Plato and Aristotle on two fundamental issues, namely their consistent materialism and their insistence on the pervasive immanence of god throughout the physical world rather than in separation from it. The Stoics' god as *logos* correlated with another aspect that belonged with the functioning of what they called *pneuma*. This was thought to be composed of a mixture of fire and air, and it was the constituent proportions of these ingredients holding the material in the appropriate 'tension' that accounted for the variety of phenomena. But the divine *pneuma* was omnipresent, and could not be separated from the earth and water which it informed, so that in this dynamic continuum god could be viewed as both active and passive, differentiated and differentiating, in a true pantheism. The old Ionian theory, long despised by more sophisticated philosophers, of a universal world 'stuff', vibrant and deathless, had found a second home in Stoic theory. Throughout the development of their theology, the Greek philosophers regarded the relationship of the divine to the world around them as a subject for secular study and debate, to be explained, criticised and modified by human reasoning according to the principles of theoretical argument, inference and deduction. God, *logos* and cosmos became an entwined trilogy as the individuals grappled with their relation to the life of the observed natural world, and attempted to bring the whole within the compass of their own intellectual range. The tendency throughout was to view the cosmos as living, eternal and self-contained, governed according to intelligible laws, with reason in control, whether immanent in its material or separate from it.

The main dissenting voice came from the early atomists, who belonged with the intellectual revolution of fifth-century Athens; their physics and cosmology were subsequently revived and revised by Epicurus, and given their greatest expression more than two centuries later by the Roman poet Lucretius. The young atheist in the tenth book of the *Laws*, cited earlier on p. 175, whom Plato represented as the main threat to the ideological foundation of the state and its stability, was especially relevant to the early atomists in that he affirmed that everything happens by nature and chance, and not as the result of any divine activity or intelligence or craftsmanship. No god generated the world in the past or caused movement within it; there is now no divine guidance or influence (so that prayer is useless); the sun, moon and stars are not gods or even alive but made of earth and rock; and, the most brazen assertion of all, mind itself is derivative rather than primary. The phenomena of life and the generation of living species could be plausibly explained as arising from an aggregation of insentient and inanimate matter with no informing intelligence. To counter such dangerous theories Plato used a complex stretch of argument, both scientific and theological, based on an analysis of the causes of change and movement. If however his legislator were unsuccessful in rational persuasion, then the unacceptable counter-philosophy would be silenced by force.

From the first, the atomists had followed Parmenides in ascribing to their version of what exists the divine characteristics of sempiternity and immutability, but accepted also the existence of not-being in the sense of eternal and limitless void. They maintained that it was in the nature of atoms to be in constant motion in this void, differentiated only by size, shape, position and later by weight. The chance congruence of atoms could bring about a vortex which would then attract further atoms, and eventually a compound of greater or less sophistication would arise. Although the first groupings might be random, the movements and generations would then settle into regular and predictable patterns according to the laws of nature. There was therefore no requirement to have creator gods or a divine cause of motion, the present world order goes through its stages of generation, maturity and eventual dissolution without divine intervention, 'miracles' have natural explanations, and the atoms themselves, the primary masses of earth, water, air and fire which they form, as well as stars, planets, sun and moon, are all lifeless and a priori without feeling, perception or intelligence. The Roman poet Lucretius is explicit on this:

> Do not imagine, in the throes of superstition, that earth and sun and sky, sea, stars and moon, have a divine body and survive for ever. . . . These are so far from having any divine power and so unworthy to be counted as gods that rather they serve to show us what it is to be lifeless and insentient.
>
> (5.114–16, 122–5)

Nature is free, and has no proud masters; a stream of rhetorical questions shows what an impossible task is assumed otherwise:

> Who can rule the immeasurable whole? who has the strength to hold in hand and control the mighty reins of the deep? who can spin all the heavens at the same time and warm the fruitful lands with fire from the sky? who can be in every place at every moment?
>
> (2.1090–9)

Epicurus did reintroduce gods into the cosmos mainly in response to the argument from univeral consensus for their existence, and to provide a source for the apparitions of them as *simulacra* in dreams, but they were placed far from the present world in the clear places between the galaxies. These were described by Lucretius in his great vision, when he sees the ramparts of this world roll back and gazes into the depths of space:

> The majesty of the gods is revealed and their quiet homes, which no winds shake or rain-clouds drench or frost-frozen, white falling snow spoils, but an air ever cloudless protects them and pours its pleasant light around. Nature supplies their wants and nothing ever disturbs their peace of mind.
>
> (3.18–24)

In these *intermundia* the gods lead perfectly happy lives (and the description is given in language derived from the Homeric account of Olympus), so the argument asks why they would need to create a world for the benefit of the human race, even if they were able to;

there is no return that humans could give gods for the trouble of their creation. And what pattern was available? What source could there be for an image of humans to be a model for what they wanted to make?

> To say that the gods deliberately created the natural splendour of the world for the sake of the human race, and that it should therefore be praised as a wonderful piece of divine workmanship, is wrong; to think that it is eternal and will be there for ever, and that this theory cannot be questioned or destroyed with arguments – this is all sheer madness.
>
> (Lucretius 5.156–65)

Finally, if a divine intelligence motivated by providential care fashioned this world to provide the best habitation for the human race, the objection was raised (which has echoed down the centuries) that it was not very efficient. Lucretius points out that most of the earth's surface is taken over by the sea, the equatorial and polar zones have temperatures too extreme to be habitable, what is left is mountainous, rocky, marshy or forest land, very little is fertile, and then human labour is ruined by rains, winds, frost or drought:

> Even if I knew nothing about atomism I would still venture to assert, on the meteorological evidence and for many other reasons, that the world was not created for us by gods: it is so very imperfect (*tanta stat praedita culpa*).
>
> (5.195–9)

GLOSSARY

Academy: Europe's first university established by Plato near Athens; sometimes used for theories put forward by the followers of Plato.

Alexandrians: scholars in science and literature associated with the museum and library of Alexandria in Egypt in the third century BC.

archē: origin and first principle.

aiōn: life-span, time generally.

aithēr: the bright upper air; Aristotle's fifth element.

anthropocentrism: the theory that the human race occupies a central position in the universe, or has a key function in it.

catasterism: transformation into a star or constellation.

chāos: 'yawning gap' or 'chasm' without boundaries; what there is before anything else; a confused mass; primeval disorder.

clepsydra: 'water-stealer', a vial-shaped device, perforated at one end and with a hole that can be plugged at the other, for transferring water between containers.

Cloud-cuckoo-land: *Nephelokokkygia*, a utopia between earth and sky invented by Aristophanes in *The Birds*.

cosmogony: an account of the formation of the cosmos.

Cynics: 'dog philosophers', followers of Diogenes of Sinope, who lived as street beggars and preached simplicity and independence.

deferent: the circular path followed by the centre of an epicycle.

Demiurge: 'low-class workman', the title Plato gives to the craftsman-god of the *Timaeus*.

dinē: a whirl or vortex in primary matter which causes the separating out of ingredients for a world-system.

eccentric circle: 'off-centre', a hypothetical planetary circle not concentric with the earth, but centred separately from it.

ekpyrōsis: a conflagration, which according to Stoic theory periodically engulfs the cosmos.

185

Eleatic: characterising the philosophy associated with Elea in south Italy, especially that of Parmenides, Zeno and Melissus.

epicycle: a circle with a centre moving round the circumference of a larger circle.

equant: a hypothetical circle proposed to reconcile the movements of the planets.

Erebus: the primeval dark space from which light emerged.

Gaia: the earth personified as universal mother.

genesis: coming into existence, being born into life, complementary 'passing away'.

geocentrism: the theory that the earth is at the centre of the solar system.

gnōmon: a type of set-square used to mark the hours of daylight from the shadow cast by the sun.

Great Year: the length of time taken by the planets to return to the same position in relation to each other, variously calculated from 1,000 to 30,000 solar years.

heliocentrism: the theory that the earth and some of the planets move round the sun.

Hellenic: relating to Greece generally.

Hellenistic: like Alexandrian, referring to the science and literature of Greece in the third and second centuries BC.

hippopede: 'horse-fetter', a figure of eight proposed as part of a complex movement to explain the apparent occasional retrograde paths of the planets.

homocentric: of spheres or circles with a common centre.

hylozoism: 'living-matter' theory, according to which everything has life, or life is a property of the material substrate.

Ionians: philosophers of nature living in Miletus on the Greek Ionic coast of Asia Minor, especially Thales, Anaximander and Anaximenes.

kosmos: orderly arrangement, world order, a particular world-system, the universe.

logos: rational account, often opposed to the unverifiable narrative of myth.

Megarians: post-Socratic philosophers, centred in Megara near Corinth, famous for dialectic argument and logical puzzles.

Milesians: see Ionians.

Necessity: compulsion imposed by logic, natural forces or the chain of cause and effect, personified as a goddess.

Neo-Ionians: those who attempted to explain plurality and

GLOSSARY

change after Parmenides' denials of them, including especially Empedocles, Anaxagoras and the atomists.

ouranos: the sky, the outer sphere or spherical shell of the world-system containing the fixed stars and revolving with them; sometimes equivalent to 'cosmos'.

Peripatetics: followers of Aristotle, so named from the covered colonnade (*peripatos*) at the Lyceum in which he walked up and down.

physis: 'nature', hence 'physicists', meaning primarily students of nature or natural science.

plenum: a bounded world-system regarded as filled with matter, with no intervening empty spaces.

pneuma: wind, breath, warm breath of life; a combination of air and fire.

sempiternity: everlasting duration, without beginning or end.

'spear' argument: a dilemma to show that the universe has no limit, by asking what happens to a spear cast at the furthest assumed boundary.

stoicheion: element.

Tartarus: the dark region beneath the earth or the earth's surface; the abode of the dead, or a place of punishment after death.

telos: 'end', the aim or purpose which organisms pursue to reach their maturity or achieve their potential.

theogony: an account of the birth of gods or of the emergence of divine forces.

Titans: the first generation of powerful gods in Greek mythology, defeated in a great battle by the younger Olympians; 'Titan star' is a name for the sun.

whorls: a nest of hemispherical bowls envisaged by Plato as a model for the arrangement and movement of the planets.

BIBLIOGRAPHY

The numbering of the Presocratic fragments and the 'A' testimonia has been taken from H. Diels and W. Kranz (*DK*), of Ancient Near Eastern Texts (*ANET*) from J.B. Pritchard, and of Stoic texts (*SVF*) from J. von Arnim.

Archer-Hind, R.D. (1973) *The Timaeus of Plato*, reprint of 1988 edn, New York: Arno Press.

Asmis, E. (1984) *Epicurus' Scientific Method*, Ithaca, NY: Cornell University Press.

Bailey, C. (1928) *The Greek Atomists and Epicurus*, Oxford: Oxford University Press.

Balme, D.M. (1939) 'Greek Science and Mechanism I. Aristotle on Nature and Chance', *Classical Quarterly* 33: 129–38.

—— (1941) 'Greek Science and Mechanism II. The Atomists', *Classical Quarterly* 35: 23–8.

Barnes, J. (1982) *The Presocratic Philosophers*, 2nd edn, London: Routledge.

—— (1987) *Early Greek Philosophy*, Harmondsworth: Penguin.

Barrow, J.D. (1991) *Theories of Everything: The Quest for Ultimate Explanation*, Oxford: Clarendon Press.

Bauval, R. and Gilbert A. (1994) *The Orion Mystery: Unlocking the Secrets of the Pyramids*, London: Heinemann.

Boas, G. (1968) s.v. 'Macrocosm and Microcosm', *Dictionary of the History of Ideas*, New York: Charles Scribner.

Brisson, L. (1974) *Le même et l'autre dans la structure ontologique du Timée de Platon*, Paris: Éditions Klincksieck.

Cherniss, H.F. (1957) *Concerning the Face Which Appears in the Orb of the Moon, Plutarch's Moralia*, vol. xii, Cambridge, Mass.: Harvard University Press (Loeb).

Clagett, Marshall (1971) *Greek Science in Antiquity*, reprint of 1955 edn, New York: Books for Libraries Press.

Cohen, N. (1988) *Gravity's Lens: Views of the New Cosmology*, New York: John Wiley & Sons.

Cornford, F.M. (1934) *Plato's Cosmology*, London: Routledge.

—— (1942) 'Was the Ionian Philosophy Scientific?', *Journal of Hellenic Studies* 62: 1–7, reprinted in D.J. Furley and R.E. Allen (eds) (1970) *Studies in Presocratic Philosophy*, 2 vols, London: Routledge, vol.1: 29–41.

Coveney, P. and Highfield, R. (1991) *The Arrow of Time: The Quest To Solve Science's Greatest Mystery*, London: Harper Collins.

Davies, Paul (1984) *God and the New Physics*, Harmondsworth: Penguin.

—— (1987) *The Cosmic Blueprint*, London: Heinemann.

Dicks, D.R. (1970) *Early Greek Astronomy to Aristotle*, London: Thames & Hudson.

Diels, Hermann (1958) *Doxographi Graeci*, reprint of 1879 edn, Berlin: de Gruyter.

Diels, Hermann and Kranz, Walther (1951–2) *Die Fragmente der Vorsokratiker*, 6th edn, Berlin: Weidmann.

Edwards, Paul (ed.) (1969) *The Encyclopedia of Philosophy*, 6 vols, New York and London: Collier-Macmillan.

Elders, L. (1965) *Aristotle's Cosmology: A Commentary on the De Caelo*, Assen: Van Gorcum & Co.

Farrington, B. (1961) *Greek Science*, revised edn, Harmondsworth: Penguin.

Ferguson, J. (1971) 'DINOS', *Phronesis* 16: 97–115.

Furley, D.J. and Allen, R.E. (eds) (1970, 1975) *Studies in Presocratic Philosophy*, 2 vols, London: Routledge.

—— (1987) *The Greek Cosmologists: Vol. 1. The Formation of the Atomic Theory and its Earliest Critics*, Cambridge: Cambridge University Press.

—— (1989) *Cosmic Problems*, Cambridge: Cambridge University Press.

Gerson, L.P. (1990) *God and Greek Philosophy: Studies in the Early History of Natural Theology*, London: Routledge.

Guthrie, W.K.C. (1952) 'The Presocratic World-Picture', *Harvard Theological Review* 45: 87–104.

—— (1953) *Aristotle: On the Heavens*, reprint of 1939 edn, Cambridge Mass.: Harvard University Press (Loeb).

—— (1962–78) *A History of Greek Philosophy*, vols 1–6, Cambridge: Cambridge University Press.

Hahm, D.E. (1977) *The Origins of Stoic Cosmology*, Athens, OH: Ohio State University Press.

Harris, J.R. (1971) *The Legacy of Egypt*, 2nd edn, Oxford: Clarendon Press.

Harrison, E.R. (1981) *Cosmology: The Science of the Universe*, Cambridge: Cambridge University Press.

Hawking, Stephen (1993) *Black Holes and Baby Universes and Other Essays*, London: Bantam Press.

Heath, Sir Thomas (1932) *Greek Astronomy*, London: J.M. Dent & Sons.

—— (1959) *Aristarchus of Samos: The Ancient Copernicus*, reprint of 1913 edn, Oxford: Clarendon Press.

Huffman, Carl A. (1993) *Philolaus of Croton: Pythagorean and Presocratic*, Cambridge: Cambridge University Press.

Hussey, E. (1972) *The Presocratics*, London: Duckworth.

Jaeger, W. (1947) *The Theology of the Early Greek Philosophers*, Oxford: Clarendon Press.

Kahn, Charles H. (1960) *Anaximander and the Origins of Greek Cosmology*, New York: Columbia University Press.

—— (1970) 'On Early Greek Astronomy', *Journal of Hellenic Studies* 90: 99–116.

—— (1979) *The Art and Thought of Heraclitus*, Cambridge: Cambridge University Press.

—— (1985) 'The Place of the Prime Mover in Aristotle's Teleology' in A. Gotthelf (ed.) *Aristotle and Nature on Living Things*, Bristol: Bristol Classical Press: 183–205.

Kendall, D.G. (1974) (ed.) *The Place of Astronomy in the Ancient World. A Joint Symposium of the Royal Society and the British Academy*, Oxford: Oxford University Press.

Kenney, Anthony (1979) *The God of the Philosophers*, Oxford: Clarendon Press.

Keyt, D. (1971) 'The Mad Craftsman of the *Timaeus*', *Philosophical Review* 80: 1–14.

Kirk, G.S. (1954) *Heraclitus – The Cosmic Fragments*, Cambridge: Cambridge University Press.

—— (1955) 'Some Problems in Anaximander', *Classical Quarterly* 5: 21–38, reprinted in D.J. Furley and R.E. Allen (eds) (1970) *Studies in Presocratic Philosophy*, 2 vols, London: Routledge, Vol. 1, 323–49.

Kirk, G.S., Raven, J.E. and Schofield, M. (1983) *The Presocratic Philosophers*, 2nd edn, Cambridge: Cambridge University Press.

Kretzmann, N. (ed.) (1982) *Infinity and Continuity in Ancient and Medieval Thought*, Ithaca, NY: Cornell University Press.

Laks, A. (1983) *Diogène d'Apollonie: La dernière cosmologie présocratique*, Lille: Presses Universitaire.

Langdon, S. (1923) *The Babylonian Epic of Creation*, Oxford: Clarendon Press.

Layzer, David (1990) *Cosmogenesis: The Growth of Order in the Universe*, Oxford: Oxford University Press.

Lee, H.D.P. (1965) *Plato Timaeus and Critias, Translated with an introduction and an appendix on Atlantis*, Harmondsworth: Penguin.

Lesher, J.H. (1992) *Xenophanes of Colophon*, Toronto: University of Toronto Press.

Lincoln, B. (1986) *Myth, Cosmos and Society*, Cambridge, Mass.: Harvard University Press.

Lloyd, G.E.R. (1966) *Polarity and Analogy*, Cambridge: Cambridge University Press.

—— (1970) *Early Greek Science: Thales to Aristotle*, London: Chatto & Windus.

—— (1973) *Greek Science after Aristotle*, London: Chatto & Windus.

—— (1979) *Magic, Reason and Experience: Studies in the Origin and Development of Greek Science*, Cambridge: Cambridge University Press.

—— (1983) *Science, Folklore and Ideology: Studies in the Life Sciences in Ancient Greece*, Cambridge: Cambridge University Press.

—— (1990) *Method in Greek Science*, Cambridge: Cambridge University Press.

Long, A.A. and Sedley, D. (1987) *The Hellenistic Philosophers*, 2 vols, Cambridge: Cambridge University Press.

Merlan, P. (1966) 'Two Theological Problems – Aristotle's *Metaphysics* Lambda 6–9 and *De Caelo* A9', *Apeiron* 1: 3–13.

Moraux, Paul (1965) *Aristote: du Ciel*, Paris: Les Belles Lettres.

Mourelatos, A. (1970) *The Route of Parmenides*, New Haven, Conn.: Yale University Press.

Neugebauer, O. (1962) *The Exact Sciences in Antiquity*, New York: Harper Torchbooks.

—— (1975) *A History of Ancient Mathematical Astronomy*, 3 vols, Berlin and New York: Springer-Verlag.

Norman, R. (1969) 'Aristotle's Philosopher-God', *Phronesis* 14: 163–74.

Parker, R.A. (1950) *The Calendars of Ancient Egypt*, Chicago, Ill.: Chicago University Press.

—— (1974) 'Ancient Egyptian Astronomy', in D.G. Kendall (ed.), *The Place of Astronomy in the Ancient World*, Oxford: Oxford University Press.

Popper, Sir Karl (1958–9) 'Back to the Presocratics', *Proceedings of the Aristotelian Society* 59: 1–24, reprinted in D.J. Furley and R.E. Allen (eds) (1970) *Studies in Presocratic Philosophy*, 2 vols, London: Routledge, Vol. 1, 130–53.

Pritchard, J.B. (ed.) (1955) *Ancient Near Eastern Texts*, Princeton, NJ: Princeton University Press.

Robert, Charles (1963) *Eratosthenis Catasterismorum Reliquiae*, Berlin.

Sachs, A. (1974) 'Babylonian Observational Astronomy', in D.G. Kendall (ed.), *The Place of Astronomy in the Ancient World*, Oxford: Oxford University Press.

Saggs, H.W.F. (1989) *Civilisation before Greece and Rome*, London: B.T. Batsford.

Sambursky, S. (1956) *The Physical World of the Greeks*, reprinted 1987, London: Routledge.

—— (1959) *The Physical World of the Stoics*, reprinted 1987, London: Routledge.

—— (1962) *The Physical World of Late Antiquity*, reprinted 1987, London: Routledge.

Schofield, M. (1980) *An Essay on Anaxagoras*, Cambridge: Cambridge University Press.

Sedley, D. (1982) 'Two Conceptions of Vacuum', *Phronesis* 27: 175–93.

Sorabji, Richard (1983) *Time, Creation and the Continuum*, London: Duckworth.

Stokes, M.C. (1962–3) 'Hesiodic and Milesian Cosmogonies', *Phronesis* 7: 1–37 and 8: 1–34.

Taton, R. (1963) *Ancient and Medieval Science*, trans. A.J. Pomerans, London: Thames & Hudson.

Tigner, S. (1974) 'Empedocles' Twirled Ladle and the Vortex-Supported Earth', *Isis* 65: 433–47.

Toomer, G.J. (1984) *Ptolemy's Amalgest*, London: Duckworth.

Van der Werden, B.L. (1974) *Science Awakening, II: The Birth of Astronomy*, Leiden: Noordhoff.

Vlastos, G. (1947) 'Equality and Justice in Early Greek Cosmologies', *Classical Philology* 41, reprinted in D.J. Furley and R.E. Allen (eds) (1970) *Studies in Presocratic Philosophy*, 2 vols, London: Routledge, Vol. 1, 92–129.

—— (1975a) 'One World or Many in Anaxagoras', in D.J. Furley and R.E.

Allen (eds), *Studies in Presocratic Philosophy*, 2 vols, London: Routledge, Vol. 1, 354–60

—— (1975b) *Plato's Universe*, Seattle, Wash.: University of Washington Press.

Von Arnim, J. (1903–24) *Stoicorum Veterum Fragmenta*, 4 vols, Leipzig: Teubner.

West, M.L. (1966) *Hesiod: Theogony*, Oxford: Clarendon Press.

—— (1971a) *Early Greek Philosophy and the Orient*, Oxford: Clarendon Press.

—— (1971b) 'The Cosmogony of [Hippocrates] *De Hebdomadis*', *Classical Quarterly* 21: 365–88.

Whitrow, G.J. (1988) *Time in History: Views of Time from Prehistory to the Present Day*, Oxford: Oxford University Press.

Wiener, Philip P. (ed.) (1973) *Dictionary of the History of Ideas*, New York: Charles Scribners.

Wright, M.R. (1981) *Empedocles: The Extant Fragments*, New Haven, Conn.: Yale University Press.

—— (1985) *The Presocratics*, Bristol: Bristol Classical Press.

Zuntz, G. (1971) *Persephone*, Oxford: Oxford University Press.

INDEX OF CLASSICAL
SOURCES

Diogenes Laertius: 2.8–10: 171; 2.7: 73; 7.134: 180; 9.30–2: 85; 10.39–40: 88; 10.45: 89

Empedocles: fr. 6: 98; fr. 16: 130; fr. 17.1–13: 142; frs 17.1–2, 17.6–8, 2.21–3: 64; frs 17.34–5: 99; fr. 21: 105; fr. 22: 64, 99, 113; fr. 23: 53; fr. 26.5: 4; fr. 30: 73; fr. 34: 53; fr. 35: 83; fr. 38: 112; fr. 53: 83; fr. 55: 67; fr. 73: 53; fr. 82: 66; frs 87, 91, 93: 53; fr. 100: 109, 112; fr. 109: 67; frs 110, 129: 130; fr. 115: 73; frs 131–2: 170; fr. 134: 4, 170
Eudemus: *Physics* fr. 51: 143
Euripides: *Bacchae* 393–4: 112; *Helen* 1014–16: 122; *Suppliants* 531–4, 1104: 122; fr. 877: 112

Genesis 1.10: 76, 165

Heraclitus: frs 5, 14–15: 168; fr. 30: 4, 62, 168; fr. 31: 97, 112; fr. 36: 112; frs 40–2, 50: 168; fr. 51: 52; fr. 52: 53, 130; fr. 53: 71, 168; frs 56–7: 168; fr. 60: 52; frs 62, 64, 67, 78–9: 168; fr. 80: 72; fr. 88: 53; fr. 90: 52, 97; fr. 94: 72; fr. 96: 168; frs 102, 114: 72; fr. 120: 112; fr. 125: 52
Herodotus: 1.65: 3; 2.25, 68, 3.86: 112; 7.16.1: 116
Hesiod: *Theogony* 116–27: 77; 124, 127: 112; 519–21: 38; 721–5: 39; 738: 112; *Works and Days* 383–4, 564–7: 18; 548–9: 112
Hippocratic Corpus: *On Human Nature* 7: 105; 7.58–60: 5; *Regimen* 1.2: 5; 1.10: 66; *On Sevens* 6.1–2, 11: 66
Hippolytus: *Refutations* 1.6.3: 39; 1.6.4–5: 42; 1.7.2–3: 96; 1.7.5: 46; 1.13.2: 89
Homer: *Iliad* 1.70: 126; 590–604: 38; 2.204: 70; 214: 3; 412: 112; 3.381: 111; 5.696: 130; 7.422: 59; 8.50: 111; 10.472, 14.187: 3; 200, 244: 59; 288: 111; 15.187–93: 93; 15.192, 16.365: 112; 17.447: 116;

18.487: 17; 21.194–8: 59; *Odyssey* 1.52–4: 38; 6.42–6: 112; 7.143: 111; 13.77: 3

Lucretius: 1.290–4: 110; 968–73: 51–2; 1002–7: 39; 2.116–20: 86; 312–32: 54; 731–8: 107; 1052–7: 89; 1090–9: 183; 1161–74: 91; 3.18–24, 5.114–16, 122–5: 183; 156–65, 195–9: 184

Marcus Aurelius: 4.23: 74
Melissus: fr. 6: 88; fr. 7: 4

Nemesius: *On Human Nature* (*SVF* 2.625): 143

Origen: *Against Celsus* (*SVF* 2.626): 144
Ovid: *Metamorphoses* 1.548–52, 4.657–62, 8.609–10: 68

Parmenides: fr. 8.5–6: 126, 169; fr. 8.6–10: 79–80; fr. 8.56–9: 97; fr. 9: 98; fr. 12.3: 169; fr. 13: 64; fr. 14: 44
Philolaus: frs 2, 6: 5
Plato: *Apology* 18–19: 174; *Cratylus* 389a–d: 48; 402b: 59; *Gorgias* 508a: 6; *Laws* 896d: 166; 891c: 175; 898b: 176; 899b: 167; *Phaedo* 81a: 124; 97b–98c: 172; 98a: 6; 98c: 174; 108e–109a: 40–1; 114b–c: 124; *Phaedrus* 247c: 125; 249c: 25; *Republic* 525–31: 145; 529b–c: 42; 530b–d: 46, 135, 145; 546b: 139; 616b–c: 46; 616d–617b: 149; 617b–c: 25, 137; *Statesman* 269c–d, 270–1: 140; *Theaetetus* 152e: 59; *Timaeus* 28b–d: 80; 31a–b: 87; 32b–c: 101; 33b: 64–5; 34c: 131; 34e–37a: 48; 36b–d: 148; 36e: 65; 37d–e: 130–1; 39b–d: 138–9; 40a–e: 47, 59, 113, 148; 41b: 177; 41d: 48; 41–2: 124; 42b: 177; 43b–c, 49b–c: 101; 47a: 131; 52b–c: 81; 53a: 82;

GENERAL INDEX